SWINDON:
THE LEGACY OF A RAILWAY TOWN

A watercolour panorama of New Swindon painted by Edward Snell in 1849. The viewpoint is from the western side of the works and railway village, looking in an easterly direction. Compare this view with one taken from a similar position in 1994 (opposite).

SWINDON:
THE LEGACY OF A RAILWAY TOWN

John Cattell and Keith Falconer

ENGLISH HERITAGE

Published by English Heritage at the National Monuments Record Centre,
Great Western Village, Kemble Drive, Swindon SN2 2GZ

© Crown copyright 1995

Applications for the reproduction of images should be made to Enquiry and
Research Services, National Monuments Record. The National Monuments
Record is the public archive of English Heritage. The Royal Commission on
the Historical Monuments of England and English Heritage merged on 1
April 1999.

First published 1995 by HMSO on behalf of the RCHME (ISBN 0 11 300053 7)

Reprinted in paperback with slight revisions 2000

ISBN 1 873592 54 X
Product code XC20048

British Library Cataloguing in Publication Data
A CIP catalogue record for this book is available from the British Library

Designed by Chuck Goodwin, 27 Artesian Road, London W2 5DA

Reprinted in Belgium by Snoeck-Ducaju & Zoon

Contents

Foreword to the paperback edition (2000)

As Chairman of English Heritage, it gives me particular pleasure to welcome this paperback edition of *Swindon: the legacy of a railway town.* Swindon, and especially its railway heritage, holds a very special place in my heart, as part of my early career in museums was spent at the GWR Museum a great many years ago. And such was my interest in this book, that when it first appeared I made my order through the RCHME's new Web site as one of its first customers. That the book went on to be the Royal Commission's best seller and that it has helped to fashion the redevelopment of the railway works site was no surprise. The Royal Commission led the way in the regeneration of the site in 1994 with the relocation of its headquarters to the redundant, but historically important drawing offices and with the construction of the adjoining archive building. The transformation of the railway works since then has been one of the success stories in the regeneration of historic industrial sites.

The rehabilitation of the site has not always been easy. English Heritage had to endure criticism in 1984 when it listed most of the buildings in the historic core of the works. But that decision was fully vindicated fifteen years later when the Great Western Railway line and these works were included on the list of sites nominated for World Heritage status. The turning point proved to be the conversion of the huge workshops into a shopping mall by BAA McArthurGlen. As HRH The Prince of Wales commented in his address to the conference on 'Making Heritage Industrial Buildings Work', held in Swindon in 1999, 'it took courage and vision to tackle a building like this'. McArthurGlen's bold and imaginative scheme, informed by *Swindon: the legacy of a railway town*, respected and retained the original structure and architecture. It applied, as The Prince of Wales remarked, a 'successful retail formula developed in the shopping malls of the New World to one of the most important heritage industrial buildings in the Old'. The subsequent expansion, in a further two phases, of the Great Western Designer Outlet Village has proved the commercial soundness of that vision.

The most recent development on the site has been the opening of STEAM: the Museum of the Great Western Railway. Replacing the old museum in Faringdon Road, STEAM has been a model partnership project. It involved the Heritage Lottery Fund, Swindon Borough Council, BAA McArthurGlen and the site owners Carillion; English Heritage staff provided advice throughout. STEAM, with the National Monuments Record, the Railway Village and the Designer Outlet Village, now constitutes one of the largest conservation schemes and visitor attractions in southern England. English Heritage is proud to have been a major player – from the outset – in this remarkable achievement, bringing back to life the buildings of an outstanding industry, the history of which is so ably recounted in this book.

SIR NEIL COSSONS

Foreword

The Royal Commission on the Historical Monuments of England (RCHME) has an especially good reason for recording and celebrating the buildings of the Swindon railway works, since one of those buildings – formerly known as the general offices – became its new headquarters building in 1994. Renamed the National Monuments Record Centre (NMRC), this important historic building, built in 1842 at the hub of Isambard Kingdom Brunel's Great Western Railway (GWR), now houses the National Monuments Record (NMR), England's primary source of information on the architectural and archaeological heritage.

The Commission's involvement with the railway works began several years before the idea of converting the GWR general offices to the NMRC was ever conceived. As early as 1984, the RCHME recognised that rationalisation within British Rail Engineering Limited (BREL) would inevitably involve drastic contraction at the railway works in the town. In the light of this threat, many of the earlier buildings on the site had already been listed, and the Commission's Threatened Buildings Section arranged for a photographic record to be made of most of the buildings belonging to BREL. The opportunity to record such an important industrial site, while it was still functioning, was a rare occurrence for the RCHME. The quality of the buildings, and their significance for railway history, were such that a more detailed study seemed to be justified. Thus, when the Commission decided to centralise its archives and many of its activities at Swindon, it was appropriate that the emergency recording exercise should be expanded into the full-scale project, of which this publication, tracing the architectural history of the railway engineering works and of the associated railway village, is the result.

The closure of the Swindon works in 1986 marked the end of an era in the life of the town and in the history of the railways, but subsequent developments mean that the public now has access to a site that for 150 years, apart from regular guided tours, was closed to all but the employees. The Commission's own headquarters building is open to all who wish to consult the archives of the National Monuments Record, and the planned use of the buildings on the site for retail outlets and a new railway heritage centre will introduce an entirely new audience to the dignified architecture of the railway works and village. We hope that many who visit the site in the future will do so with this book as their guide.

The book could not have been produced without the co-operation and assistance of a great many people from both within and without the RCHME. In particular, the Commissioners would like to thank the authors of the book, Keith Falconer (who wrote the sections on the railway works) and John Cattell (who wrote the sections on the station and railway settlement), and their colleagues in the Commission's former Salisbury and Swindon field offices.

Outside the Commission, thanks are due especially to John Walter, who located the relevant historic plans of the works and provided a great deal of detailed information on the functions of the works' buildings, as well as commenting on the text, and Tim Bryan, Keeper of the Great Western Railway Museum in Swindon, who provided invaluable advice and made available many historic illustrations from the museum's collection. The Commissioners are also grateful to the former staff of Tarmac Properties Ltd, and, latterly, to Gary Bond of Tarmac Swindon Limited, for unrestricted access to all the works' buildings and for financial support towards the production of this volume; and to Thamesdown Borough Council for its financial contribution and for the advice given by its present and former staff.

FARINGDON

Chairman of the RCHME, 1994–9

Acknowledgements

The authors wish to thank the many people who have helped in the production of this book. Their assistance was always given without reservation and, in many instances, has led to close working friendships. In particular the authors wish to reiterate the debt owed to John Walter and Tim Bryan for their help throughout the project.

Amongst their colleagues the authors wish to mention the assistance given by Allan Brodie and the Commission's Swindon-based field-survey staff in investigating the buildings, and by Helga Lane and Peter Spencer of the former Salisbury office for, respectively, typing the text and overseeing the collation of illustrations. Peter Spencer also drew the new illustrations, while Andy Donald, of the London office, contributed measured survey work.

The archive photography was carried out over a period of some ten years, firstly by Derek Kendall and then by the Swindon-based photographers Len Furbank and Mike Hesketh-Roberts, with assistance from Peter Williams and James Davies. Diane Kendall and Ian Savage supervised the processing and printing of the photographs, while air photography was supervised by Roger Featherstone. Janet Atterbury, of the National Monuments Record, provided initial information on the location of documentary and photographic sources.

Kate Owen and Dr Robin Taylor provided editorial guidance while Dr John Bold and Commissioners Dr Marilyn Palmer, Dr Anne Riches and Dr Malcolm Airs commented most helpfully on the text. The advice and comments of a former Commissioner, Professor R A Buchanan, and the former Head of Architectural Survey, Dr Robin Thornes, were also very much appreciated.

Outside the Commission, assistance was freely given by David Pollard, curator of the Underground Quarry Museum at Corsham, who advised on the many and varied types of building stone used at the works and railway village; by Alan Peck, former works' manager and author of the classic book on the history of the works, who commented authoritatively on the text; and by George and Susan D'Amico for helping to uncover information on the early history of Cambria Place and for allowing their house to be measured and photographed.

Thanks are also due to present and former staff of Thamesdown Architects and Planning Departments, especially Robert Bruce, Dick Bailey and Bob Perkins; the staff of Wiltshire County Council Libraries, Museums and Arts, especially Roger Trayhurn at Swindon Reference Library and Michael Marshman at the Local Studies Library, Trowbridge; Steve Hobbs and John d'Arcy at the County Record Office at Trowbridge; Nicholas Lee of the University of Bristol Library for allowing access to material in the Brunel Collection; Ian Nulty, Records Manager, Railtrack PLC, Swindon, for the use of newly discovered plans of the works and village dating from the 1840s; G R Hatherill and J C Morgan of the Permanent Way Institution for assistance with the caption for Figure 142; Dieter Hopkin and Christine Heap of the National Railway Museum, York, and Jean Allen and Brian Bridgeman of the Swindon Society for permission to reproduce some early photographs.

Special thanks should be made to Mrs Margaret Snell and her daughter Mrs Gillian Burrough, the descendants of Edward Snell, for allowing access to Snell's unpublished diary of 1842–9 and for permitting some of the charming sketches to be copied. This diary was traced with the assistance of Dr Alan Platt, and Shona Dewar of the State Library of Victoria, Melbourne. Lastly, thanks are due to Christopher Catling and Susan Whimster for their various editorial contributions to the text, and to Chuck Goodwin for the book's design.

Illustration Credits

Figures are reproduced by kind permission as follows:

Wiltshire and Swindon Record Office
1, 20, 21, 23, 24, 25, 26, 27, 28, 30, 49, 69, 90, 94, 96, 100, 101, 106, 107, 115, 116, 122 (WRO 700/248H), 123 (WRO G24/760/60), 124 (WRO G24/760/80), 125 (WRO G24/760/80), 126 (WRO G24/760/122), 129 (WRO G24/760/149), 133 (WRO G24/760/410), 136 (WRO G24/760/251), 150 (WRO County Architect's Dept, Swindon Schools); Figs 20–116 are from the GWR archive (WRO 2515), but are still being catalogued and are not readily accessible

STEAM: Museum of the Great Western Railway, Swindon
2, 29, 97, 102, 127, 132, 134, 142, 155, 161, 164, 167, 168, 201, 203, 204, 205, 206, 215, 217

STEAM: Museum of the Great Western Railway, Swindon/British Railways Board
46, 47, 48, 51, 52, 54, 59, 60, 61, 64, 66, 67, 68, 84, 87

University of Bristol Library
5 (Sketchbook GWR 10), 12 (Sketchbook GWR 9), 13 (Sketchbook GWR 9), 14 (Sketchbook GWR 11), 16 (Sketchbook GWR 13), 76 (Sketchbook Small 25)

Wolverton and District Archaeological Society
11

Railtrack plc
17, 18, 32, 37, 38, 42, 44, 70

Swindon Museum & Art Gallery
19, 56, 57, frontispiece

Wiltshire County Council, Libraries and Heritage
31, 78, 91, 92, 93, 95, 98 (Hawksworth Plans), 99, 108, 109, 110, 112, 114, 128, 138 (Hawksworth Plans), 139, 141, 147 (Hawksworth Plans), 163 (Hawksworth Plans), 166 (Hawksworth Plans), inside front cover plan of the works

National Railway Museum, York
40 (S2/42 1911?), 162 (F3/136), 165 (S1/519 1930), 196 (S1/266 1933), 199 (F4/43 1938), 218 (B2/37 1892), 219 (S3/22 1927), 220 (S3/35 1927)

The British Library
43 (506.99.9 Vol II No 21)

Ordnance Survey on behalf of the Controller of Her Majesty's Stationery Office, © Crown copyright GD 03133G
45, 193, inside back cover streetplan of Swindon

Mrs Gillian Burrough
63, 73, 74

British Architectural Library, RIBA, London
72

The Swindon Society
77, 131, 137

R C H Nash
88

Swindon Borough Council
169, 170

John C Robinson
197 (photograph by John Henry Davy James)

Geographers' A–Z Map Co Ltd. Licence No B0784
inside back cover streetplan of Swindon

The Swindon Reference Library (Wiltshire County Council, Libraries and Heritage) and the Bristol Reference Library made a number of published sources available to us for copying which are out of copyright. Figures 6 and 216 are reproduced from out of copyright papers held at the Public Record Office (PRO).

All other illustrations are © Crown copyright; applications for reproduction should be made to the National Monuments Record. English Heritage has endeavoured to ensure that full permission has been sought and given for all material used in this publication.

Preface

This book is concerned with the architectural legacy of the Great Western Railway's works and village at Swindon, as represented by the surviving buildings. At its peak, in the second quarter of the 20th century, the works occupied an area of 326 acres (130·4 hectares), of which more than 77 acres (30·8 hectares) were covered by buildings. As the Great Western Railway was itself to claim with pride, the combined locomotive, carriage and wagon works at that time comprised one of the largest engineering complexes in the world, with a total workforce of over 10,000. The workforce was boosted to over 14,000 by the staff of the mechanical and electrical engineers' department, the carriage and wagon department, and the central stores, all of which had their headquarters at Swindon. The Great Western Railway was thus by far the largest employer in the region and, with such a large proportion of the population dependent on the railway throughout the first century of its development, the fortunes of the town were inseparably linked with it.

World War II was to prove a watershed both for the Great Western Railway and for Swindon. The former was to lose its separate identity with the nationalisation of the railways in 1948, while the latter was to be designated an overspill town for London under the provisions of the 1951 Town Development Act. The character of the town was to change completely over the next three decades as its population doubled at the very same time as the railway works were withering away. The industrial centre of gravity shifted to the north and east of the works, while new office developments replaced much of the 19th-century housing to the south of the railway.

The works themselves were drastically reduced in size during the last two decades of their operating life, and this process has continued until the present day, when the remaining buildings occupy a site which has shrunk to an area of 38 acres (15·2 hectares) clustered around the historic core.

Substantial parts of early railway engineering works also survive at Derby and Ashford and to a lesser degree at Crewe, Doncaster and York, but only Derby rivals Swindon in the historic interest of its individual buildings. At Derby the future of many of the earliest buildings is uncertain, so Swindon looks set to become the country's main railway engineering heritage show-piece. Increased public access to the site may well lead to a wider appreciation of the surviving works' buildings, and of those belonging to the associated railway village.

At present it is easy to overlook the village, tucked away amongst a jumble of later brick buildings in an area to the north of Swindon's main shopping centre. However, what remains is an almost complete planned railway settlement of the 1840s and early 1850s, unrivalled in its state of preservation by Crewe, Wolverton and Derby, England's other surviving railway company settlements, all three of which have seen the loss of many of their early buildings.

Now that the buildings of the works and village have been listed, there is a greater chance that they will be preserved for posterity. At present private developments associated with the railway village, such as Cambria Place and the remnants of the estate of the Swindon Permanent Benefit Building and Investment Society, are under threat. Selective listing of some of the remaining and less well-known buildings would do a great deal to help preserve an important part of Swindon's character. It is indeed remarkable that, despite the depredations of a century and a half of relentless development, and equally remorseless contraction, so much of the works and railway village has survived. Together they constitute one of Britain's finest monuments to the early days of the railway age.

Swindon, with its population of over 170,000, is by far the largest and most dominant town in Wiltshire. A mere century and a half ago, it consisted of nothing more than a small hilltop market town, overlooking the thinly populated western end of the Vale of the White Horse, with only 2,459 inhabitants. The transformation was wrought by the coming of the Great Western Railway (GWR), and its engineering works, in the 1840s. The Swindon railway works were located in the Vale to the north of the market town and, at their peak in the middle of the 20th century, stretched for over 1½ miles (2·4km) alongside the mainline railway, employing a workforce of over 14,000. How very different this was from a century earlier, when the site chosen for the works was described by Richard Jefferies, the naturalist, author and local historian, as 'the poorest in the neighbourhood; low-lying, shallow soil on top of an endless depth of stiff clay, worthless for arable purposes, of small value for pasture, covered with furze, rushes and rowen [*sic*]'.[1]

The story of the development of the works and their associated railway village, long known as New Swindon, is dominated by the involvement of a succession of outstanding GWR engineers. The individual contributions of Isambard Kingdom Brunel, Daniel Gooch, Joseph Armstrong, William Dean and George Churchward are still clearly evident in the fabric of the town and it is with their legacy that this book is concerned.

A GREENFIELD SITE

New Swindon was developed on a greenfield site over 1 mile (1·6km) to the north of the existing town. The site was chosen for purely operational and engineering reasons and, at the time, there were few buildings in the vicinity (**Fig 1**). The hamlet of Upper Eastcott lay to the south, about halfway between the proposed works' site and the town of Swindon. About twenty cottages were spread out along the road that connected Upper Eastcott with the town, and, further to the north, a few more dwellings were grouped around Lower Eastcott Farm.[2]

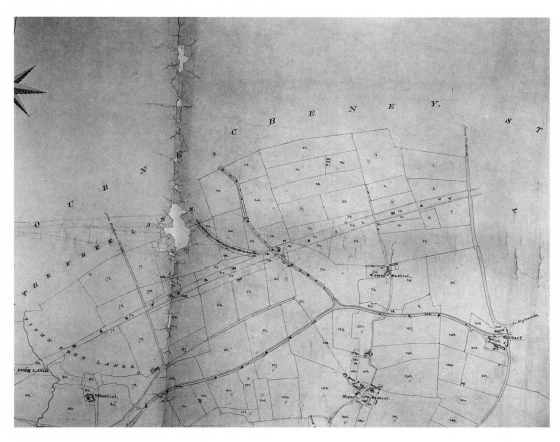

Fig 1 *Part of the 1841 tithe map of Swindon parish, showing the line of the Great Western Railway, the Cheltenham & Great Western Union line and the surrounding hamlets.*

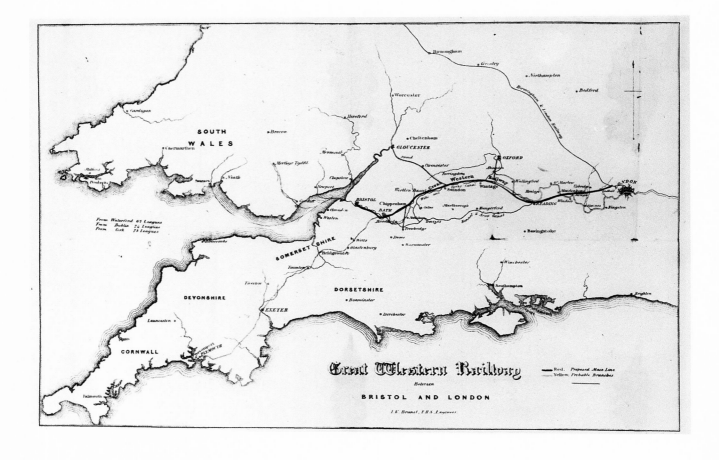

Fig 2 *The proposed route of the Great Western Railway as shown on the map accompanying the revised prospectus of September 1834.*

To the south west was another hamlet, Westcott, which at the time of the 1841 census consisted of about ten houses. It is possible that some of the cottages at Westcott were associated with the Wilts & Berks Canal, which had been cut through the area between 1802 and 1805. The canal branched off from the Kennet & Avon Canal at Semington and continued northwards, passing in a north-easterly direction just to the south of the site of the new works and to the north of old Swindon. A quarter of a mile (400m) south of the proposed station site, the Wilts & Berks joined the North Wilts Canal, which had been completed in 1819 and which linked with the Thames & Severn Canal some 12 miles (19km) to the north west at Latton. A wharf and small settlement existed a short distance to the east of the junction of the Wilts & Berks and North Wilts canals. The settlement consisted of a substantial house occupied by the canal superintendent, William Dunsford, and

several ancillary buildings (possibly warehouses). A road ran from the wharf southwards to Swindon.

Present-day Fleet Street was once an ancient track known as the Fleetway (in the 19th century it was also known as Bleat Lane). This ran from an area of boggy ground called Rushey Platt, to the south west of Westcott, through to a point just west of the North Wilts Canal. The Fleetway passed between Eastcott and the site of the proposed railway village to the north. The only direct communication with old Swindon was a footpath, which ran down the hill from Upper Eastcott. This crossed the Wilts & Berks Canal by means of a drawbridge, and joined the east end of the Fleetway.

The whole area was thus truly a greenfield site in 1841, at the time when the GWR began to consider possible locations for its principal engine-making and maintenance establishment.

THE BIRTH OF
THE GREAT WESTERN RAILWAY

The account of the protracted birth of the GWR has been told many times, though E T Mac-Dermot's classic *History of the Great Western Railway* (as revised by C R Clinker in 1964) has never been bettered. Most of the initial manoeuvres did not impinge directly on Swindon and need only be summarised here.[3] Abortive efforts were made in 1824, and again in early 1832, to form a railway but these were of little substance. By the end of 1832, however, commercial pressure in Bristol for a railway link to the capital was becoming irresistible. Accordingly, a committee was formed of prominent Bristol merchants and representatives of the city's five corporate bodies to investigate the matter.

The committee first met in January 1833 and appointed a subcommittee, called the Committee of Deputies, to arrange a preliminary survey and to select an engineer. The twenty-six-year-old Isambard Kingdom Brunel was chosen in preference to several local candidates and took up his appointment on 7 March. Brunel, accompanied by W H Townsend, a land surveyor and valuer, reconnoitred two routes between Bath and Reading and recommended the northerly route, via Chippenham and Swindon.

The Committee of Deputies then presented a detailed report to a public meeting on 30 July 1833 in the Bristol Guildhall, whereupon it was resolved to form a company to obtain an Act of Parliament to effect railway communication between Bristol and London. Directors were to be drawn from both Bristol and London and represented by respective committees. In August a joint meeting of these committees adopted the title Great Western Railway and a prospectus was issued, seeking to raise the capital sum of £3 million. The accompanying map showed three probable branch lines – minor ones from Didcot through Abingdon to Oxford and from Chippenham to Trowbridge, and a much more important, and longer, line to Gloucester, branching from the main line near Swindon (**Fig 2**). Albeit unwittingly, the die had already been cast for the future development of Swindon.

ROUTES, INCLINES AND THE
BROAD GAUGE

Opposition from local landowners at the eastern end of the line (including Eton College), and from rival railway promoters, caused the Great Western Railway Bill to have a lengthy and troubled passage through parliament. Indeed, after a very thorough examination by a committee, lasting fifty-seven days, the Bill was passed by the House of Commons, only to fail in the House of Lords in July 1834. An amended Bill was published the following year, and this, bolstered by well-marshalled public support, finally received royal assent on 31 August 1835. The following year the Cheltenham & Great Western Union Company obtained its own separate Act of Parliament for a railway line meeting the Great Western at Swindon.

J C Bourne, in his lavishly illustrated *History and Description of the Great Western Railway*, published in 1846, was most impressed by the route selected, commenting on the fact that it not only connected or passed close to many important towns, but that it also had an 'unusually favourable gradient' and an 'absence of objectionable curves'.[4] He included a long section of the entire line in the illustrations (**Fig 3**) and remarked that 'the greater part of the rise upon this line is concentrated within a comparatively short space by means of two inclined planes, upon one of which assistant power is employed, and the remainder of the line is thus left free to be more economically worked'. He also commented on the fact that there was 'but one summit level' – at Swindon – only 270ft (82·3m) above the London depot and 290ft (88·4m) above that at Bristol, and that the general gradient for the first 56 miles (90km) from London never exceeded 1:1 320.[5]

The two inclines referred to, at Box and at Wootton Bassett, had concerned the parliamentary committee in 1835, but expert witnesses, including George Stephenson, agreed that, worked by a stationary or 'assistant' engine, they should not present any particular problems. Such were the advances in railway technology at this time that little more was heard of the suggestion of a stationary engine to help overcome these inclines. The grouping of the most severe gradients at the western end of the line was, however, to bear on the selection of Swindon as the site for the main locomotive establishment.

When negotiations to make a junction with the London & Birmingham Railway, and to share facilities at Camden and Euston, collapsed, Brunel was free to pursue the adoption of his revolutionary 7-ft (2·2-m) gauge (known as the broad gauge) and this was sanctioned by the GWR board in October 1835.[6] This decision, which was taken on engineering grounds, was to have profound operational consequences for the GWR over the next fifty years. Indeed, the issue had become so contentious by the mid 1840s that the government appointed a Royal Commission to investigate the merits of the rival broad and standard gauges and the Commissioners held a series of trials to examine rival locomotive performance

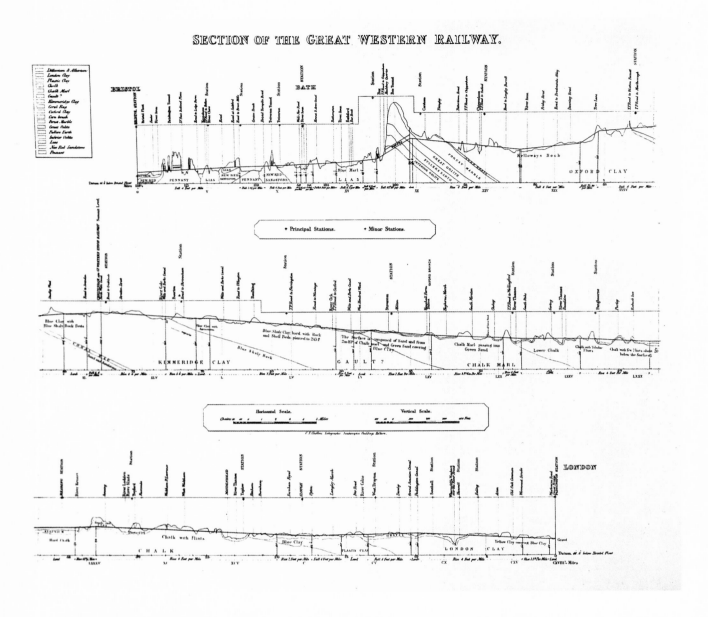

SECTION OF THE GREAT WESTERN RAILWAY.

Fig 3 *J C Bourne's long section of the line of the Great Western Railway, showing Swindon at the summit level (1846).*

claims. Though the Commissioners conceded that there were speed advantages on the broad gauge, for practical reasons they suggested that it should be limited to a region focused on the London to Bristol main line. This was to reinforce the already existing tendency within the GWR to go its own way in most civil and mechanical engineering matters and was to have great bearing on the insularity of its workshops.

By the close of 1835, the construction of the line had started at each end and the first section, from Paddington to Maidenhead, opened on 4 June 1838. Nevertheless, some uncertainty remained as to the exact line to be followed to the west, for in the same month Brunel commented on the two options 'in the neighbourhood of Swindon'.7

THE APPOINTMENT OF DANIEL GOOCH

The ultimate selection of Swindon as the site of the main depot was the result of Daniel Gooch's intervention. Gooch (**Fig 4**) had been born and brought up in Bedlington, Northumberland, where his father was employed at the local ironworks. He was only twenty years old when he was interviewed by Brunel for the post of superintendent of locomotive engines, but he had considerable experience of engine-building and foundry work in various parts of the country, as his letter of application to Brunel stressed. This letter, preserved in the Great Western Railway Museum at Swindon, summarises very adequately his career to date:

Manchester & Leeds Railway Office
Rochdale
July 18th 1837

I. K. Brunel, Esq.,

Dear Sir

I have just been informed it is your intention to erect an Engine Manufactory at or near Bristol and that you wish to engage a person as manager. I take the earliest opportunity of offering my services for the situation.

I have until the last two months been constantly engaged on Engine Building and have worked at each branch of the business but principally at Locomotive Engine Work. The first 3 years of my time was with Mr Humphrey at the Tredegar Iron Works, Monmouthshire. I left him to go to Mr R. Stephenson and was at the Vulcan Foundry 12 months when I obtained leave from Mr Stephenson to go down to Mr Stirling at the Dundee Foundry Company, Dundee to get a knowledge of steam boat work. I remained with him 12 months and returned to Mr Stephenson's works at Newcastle where I remained until last October, when I left having had an offer from a party in Newcastle to take the management of a Locomotive Manufactory which they intended erecting, but which owing to some unavoidable circumstances they have now given up the idea of proceeding with, and we have counter-manded the orders for the Machinery.

This has left me without a situation and I am anxious to engage Myself to some company where I will have the management of the building of Engines. At present I am with My brother on the Manchester & Leeds line where I have employment until I meet with something suitable.

I will be glad to refer you to any of the former-tioned places for testimonial.

I trust you approve of my application. I shall be glad to hear from you stating the Salary and any other information you may think necessary.

I am, Sir,

Yours Obediently,
Danl. Gooch

Gooch was appointed in August 1837 and initially based at West Drayton, halfway between Paddington and Maidenhead, where the railway crossed the Grand Junction Canal. The canal was to be used for transporting locomotives from their various northern manufacturers and one of Gooch's first tasks was to provide accommodation for the engines at Maidenhead and West Drayton. He also had to build a running shed, repair shops and an engine shed at Paddington. It seems that, for the detailed design of these buildings, he was able to call on the expertise and draughting facilities of Brunel's office. The largest structure was the octagonal engine house at Paddington, which

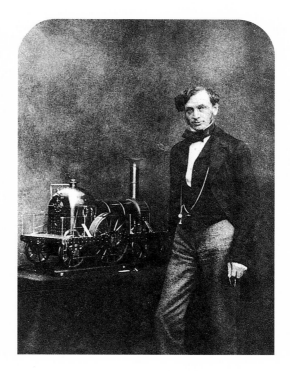

resembled that already built by the North Midland Railway at Derby (see pp 9–10). Contemporary illustrations show a mainly wooden structure with a central turntable serving seven inspection pits.

In November 1837, the first two engines, *Premier* and *Vulcan*, arrived from one of seven suppliers, the Vulcan Foundry of Warrington. On 28 December, *Vulcan* became the first locomotive to run on Great Western rails, being driven by Jim Hurst, who was previously employed as an engine-driver on the Liverpool & Manchester Railway.[8] However, all the early engines, with the exception of *North Star* (built by R Stephenson & Co), performed poorly in the trials and it was with some relief that the second generation 'Firefly'-class engines, designed by Gooch, were available for the opening of the line to Reading in March 1840.

THE CHOICE OF SWINDON

Meanwhile, such were the difficulties, both constructional and contractual, at the western end of the line, that construction of the 16½-mile (26·4-km) stretch past Swindon, which was nominally in the Bristol division, was switched to the eastern division, starting at the temporary Faringdon terminus. This section was still unfinished when the Inspector-General of Railways, Sir Frederick Smith, reported on it in December 1840.[9] He commented on the new temporary terminus, officially called Wootton Bassett Road, that had been created at Hay Lane, some 2 miles (3·2km) to the west of Swindon,

Fig 4 *Daniel Gooch, at the height of his involvement at Swindon, photographed in 1845 with a model of a 'Firefly'-class locomotive, which he designed.*

Fig 5 *Brunel's preliminary sketches of early 1840, showing possible layouts for an engine house at Wootton Bassett Road ('W B Road'). The sketches show (top) the dimensions of the various elements required by Brunel, and (bottom) those elements arranged approximately as they were later to be built at Swindon.*

saying that 'Although Hay Lane Station is merely intended as a temporary terminus, the Company are forming it, in regard to sidings, switches and other mechanical arrangements, in the same extensive and substantial manner as is their ordinary practice at permanent terminals'.[10]

The line to Hay Lane opened on 17 December 1840, but, some time before this event, both Brunel and Gooch had been exercised as to the most suitable location for their principal engine shed. A letter of 18 June 1839 from Brunel to the directors indicated that he had not yet considered Swindon for the main depot. Reading seems to have been the first suggestion, but Brunel preferred 'a point more central' than Reading, such as Didcot.[11]

Early in 1840 Brunel made preliminary sketches in his notebook of possible engine-house layouts for Wootton Bassett Road (Hay Lane), anticipating the need for a locomotive establishment located at some point where the engines could be changed to overcome the steeper gradients to the west (**Fig 5**).[12] In the event, a temporary works was erected there alongside the temporary terminus and it was perhaps the groundwork for this that Sir Frederick noted in his December 1840 report.

In September 1840, Gooch wrote to Brunel suggesting Swindon as the most suitable location for the principal engine establishment, enclosing a sketch plan showing a roundhouse in the triangle formed by the main GWR line and the Cheltenham branch (**Fig 6**). This letter is of such significance for Swindon that it is here reproduced in full.[13]

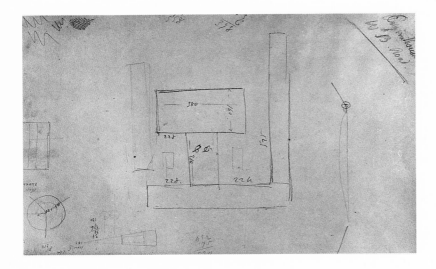

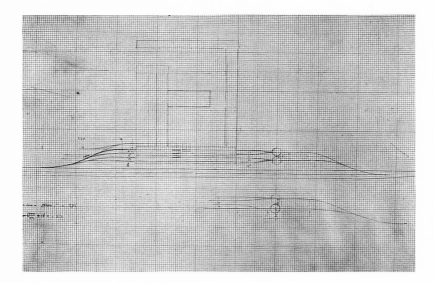

BRISTOL
13th September 1840

My Dear Sir,

According to your wish I give you my views of the best site for our principal engine establishment, and in doing so I have studied the convenience of the Great Western Railway only, but also think the same point is the only place adapted for the Cheltenham and Great Western. The point I refer to is the Junction at Swindon of the two lines.

The only objection I see to Swindon is the bad supply of water. There is also an apparent inequality of distance or duty for the engines to work – but which is very much equalized when the circumstances attending it are taken into account. I find the actual distances are as 76½ miles [122·4km] to 41 [65·6] and the gradients are for the short distance of 41 miles a rise of 318 feet [97m] or 7·75 feet per mile [1·5 m per km], and for the 76½ miles a rise of 292 feet [89m] or 3·8 feet per mile [2·4 m per km]. Swindon being the point at which these gradients change, the different gradients necessarily require a different class of engine, requiring for the Bristol end a more powerful one than for the London end.

That power can only be obtained conveniently by reducing the diameter of the Driving Wheels, therefore, supposing we work between Swindon and Bristol with 6 feet [1·8m] wheels, and between Swindon and London with 7 feet [2·1m] wheels, there will actually be very little difference between the work required of the two engines, when the additional gradients and curves, and the increased number of revolutions per mile which the small wheeled engine makes are taken into account. It would also divide the pilot engines very nearly equally, as Reading being the first Station where a pilot engine would be kept, say 36 miles [57·6km], the next distance, to Swindon, would be 41 miles [65·6km], and on to Bristol another 41 [65·6km], and which I think would be sufficiently near for pilot engines to be constantly ready, and with this arrangement the watering stations would work very well. Steventon, where plenty of water can be had, forming a central station between Reading and Swindon, and as our Oxford Traffic comes on there I should think it likely that all trains will stop there. A large station at Swindon would also enable us to keep our Bank engines for Wootton Bassett incline at Swindon instead of having a separate station for that purpose at the bottom of the incline, and in addition it would at any rate be necessary to have a considerable Station at Swindon to work the Cheltenham line, which would be saved if Swindon was our principal station.

It has also the great advantage of being on the side of a canal communicating with the whole of England, and by which we could get coal and coke, I should think at a moderate price. I am not sufficiently acquainted with the place to know how far we would be affected by the want of water, it might probably be collected in the neighbourhood, and as we have a great deal of side cutting they might be converted into reservoirs, and would even this fail us we have the canal. These reasons lead me to think

Swindon by far the best point we have for a Central Engine Station. From the plans and sections there appear little or no difficulties with the nature of the ground for building upon, and by placing the Station somewhere as shown in the enclosed sketch, it might be made in every respect very complete. I have not thought of the Bristol and Exeter line in the arrangement, as it is quite possible to work it very well by engines kept at Bristol as long as they are fit for work. In the same way we could work the additional Bath traffic, for when necessary they could always work their way to Swindon when any heavy repairs were required. The Engine House we are building at Bristol would be ample for any slight repairs that might be required during the time the engine was in working order, and that without any outlay of machinery beyond a few hundred pounds. I am not aware of any difficulties connected with Swindon more than the water.

I am, my dear Sir,

Yours very truly,
DANIEL GOOCH.

I. K. Brunel, Esq.

Fig 6 *Gooch's sketch, accompanying his letter to Brunel in September 1840, of the possible location and layout of a central engine station. The central 'Principal Engine House' is approximately 200ft (61m) in diameter. The other structures (reading clockwise from the top) are the 'Cheltenham Engine House', the 'London Engine House', the 'Erecting Shop' and the 'Bristol Engine House'. (PRO RAIL 1008/82)*

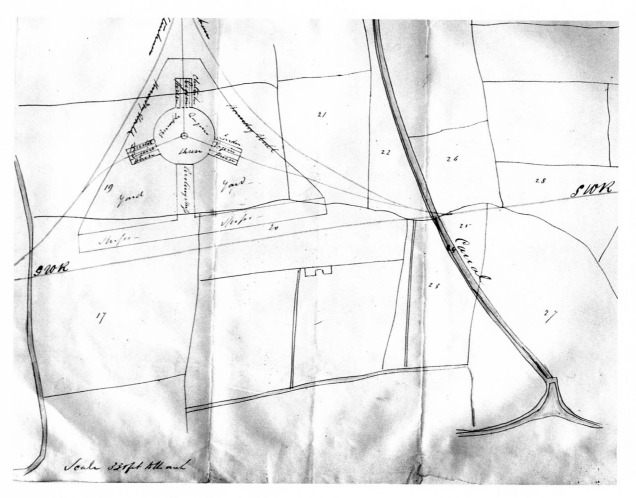

Fig 7 *J C Bourne's lithograph of the Camden Locomotive Engine House, London & Birmingham Railway, 1838.*

Gooch, on the strength of this letter, should certainly get the credit for the reasoned choice of Swindon as the location of the main works, especially since the tone of the letter indicates that he was making a fairly novel suggestion. Brunel, as we have seen, had already sketched the facilities he might require, but as he titled these 'W B Road' (ie the Wootton Bassett terminus) in his sketchbook, it would seem that he was still considering Hay Lane as a possible site. In the event, he endorsed Gooch's Swindon recommendation and forwarded it to the board. Accordingly, on 6 October 1840 the GWR directors resolved that 'the principal Locomotive Station and Repairing Shops be established at or near the Junction with the Cheltenham and Great Western Union Railway at Swindon'.[14] By the end of the same month Brunel had met with, and persuaded, the directors of the Cheltenham & Great Western Union Railway to 'make over' the land purchased by that company from Mr Sheppard 'for the engine house for both companies'.[15] Platt, in his biography of Daniel Gooch, implies that the availability of this land may have been a contributory factor in Gooch's recommendation of Swindon. Some have also suggested that Gooch may have been person-ally involved in the land speculation, but there is no documentary evidence to confirm this.[16]

PRECEDENTS FOR THE SWINDON WORKS

What precedents could Brunel draw upon for a 'locomotive establishment' to service a railway of the length of the GWR? Scrutiny of Whishaw's *Railways of Great Britain and Ireland*, first published in December 1840, provides a summary of facilities on comparable railways and gives an insight into contemporary thinking on these matters. Whishaw makes no mention of any company manufacturing its own locomotives. Indeed, after an initial false start by the Stockton & Darlington Railway from 1827 to 1832 (by which date they had constructed eight engines), all locomotive manufacture was undertaken by private engine builders until the mid 1840s.[17] Commenting on the need to change engines Whishaw asserts: 'we consider even fifty miles [80km] too great a distance to run an engine without examination ... we should prefer about thirty miles' [48km] stages.'[18] Clearly, the amount of attention required by these early locomotives, and their limited operational range, had to be borne in mind when the siting and fitting out of engine sheds was discussed.

Whishaw pays considerable attention to the London & Birmingham Railway, since it was the longest, and arguably the most significant, line opened by 1840. After commending the passenger facilities he gives details of the engine sheds at Camden Town, London and Birmingham and the 'locomotive establishment' at Wolverton. All three were built on a rectangular plan, with turntables to manoeuvre the engines. The Camden shed is illustrated by Bourne (**Fig 7**) but not, unfortunately, the Wolverton building, as the line was not complete when Bourne made his initial survey in 1837.[19] Whishaw's description of Wolverton (given below) is therefore highly relevant, especially as we know that Brunel was familiar with Wolverton at the time he was involved with the design of the Swindon facilities:

> The buildings lately erected at Wolverton, as the principal station for the locomotive engines, form, perhaps, one of the most complete establishments of the kind in the world. The site of this establishment is ... at a distance of about 52½ miles [84km] from the London terminus, and 59 miles [94·4km] from that of Birmingham, having a frontage on the Grand Junction Canal. The buildings, which are of plain but neat design, and constructed chiefly of brick, surround a quadrangular space ... the entrance of which is under an archway in the centre of the principal front. The whole length of the buildings is 221 feet [67·4m], the depth 314 feet 6 inches [95·9m], and the height 23 feet [7·0m] ... Besides the central gateway ... there are two side-entrances: the one to the large erecting-shop, the other to the repairing-shop.
>
> The erecting-shop is on the right of the central gateway, and occupies one half of the front part of this building. It has a line of way down the middle, communicating with a turn-table in the principal entrance, and also with the small erecting-shop, which is on the left of this entrance. Powerful cranes are fixed in the erecting-shops for raising and lowering the engines when required.
>
> Contiguous to the small erecting-shop, and occupying the principal portion of the left wing, is the repairing-shop, which is entered by the left gateway. One line runs down the middle of this shop, with nine turn-tables, and as many lines of way at right angles to the central line. This shop ... will hold eighteen engines and tenders, or thirty-six engines.
>
> In the same wing, and next to the repairing-shop, is the tender-wrights's shop, having the central line of way of the repairing-shop running down its whole length, with a turn-table and cross line, which runs quite across the quadrangle, and intersects a line from the principal entry to the boiler-shop in the rear of the quadrangle.
>
> The remainder of the left wing is occupied by a

room for stores on the ground-floor, with a brass-foundry and store-roof over; and the iron-foundry, which extends to the back line of the buildings.

> The right wing contains the upper and lower turneries, each 99 feet [30·1m] long and 40 feet [12·2m] wide; the upper floor being supported in mid-line by nine iron columns. There are fourteen lathes in the lower, and eight in the upper turnery.

The installations at Derby might have been a second source of influence. Here, in 1839, Francis Thompson, the North Midland's architect and one of Brunel's professional contacts, had designed the station that served three separate railways, the North Midland, Midland Counties and Birmingham & Derby Junction (B&DJR). All three companies had also opened workshops at Derby by 1840.[20] The B&DJR workshop comprised a single rectangular shed 150ft (45·7m) long and 48ft (14·6m) wide, built by T & W Cooper at a cost of some £4,000 and accommodating three lines of track, a blacksmith's shop and some offices.

The Midland Counties' workshop was built in 1839. By 1844, when the building was shown on a plan of the three companies' properties, its facilities comprised all the elements necessary for maintaining a small fleet of rolling stock with a degree of self-sufficiency. The running shed to the north was rectangular, 134ft (40·8m) long by 52ft (15·9m) wide, with an adjoining repair shop 93ft (28.4m) long and widening to 88ft (26·8m). The main workshop to the south was some 200ft (61·0m) long by 93ft (28·4m) and its southern section, containing the fitting and turning shops, was of two storeys.

The single-storey section was served by three lines of track. To provide clear working space, the ground-floor workshop of the two-storey section had an arcaded central brick wall with only two cast-iron columns in each half supporting a matrix of metal-trussed, composite wooden beams. The upper floor had a central rank of columns to support the valley of the twin queen-post roof; on either side of the columns there was clear space. The workshops were driven by a beam engine in an integral engine house in the southern bays of the building, which also accommodated offices and stores. The complex also included a long narrow range, identified as 'shops' on a plan of 1844, that would have contained the smiths' forges.

The North Midland's facilities were designed by Thompson and were on an altogether grander scale, costing some £62,000 in total. The main element was a polygonal engine house 130ft (39·6m) in diameter with sixteen lines radiating from a central turntable. As each bay would have been able to accommodate two engines, there would have been a stabling capacity for up to

thirty engines (**Fig 8**). The engine house was over 48ft (14·6m) high to the top of its lantern and access was provided via ornamented portals in the office ranges to the north and west.

The engine and carriage workshops formed oblique wings to the roundhouse and were 184ft (56·1m) by 70ft (21·3m) and 191ft (58·2m) by 70ft (21·3m) respectively with smiths' shops attached to both ranges. Further ranges of workshops and smiths' shops to the east completed an open court-yard plan. The construction throughout was surpris-ingly sophisticated for its date. The workshop ranges were constructed with three tiers of massive cast-iron columns supporting cast-iron beams and their windows were very generous in their propor-tions. Although the roof of the engine house was wooden framed it was of elegant design and considerable use was made of tall cast-iron columns for intermediate support.

The form and the dimensions (**Fig 9**) of the facilities at Wolverton and Derby are especially significant as they provide contemporary models of which Brunel had first-hand knowledge. This was recognised by Bourne who, in the commen-tary to his 1845 illustrated history of the GWR, remarked on the similarity between the facilities provided at Swindon and those at Wolverton: 'Swindon has been selected as the principal depot and place of repair for the locomotive engines ...

as well as for the stopping place of all the trains for the refreshment of the passengers, answering in these respects to the Wolverton station upon the London and Birmingham Railway'.[21]

Two other railway companies whose facilities may have influenced the design of those at Swindon were the Liverpool & Manchester Railway and its sister company, the Grand Junction Railway. The former's engine depots at Edgehill, Liverpool, and at Salford, near Manchester, were comparatively long established by 1840 and were soon to be run down, the staff from Edgehill being moved to the Grand Junction's new works at Crewe. Crewe, despite being Swindon's closest parallel in date and scale, had little, if any, influence on the plans for Swindon in this initial phase. It was too close a contemporary to provide a model – indeed, it is surprising how differently the two sites were developed in response to similar demands.

THE ORIGINS OF NEW SWINDON VILLAGE

As we have seen, the site chosen by Brunel and Gooch in 1840 for the new locomotive establish-ment was an area of open ground 1 mile (1·6km) north of the old market town of Swindon. The choice of a greenfield site in an agricultural area had important implications for the supply of

Fig 8 *The 1840 round-house at Derby, North Midland Railway.*

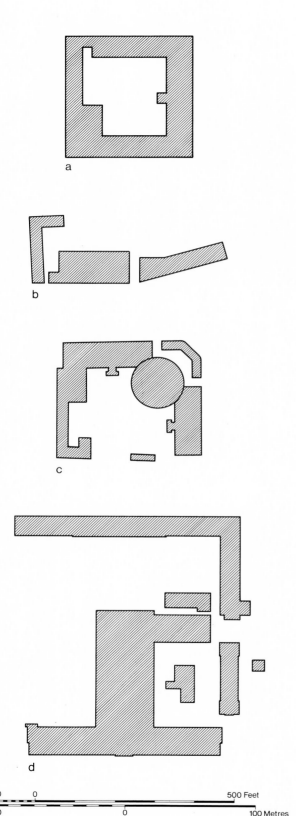

100 0   500 Feet
100   0   100 Metres

labour. There was no history of heavy industry in the Swindon area and skilled workers had to be brought in to operate the new establishment from Bristol, London, northern England and Scotland. Some local agricultural workers were able to take up better-paid positions as unskilled labourers in the new factory. The bulk of the workforce had to be imported, however, and one of the company's first priorities was to provide sufficient accommodation for them.

A new settlement, incorporating good-quality housing, churches, schools and social institutions, was necessary in order to induce skilled workers and their families to leave positions in other parts of the country and come to Swindon. It was thought that, without adequate housing and social facilities, the workmen would resort to drink and disorderly conduct, the type of behaviour usually associated, sometimes unfairly, with the itinerant navvies who were building the line. The navvies were dreaded by local landowners, many of whom had opposed the routing of the line through their area, fearing the damage that might be inflicted on their lands and the consequent depreciation in property values. In 1851 John Francis wrote of the trepidation that the navvies 'spread throughout a rural community … Depredations among the farms and fields in the vicinity were frequent. They injured everything they approached. From their huts to that part of the railway at which they worked, over corn or grass, tearing down embankments, injuring young plantations, making gaps in hedges on they went in one direct line, without regard to damage done or property invaded … They often committed the most outrageous acts in their drunken madness.'[22]

Precedents for company housing
The task of planning the new settlement fell to Brunel as the company's engineer. In doing this he was able to draw on the tradition of workers' housing that existed in the industrialised north of England and Scotland from the late 18th century. One well-known example was the village built around the cotton mills at New Lanark, on the River Clyde, from the 1780s, consisting of rows of three-storey tenement houses, along with shops and schools. In the 1770s at Cromford, in Derbyshire, Arkwright had provided his labourers with a public house, market buildings and a choice of terraced houses, some with workshops on their upper floors. At another Derbyshire cotton town, Belper, terraced rows of back-to-back houses were laid out on a grid pattern. There were also smaller blocks separated from each other by gardens. Each block consisted of four interlocking houses made up of two units of back-to-back houses. These more desirable semi-detached houses, known as 'cluster houses', were probably occupied by more

Fig 9 *Early railway workshops – comparative layouts to the same scale: a) Wolverton, London & Birmingham Railway, 1838, conjectural reconstruction; b) Derby, Midland Counties Railway, 1839, from a company plan of 1844; c) Derby, North Midland Railway, 1840, from a company plan of 1844; d) Swindon, Great Western Railway, 1842–3, from a company plan of 1849.*

Fig 10 *Railway Terrace, Derby, built around 1840. These houses are thought to be the work of Francis Thompson, architect for the North Midland Railway.*

Fig 11 *Railway workers' cottages in Glyn Square, Wolverton, built around 1840 and demolished around 1966.*

highly skilled workers. Similar houses were provided for officers of the Grand Junction Railway at Crewe in the early 1840s.

When the directors of the Great Western Railway decided to establish their works at Swindon in 1840 the railway age was still in its infancy. There were very few precedents for railway housing upon which the company could draw when planning its new settlement. A small railway town had been built at Shildon, Durham, by the Stockton & Darlington Company from 1826, but this was a tiny establishment, with informally laid-out streets, and it was therefore unlikely to have influenced the GWR directors to any significant degree.

The locomotive works at Derby were established very close to the outskirts of the town in 1838. In this case, there already existed a local supply of workmen with experience of similar forms of heavy engineering. There was still a need to attract more highly skilled mechanics to Derby from railway works elsewhere, however, and the North Midland Railway built a triangular block of terraced cottages opposite the station for their accommodation. The houses in the new settlement are thought to have been designed by the company's architect, Francis Thompson, and built in 1840. A shop and a public house were also provided. The blocks of two-storey brick houses are Georgian in style with multi-pane sash windows, a parapet and simple cornice to the street elevation, and paired doors in neo-classical surrounds (**Fig 10**).

As we have already seen with the railway works, Crewe was too close a contemporary to have had any influence on the planning of the Swindon settlement.

Wolverton and Swindon

The most important precedent for Swindon was the town of Wolverton, built by the London & Birmingham Railway Company from 1838. Like Swindon, it was built on a greenfield site close to the medieval settlement of old Wolverton and near to an important inland waterway, the Grand Union Canal, which provided an alternative means of transporting raw materials. Wolverton, like Swindon, was also the point on the line where engines had to be changed.

It is clear that the GWR looked upon Wolverton as a possible model for its new settlement and there are several instances of information being exchanged between the two companies prior to the construction of the first houses at New Swindon in 1842. Brunel was in contact with the London & Birmingham Railway in 1837 regarding the need for higher wages to be paid to railway workers in southern England compared with those in the north, and in 1839 he visited Wolverton by train.

In December 1841 an unsigned report was sent from the Grand Junction Railway's offices at Liverpool to either Brunel or Gooch detailing the buildings existing at Wolverton at that time.[23] This shows that 165 cottages had been built there for railway workers, together with nine shops, a market square, a library, a school containing a temporary chapel, a substantial piggery and 120 allotments.[24]

There were six classes of dwelling let by the company to its employees at varying weekly rentals. This accommodation ranged from small cottages, probably containing only two rooms, to substantial three-storey dwellings for clerks and other officers. The majority of the cottages (**Fig 11**) were two-storey terraced structures constructed of red brick and arranged in streets to form a grid pattern. They were built on three sides around the quadrangle formed by the engine shed and workshops.

The establishment and surrounding settlement appear to have achieved considerable fame by 1840. According to Drake, 'the town of Wolverton, hitherto unnoticed on the map of Great Britain, is now rapidly rising into importance; houses are springing up on every side, streets are being laid out, and a large and busy population is rapidly gathering, whilst its fame as the birthplace of English fire steeds is spreading through the civilised world'.[25]

Brunel as architect

Although Brunel must have been influenced by Wolverton, he had also been designing houses of his own for railway employees from 1839. At Twerton, on the outskirts of Bath, he built small, two-room houses under the arches of a Bath-stone viaduct that formed part of the Bristol to Bath section of the line opened on 31 August 1840. The use of the arches for dwellings was probably suggested to him by the 3-mile (4·8-km) viaduct making up the London & Greenwich Railway which had been built in 1836 with premises to let in the arches. The Twerton Viaduct houses were designed in a simplified Elizabethan style; the chamfered arches, buttresses and slit openings evident here would reappear in his later work.

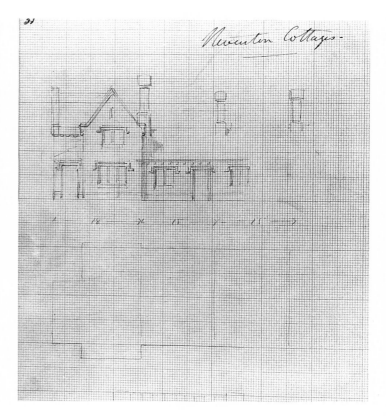

In early 1840 Brunel produced elevational sketches (**Fig 12**) for a terrace of nine brick cottages at Steventon, on the main line to the east of Swindon. Steventon was located midway between Paddington and Bristol and was regarded as an important station. Along with the station and the cottages there were also two substantial stone buildings which still survive. One of these, a hotel, was converted into a dwelling for the station superintendent in early 1842 by Samuel Whitfield Daukes, a Gloucestershire architect and friend of Brunel.[26] The contractor was J H Gandell, one of Brunel's former assistants. Daukes converted part of the ground floor of the superintendent's house into two committee rooms for the company's directors. The board of directors at that time comprised two committees, one based at Paddington, the other in Bristol, and Steventon was felt to be a convenient, central meeting-point.

The cottages at Steventon were built in a vaguely Elizabethan style with gabled projections and flat-arched window and door openings under drip moulds. There were also slit openings in the gable ends, and mullion windows with chamfered surrounds. The cottages were single storey except for two houses of two storeys used to emphasise the ends of the terrace. Brunel's predilection for taller end houses would become apparent in his designs for buildings in the new settlement at

Fig 12 *Brunel's sketch of 1840 for a terrace of nine brick-built cottages at Steventon, Berkshire.*

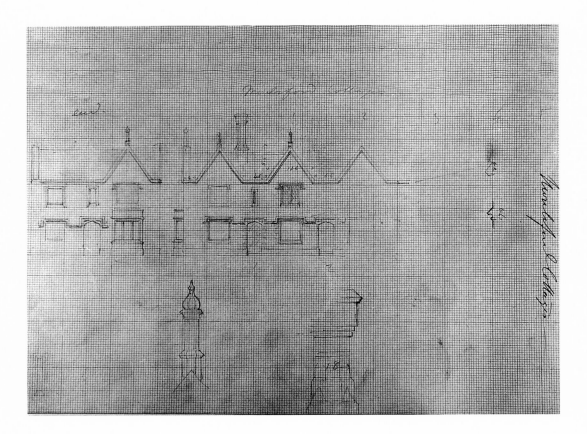

Fig 13 *Brunel's sketch of 1840 for a terrace of railway cottages in the Elizabethan style at Moulsford, Oxfordshire. The nearby station was known as Wallingford Road.*

Swindon. The Steventon cottages were built by Gandell and demolished in the late 1960s.[27]

Early in 1840, Brunel designed a virtually identical cottage terrace for the station at Moulsford, to the south east of Didcot (**Fig 13**), but it is not known whether they were ever built. A gabled former hotel building in simplified Elizabethan style, now called 'The Gables', was built close to the line, however, along with a flint-faced house. Both buildings are said to be by Brunel.

The first plan for New Swindon

The Steventon and Moulsford buildings are important precursors of the cottages Brunel was to build at New Swindon from 1842. Many of the motifs evident at the two earlier stations – such as the elaborate chimneys, gabled projections, flat-arched doors and windows and slit openings – were to be repeated there.

At the board meeting of 6 October 1840 Brunel was instructed to have cottages, stabling and refreshment rooms built at the temporary Hay Lane (Wootton Bassett Road) station. He designed a row of twelve wooden cottages which were erected by Gandell. The single-storey cottages were designed to be removed to Swindon upon completion of the permanent station building there, but they remained at Hay Lane until the

1850s, when they were relocated to a site just off Eastcott Lane. They were demolished prior to 1939.[28] There is no known photographic record of them, but they were probably of very basic construction.

The first reference to the need for cottages at Swindon appears in the board minutes of 3 November 1840 when Brunel outlined his plans for housing the workforce and identified the best position for the new settlement.[29] Two pages in one of his sketchbooks of 1840, which probably predate the November meeting and are simply labelled 'Village', show him experimenting with possible layouts for the proposed cottage estate.[30]

One sketch shows small blocks of cottages with each block enclosing space for backyards. The blocks are packed tightly together and aligned so that their principal elevations would seem to be orientated east–west. The other sketch (**Fig 14**) shows long rectangular cottage blocks arranged in parallel lines either side of a central open space. Each block consists of two parallel terraces separated from each other by rear yards. The ends of each block facing the open space are shown hatched. Brunel's intention may have been to use these areas for shops or officers' dwellings. It is possible that he also intended these end blocks to be given a more elaborate architectural

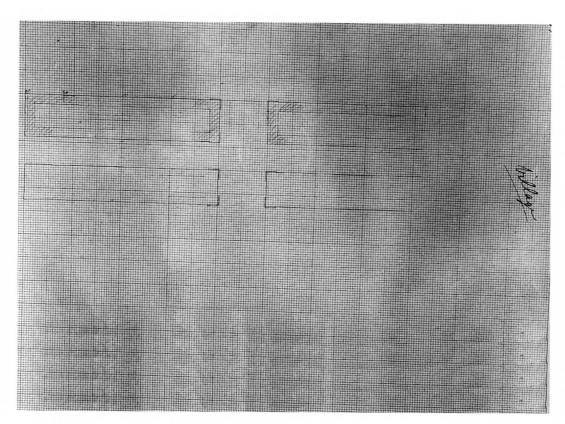

Fig 14 *This 1840 sketch by Brunel, simply labelled 'Village', shows terraces of cottages laid out to either side of a central open space to form a grid. The ends facing the centre are shown hatched, possibly indicating an intention to build officers' houses or shops in these positions. A larger version of this scheme was adopted by the GWR and built over the next fifteen years.*

treatment. Except for the ends of the blocks, the principal elevations appear to be aligned to face north or south.

This second scheme was the one Brunel submitted to the company, and a revised and expanded version of it was to be built over the next fifteen years. When complete, the plan of New Swindon was remarkably similar to Brunel's original concept. To him, therefore, must go the credit for the layout of one of Britain's best-preserved and architecturally most ambitious railway settlements.

Early in 1841 Brunel reported on the unfinished sections of line between Bath and Chippenham and expressed optimism that despite the 'continued wet weather at a critical period of the Works' the remaining 27 miles (43km) of the Great Western Railway, including Box Tunnel, would be completed by June.[1] In the event, the section from Hay Lane (Wootton Bassett Road) to Chippenham was opened separately on 31 May and the line was opened throughout on 30 June 1841.

Earlier in the year the directors had reported that the agreement to work both the Bristol & Exeter and the Cheltenham & Great Western Union railways would entail an increase in rolling stock and in its maintenance. They also confirmed their intention of siting the engine establishment and repairing shops and main refreshment rooms at Swindon, and arranging 'for the building of Cottages etc for the residence of many persons employed in the service of the company'.[2] The cottages and the station, with their refreshment

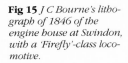

Fig 15 *J C Bourne's lithograph of 1846 of the engine house at Swindon, with a 'Firefly'-class locomotive.*

rooms, were to be built by the contractors, J D & C Rigby of Holywell Street, Westminster, at their own expense while the company was to pay only for the land and the works' buildings. At the time, this arrangement must have seemed an ingenious financial ploy, although it was to prove far from successful (see Chapter 3).

BRUNEL'S DESIGNS FOR THE WORKS

Over the next two years, Brunel and (to a lesser extent) Gooch were thus faced with several tasks: they had to design, construct and fit out a substantial engineering works, to be used for the maintenance and heavy repair of locomotives, and they had to provide a running shed for engines serving Bristol, London and Cheltenham. Brunel seems to have been open-minded on the question of the shape of the engine house. His sketchbooks show that, as well as a combination of rectangular elements, he was also considering 'round' engine houses with rectangular annexes

for the Bristol depot, similar to the 'round house' of over 200ft (61m) diameter sketched by Gooch to accompany his letter of September 1840 (see pp 6–7). However, he used only rectangular elements in his 1840 sketches for 'an engine house at W B Road' – the site where temporary workshops were to be built the following year. These preliminary sketches appear to show a running shed some 500ft (152·4m) long, backed by workshop blocks 210ft (64m) by 80ft (24·4m) and 380ft (115·8m) by 140ft (42·7m) with a further narrow workshop range 525ft (160m) long. The final sketch of the sequence shows similar elements arranged in a courtyard to the rear of the running shed (see Figure 5).

Whether the temporary facilities at Hay Lane followed these lines is not known, but it was certainly this arrangement that was translated, rather loosely, to Swindon as Bourne's description of 1845 verifies:

> At some distance west of the passenger station, on the north side of the line, is the Engine depôt; its arrangements are upon a large scale, and capable of accommodating about a hundred engines: these consist of the engines in actual use, of the stock of spare engines, and of those undergoing repair. At this station every train changes its engine, so that from this circumstance alone, at least twice as many engines are kept here as at any other part of the line.
>
> The engine shed is a rectangular building 490 feet [149·6m] long by 72 feet [21m] broad, and capable of holding upon its four lines of rails forty-eight engines and tenders; the two ends are open, the roof is of wood, slated, with louvres at intervals for the escape of the steam. The engines standing here are all in serviceable condition, and sufficient number of them are ready, with their steam up, to carry on the business of the Railway. In the centre of and at right angles to this shed, and abutting against its northern side, is the Engine house; this is an oblong room, 290 feet [88·4m] by 140 [42·7m], and divided by two rows of columns into three compartments; the engines stand in the side compartments, transversely, as horses in the stalls of a stable; and the central part, 50 feet [15·2m] broad, is occupied by a large platform, travelling on wheels from one end of the house to the other, and by means of which an engine can be readily transferred between the central part and any one of the stalls. Here the engines receive their lighter repairs, those which the enginemen themselves are for the most part capable of executing. The roof of this shed is of timber and wrought iron, covered in with slating; the stalls will contain thirty-six engines and tenders. At the northern end of the Engine house, are placed the buildings employed in the repairs of locomotive engine. The Erecting house in which the parts of the engine machinery, when repaired, are put together, is

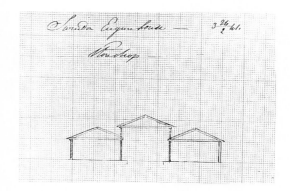

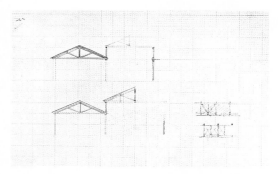

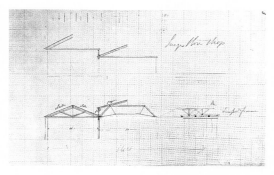

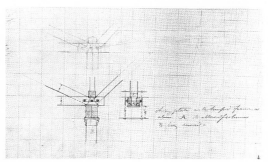

a building communicating with the Engine house, and capable of holding eighteen engines.[3]

Bourne's accompanying illustration (**Fig 15**) shows the working arrangement of the engine house or 'stable' while Brunel's private sketchbooks trace the evolution of the design of this building from a thumbnail sketch to some worked up in detail (**Fig 16**).[4] No clearer proof is needed

Fig 16 *A sequence of Brunel's 1841 sketches for the Swindon works' engine house, showing the development of his ideas, beginning with the main structural elements and proceeding through various arrangements of roof trusses, arriving at an approximation of the structure as actually built. Even at this stage Brunel was concerned with detail, as the dimensional sketch of the roof junction shows.*

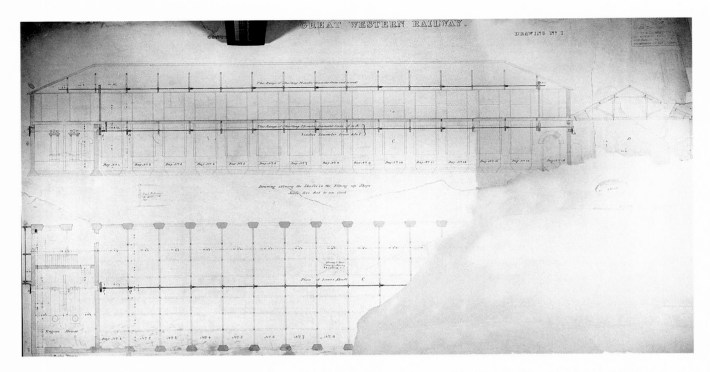

Fig 17 *A plan and section of the original fitting shop, showing the layout of the steam engines and line shaft.*

of Brunel's personal involvement in the initial design of the workshops.

Brunel's drawing office in Duke Street, Westminster, was responsible for translating these concepts into final contract-design drawings. It is intriguing to speculate on the extent of Gooch's input at this stage, for he certainly would have been concerned with the mechanical fitting-out of the workshops. In April 1841, to assist him in this task, he engaged the twenty-four-year-old

Archibald Sturrock, a friend from his days in the foundry at Dundee.

Machinery and fitting out

On 20 May 1841 a Memorandum of Agreement was made between the GWR and Joseph Whitworth & Co of Manchester 'to make, deliver and fix complete and in proper working order [machinery] at … the GWR Company's Engine Works at or near the Swindon junction of the

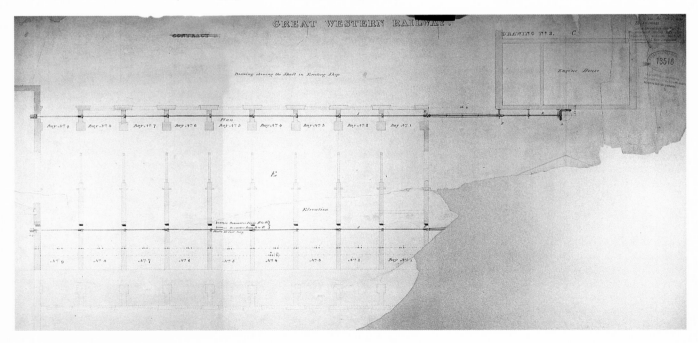

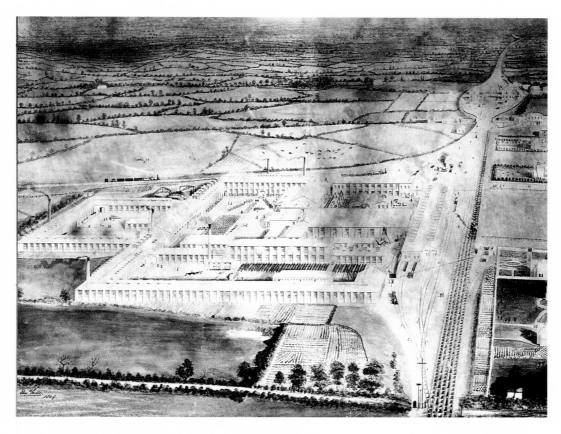

Cheltenham & Great Western Union Railway'. The memorandum specified that deliveries of light tools were to commence in January 1842 and that the whole of the machinery was to be delivered and fixed by March. There followed a detailed statement of the machinery, to a total value of £8,442, which included numerous common and self-acting slide lathes supplied by Joseph Whitworth & Co themselves, planing and drilling machines supplied by Messrs Nasmyth & Co and shearing and punching machines supplied by Messrs Sharp Roberts & Co. The GWR was responsible for all the necessary foundations and 'woodwork for hanging the shafting' and drawings have survived which were copied to Joseph Whitworth & Co to show these shafts in both the fitting shops and the erecting shop (**Figs 17** and **18**).[5] The erecting shop (see Figure 18) was equipped with a hand-operated, hydraulic, overhead travelling crane (see Figure 24) supplied to GWR specifications.

THE FIRST THREE BUILDING PHASES

No details have survived of the station and locomotive facilities provided at Hay Lane but J D & C Rigby, the contractors, were paid at least £1,200 between April and June 1841 for work at that site, while payments to them on 'account of Swindon

Engine House' started on 11 June.[6] However, *Herepath's Railway Magazine* noted in November 1841 that 'the whole of the locomotive department of the GWR [ie the running shed] has been removed from Wootton Basset [*sic*] to Swindon'.[7] As this move predated the delivery of the Whitworth machinery, it appears that the Hay Lane facilities must have been rather rudimentary at this time.

In the previous month Brunel had written to Gooch to the effect that, as 'the front shed of the Engine House at Swindon will be ready next week, all the lumber which now crowds the other Engine houses had better be sent there. The two front lines alone will hold 24 Engines and Tenders'.[8] Although the running shed was in operation by the end of 1841 the remainder of the works was still being built throughout 1842. The machinery was first started up on 28 November and the works were officially opened on 2 January 1843.

The works are shown in great detail in Edward Snell's two 1849 watercolour paintings of New Swindon. The earlier of the two paintings (**Fig 19**), which contains slightly more detail and may have been intended for Gooch, forms part of the collection of the Swindon Museum and Art Gallery in Bath Road. The other work is painted from the same viewpoint and would appear to be a copy

Fig 18 *(opposite) A part-plan and elevation showing the line shaft from the fitting shop beam-engine house to the locomotive-erecting shop. The drive spanned the gap between the buildings by what seems from the drawing to be a cruciform-sectioned shaft, 28ft 9in (8·8m) long. The instructions to Joseph Whitworth & Co, who installed the machinery, specify that the diameter of the shaft must decrease, in 30-ft (9·1-m) sections, as it progresses along the erecting shop.*

Fig 19 *(above) The Swindon works, as depicted in Edward Snell's painting of 1849 (detail).*

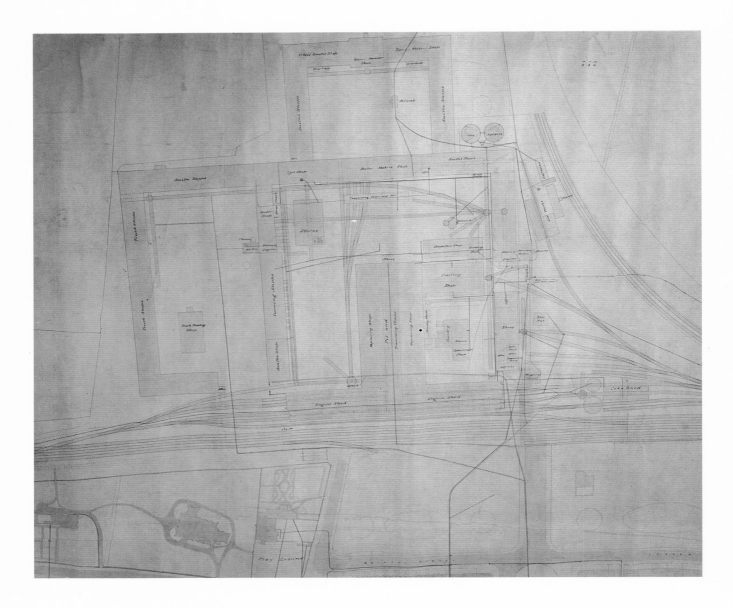

Fig 20 *A plan of the works, dated June 1846, but incorporating additions up to May 1847 (possibly the work of Edward Snell).*

made slightly later in the year for Brunel. The latter is deposited in the Great Western Railway Museum, Swindon. In the past, these paintings have been generally accepted as depicting the works in their original state. In fact, the paintings, which seem to be extremely accurate, show the works as they were after at least three separate building campaigns, involving numerous major and minor additions.

The buildings at the core of the works were originally built as a stabling, maintenance and heavy-repair facility for locomotives, with no provision for their manufacture. This complex, which also housed the locomotive department, comprised a three-sided courtyard open to the west. However, an urgent need for wagons meant that some of the facilities were used for wagon manufacture to the exclusion of their original purpose.

The second building campaign involved closing the courtyard by the provision of a range of new machine, fitting and smiths' shops to the west, and the addition of a courtyard to the north of the core quadrangle to house the smithies and steam hammers needed for locomotive construction. These additions were not completed until 1847. The third campaign, which overlapped the second, was to provide additional capacity, and this required further ranges of smiths' shops forming a second courtyard to the west of the core quadrangle.

All three building phases are shown on a plan first drawn in June 1846 (but incorporating additions up to May 1847) **(Fig 20)**, though the detailed drawings for the 'New

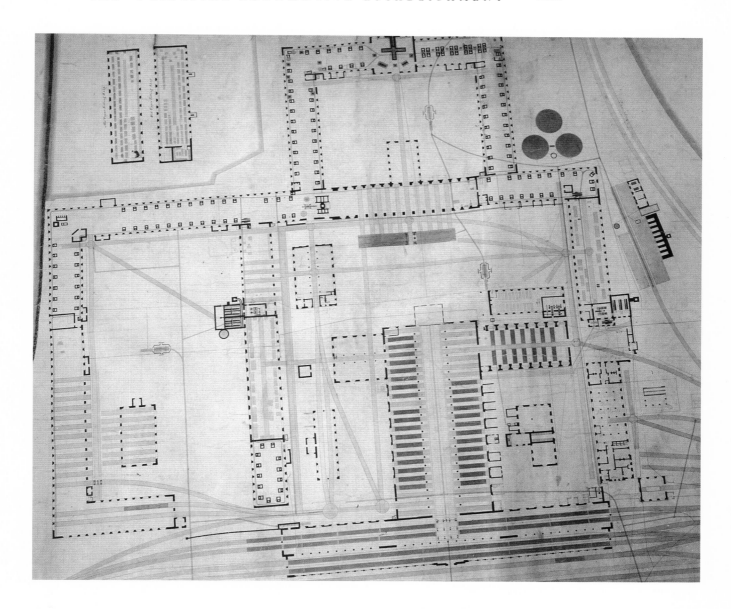

Works' of the third phase were only prepared at the end of April 1846 and it seems that construction continued until 1848.[9] For economic reasons, building work slowed drastically thereafter and only minor additions appear on a definitive plan of 1849 which corresponds to the Snell paintings (**Fig 21**).

These separate phases of development are illustrated in **Figure 22** and the various functions ascribed in the following sections are derived from annotations on the original design drawings allied to those on the 1846 plan. As the function and nomenclature of individual buildings changed over time, especially when extensive reorganisations took place within the works, caution must be exercised when dealing with sources of different dates.

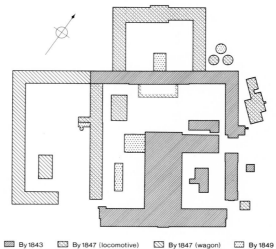

Fig 21 *(above) A plan of 1849, showing the interior layouts of all the Swindon workshops (possibly Edward Snell's last work for the GWR). The inset detail (top left) shows the upper floors of the old and new fitting shops.*

Fig 22 *(left) The development of the Swindon works, 1842–9.*

By 1843   By 1847 (locomotive)   By 1847 (wagon)   By 1849

THE LAYOUT OF THE WORKS IN 1843

Fig 23 *The running shed of 1841: (top) half-plan and elevations; (bottom right) east elevation and cross-section.*

Fig 24 *(bottom left) The hand-operated hydraulic overhead crane installed in the 1842 erecting shop.*

As we have seen, the earliest workshop complex at Swindon consisted of buildings ranged around three sides of a large square courtyard, measuring some 540ft (165m) square, based on the running shed (**Fig 23**) to the south and enclosing the engine shed and erecting shop described by Bourne, along with some ancillary structures at its eastern end.

The eastern side of the courtyard was formed of two distinct ranges, both of two storeys and 51ft (15·5m) wide, with the southern range 186ft (56·7m) long and the northern 202ft (61·6m) long. Despite the similarity in size these ranges were quite different in massing, arrangement and function. The original design drawings survive for these buildings (**Figs 24** to **27**) and subsequent plans show that the designs were adhered to fairly closely.

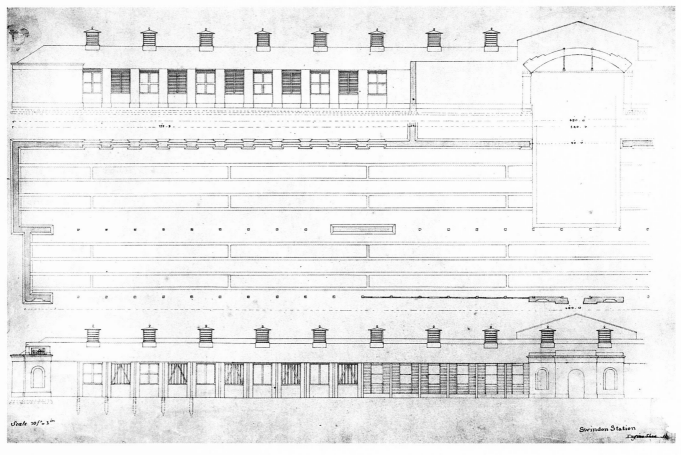

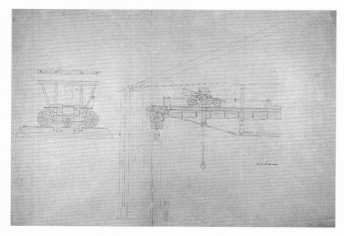

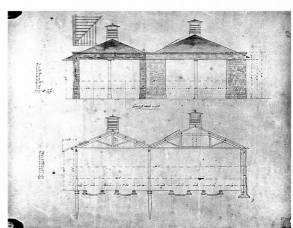

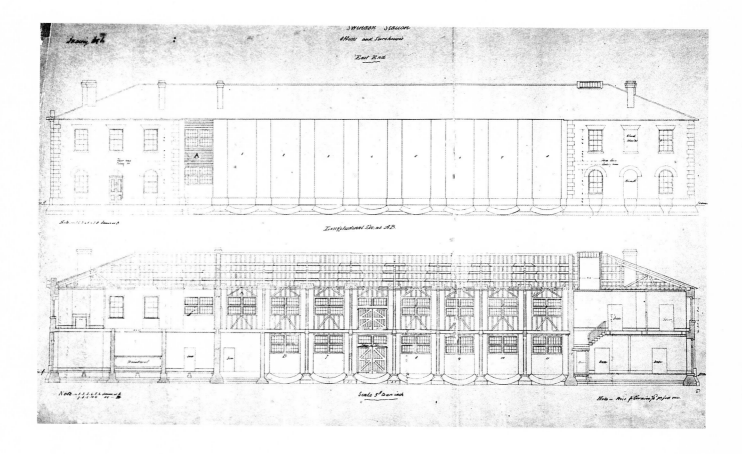

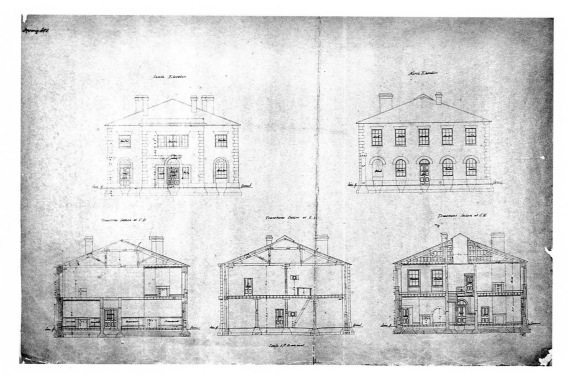

Fig 25 *(above) Design drawings of the general offices and storehouse: east elevation and long section.*

Fig 26 *(left) Design drawings of the general offices and storehouse: end elevations and cross-sections.*

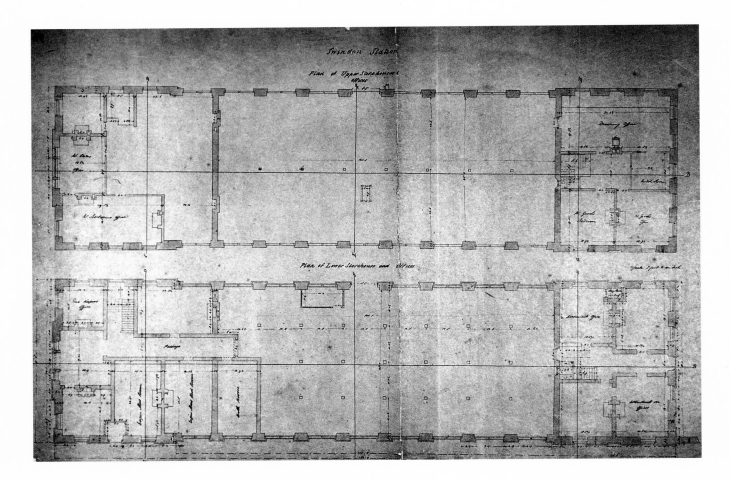

Fig 27 *Design drawings of the general offices and storehouse: plan at both levels.*

Offices, accommodation and stores

The southern range comprised three elements: pavilions of offices at each end separated by a store built in the distinctive pier-and-panel construction common to all the workshop buildings on the site. The composition was arranged to appear symmetrical with break-backs three bays from either end but the rooms in the southern pavilion extended one bay into the storehouse section.

The ground floor of the southern pavilion contained six rooms which included a time-keeper's office, a mess room and bedroom for 'enginemen' and, encroaching into the storehouse area, a large bathroom. This, if a later pencil-sketched annotation is correctly interpreted, may have contained eight bath stalls.

The upper floor housed the section of the locomotive department that was responsible for the operation of trains in the Swindon area. The plans show a large heated office for 'Mr Bertram' – the engineer with overall responsibility for the

section of line between Paddington and Swindon – and a smaller office for 'Mr Owen', local super-intendent of the section from Swindon to the Box Tunnel.[10] The main entrance was in the centre of the southern façade, while the time-keeper's office and the enginemen's suite had separate entrances.

The storehouse section occupied eight bays, and on the ground floor there were three ranks of wooden storey-posts providing intermediate support to the floor beams of 45-ft (13·7-m) span. The upper floor had only a single central rank of posts below the queen-post trusses.

The northern pavilion had a central entrance in the northern façade with a hallway leading to four offices, one of which was for the use of 'attendants on offices'. The upper floor contained an office and bedroom for Gooch himself, and a drawing office and model room. It would seem, therefore, that the original functions of these offices related to the working of the locomotive department in general rather than just the Swindon works.

The fitting shop

By contrast, the northern range on this eastern side was very much an integral part of the works. This conclusion is supported by the lettering system that was introduced as early as the 1840s to identify individual parts of the works, starting with 'A' for the running shed. In this sequence, the fitting and turning shops were ascribed the letter 'D' and, with the building of the second steam-driven fitting shop in 1846–7, the terms 'old D' and 'new D' shops were introduced. When originally built, the fitting shop held the main boilers and steam engines that provided the power and air blast to several other buildings (**Fig 28**). Built on the pier-and-panel principle, it had central rail access in its western side and was the only two-storey production building in the original works.

To carry a machine-bearing floor on the upper storey, Brunel used wooden floor trusses with underslung metal tie rods in preference to single wooden beams (**Figs 29** and **30**). These trusses have a web some 5ft (1·5m) deep with upper and lower beams 47ft (14·3m) in length and 11in by 6in (279mm by 52mm) in sections, connected by eight downward-tapering vertical struts spaced as

in Figure 29. Four of the six intermediate struts have iron vertical suspension rods against their outer faces. The intermediate struts are capped by metal plates which support longitudinal beams of 11in (279mm) depth, and there are half-depth beams in each of the wider spaces, giving a total of twelve longitudinal beams per bay. Twelve of these trusses have survived and this arrangement, though rather unsophisticated compared with later solutions engineered in metal, provides an interesting and early example of an unsupported heavy-machinery floor built over a clear-space lower floor measuring 175ft by 45ft (53·3m by 13·7m).

Engines and power transmission

This fitting shop was considerably taller than the southern range as the lower storey workshop was 18ft (5·5m) high to allow for a central line shaft supported some 14ft (4·3m) from the ground by the lower members of the floor trusses. The stairs and a pair of twin-columned beam engines were housed in separate compartments in the two southernmost bays, the engines sharing a 17ft 6in (5·3m) diameter flywheel located in a pit between them. Few technical details of the engines have

Fig 28 *Design drawings of the original fitting shop: west elevation plan, south elevation and cross-section.*

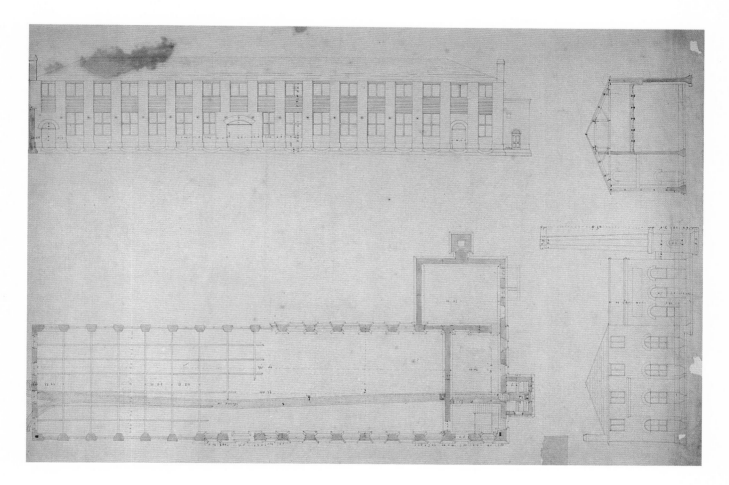

Fig 29 *(above) A 19th-century photograph showing the ground floor of the original fitting shop in use as a wheel shop. Note the deep, tensioned floor trusses and the later 'walking cranes'.*

Fig 30 *(right) A cross-section of the original fitting shop, showing a floor truss.*

been traced other than oblique references to 'the old Cornish engine and boilers' in later newspaper articles.[11] The former are described as a 'pair of large, low pressure, engines with 24-inch [609mm] cylinders and a 3-ft [914mm] stroke'. The name of the maker is known, however, for on 24 June 1842 the Bristol firm of Stothert & Slaughter was paid £900 for the 'fixed engines' at Swindon.[12]

Power was transmitted through the wall, and a drum on the horizontal line shaft drove a similar shaft in the upper floor. This arrangement was repeated in the northernmost bay, and the lower shaft continued, via a massive bearing box, through the northern gable wall to power the smiths' shops beyond. The engines also drove machinery in the erecting shop via a bevel gearing located on the outside of the southern wall. The arrangement is shown on diagrams which were copied to Joseph Whitworth & Co, the suppliers of machinery for the works (see Figures 17 and 18). It is likely that these engines also drove machinery in the adjacent carpenters' shop and grinding shop. Attached to the engine house was a blowing engine which provided blast, via a conduit below the fitting shop, to the hearths in the smiths' shops beyond.

Alongside the engine house was a stair compartment giving access to the upper floor of the fitting shop. Below the landing of this stair was a small wooden office, measuring 10ft by 10ft (3m by 3m), which, rather surprisingly, was occupied by the resident engineer, Archibald Sturrock, who was supervising the erection of the machinery. A newspaper article, admittedly written many years later, recounts an incident when a plank gave way on this landing as a heavy piece of metal was being 'lugged' across it, at which point the metal 'fell on, and smashed up, the desk at which Mr Sturrock was sitting'.[13]

The boiler house to the east of the engine house contained three Cornish boilers. Its roof carried a cast-iron water tank for which a contract was let in December 1842 to Barrett, Exall & Andrews for £830 on condition that 'they engage to complete the same in 10 weeks ... under a penalty of £10 per week for the first three weeks, £20 per week for every week afterwards'.[14] Clearly, the GWR was fairly desperate for the water supply to be assured, as by this time the works were in full operation.

Buildings to the north of the courtyard

On the northern side of the courtyard there seems to have been a continuous single-storey range some 600ft (182·9m) long, comprising a smiths' shop (198ft/60·4m long), which itself incorporated a spring shop (70ft/21·3m long), plus the boilermakers' shop (265ft/180·8m long) and a tyre shop (146ft/144·5m long). Three of the shops were a standard 50ft (15·2m) in overall width and some 17ft (5·2m) to the eaves, but the boilermakers' shop was 54ft (16·5m) wide and considerably taller, with clerestory windows above the arcading, which was designed to carry an overhead crane (**Fig 31**).

Fig 31 *The original boilermakers' shop in 1882. The travelling overhead crane appears to be the original one fitted in the mid 1840s.*

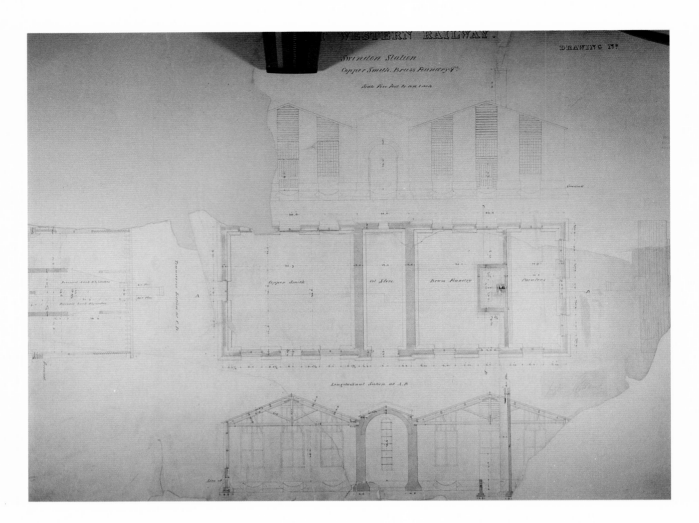

The smiths' shop contained eighteen hearths and a small foreman's office, and was ventilated by louvred wooden vents, as was the adjoining spring shop with its eight hearths. It seems, however, that the boiler shop was used for the fabrication of metal wagons soon after it was built and it was not for a couple of years that Gooch was able to reclaim it for its original purpose.[15]

In addition to the buildings in the centre of the courtyard that were described by Bourne, there was a foundry, with brass and coppersmiths' shops, in a block to the east of the engine shed (**Fig 32**), as well as a carpenters' shop and grinding shop in a block to the north of the erecting shop.

Coke and gasworks

The ancillary buildings to the east of the quadrangle consisted of a coke shed, a saw pit and a small gasworks, though probably not the one shown on the plan of 1846. Some form of gas production must have been available by April 1842 when, over seven nights, Minard Rea, the

works' manager, made 'observations on the consumption of coal gas by the eight burners in the Shed of the Engine House'.[16] The gasworks and holders shown on the 1846 plan are probably an enlarged version built around 1844 (see pp 34–5).

It is probable that coke for the locomotives was initially brought from Bristol, where the GWR had its own bank of coke ovens. These may be the coke ovens whose design appears in one of Gooch's earliest sketchbooks.[17] By April 1842 the anticipated increase in demand for coke required to supply the forges caused the GWR to seek tenders for the construction of coke ovens at Swindon, with separate tenders for the supply of the necessary ironwork. The tender for the former was let to Mr William Tiddy on condition that the whole was completed within two months. The contract for 'furnishing 32 sets of [wrought-iron] doors and [cast-iron] frames complete' was given to Messrs Bush & Beddoe on condition that they were supplied at the rate of at least six sets per week. If these contracts were successfully completed, a full bank of coke

Fig 32 *(above) Elevation, plan and section of the brass foundry and coppersmiths' shop, 1842. (opposite) Details of hearths for the coppersmiths' shop, 1842.*

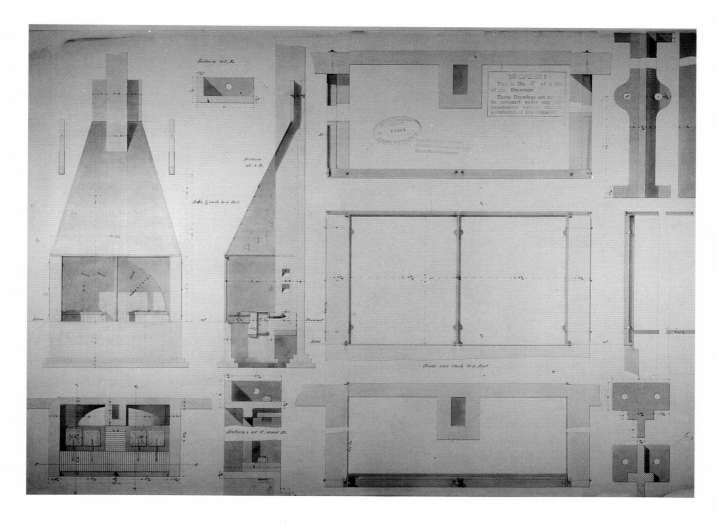

ovens would have been in operation by late summer and, as a by-product, they may also have supplied gas for the works.

THE FABRIC OF THE WORKS

The main contractors for the buildings of the Swindon railway works were J D & C Rigby. In the period from 11 June 1841 to 24 December 1842 they were paid some £35,000 in instalments, certified by company officials, for the 'Swindon Engine House'.[18] Payments were also made to subcontractors: £454 on 16 July 1841 to Barley Pegg & Co; £180 to Thomas Cooper in November 1841; £500 to Joel Spiller for ironwork (almost certainly for the iron components in the forges in the smiths' and coppersmiths' shops); and payments of £1,400, £1,000, £500 and £1,000 to E Oldham, 'on account of bricks delivered at Swindon', between October 1841 and April 1842.

Most of the works' buildings at this period were of stone, with red brick used only for the inverted arches at foundation level, the entrance arches and some window heads. It is therefore likely that most of the bricks delivered by E Oldham were destined for the coke ovens, the station and the internal walls of the railway village cottages, as well as the paving of the works, and the brick-lined drainage channels. Stone for the fabric of the original works' buildings came from the extensive quarries at the top of Kingshill, in old Swindon (see p 51), though use was also made of stone from quarries in the Bath and Corsham areas, and there are even blocks of Blue Lias and Pennant sandstone from further afield. Many, but by no means all, of the quoins are of Bath stone while most of the plinths are of Swindon stone. The office elevations facing the railway are predominantly of Bath stone, as were the panels at the ends of the running shed (see Figure 23).

The pier-and-panel construction so strikingly depicted in Snell's paintings may have been employed to save on materials and to minimise weight on rather uncertain clay foundations. The piers are connected at foundation level by inverted brick arches to give longitudinal stability. The floor beams in the store building, the floor trusses in the fitting shop and all the roof trusses were carried on these piers. The panels were originally infilled with weather-boarding and glazing, the latter being formed of vertical window bars with small overlapped glass panes.

The standard roof framing used in the works was a queen-post truss of 45-ft (13·7-m) span, of which examples survive in the fitting shop. For the wider span of the nave of the engine house, Brunel designed the elegant metal-tied wooden truss illustrated by Bourne (see Figure 15). As we have seen, Brunel's sketchbooks of 1841 show the evolution of this arrangement from a simple thumbnail sketch, showing only the relative proportions, to drawings which loosely resemble the roof as built (see Figure 16). The resident engineer was R J Ward who, from August 1841, submitted regular reports on building progress to the company, while Brunel's assistant, J W Hammond, was involved intermittently. Brunel himself was ultimately responsible for supervising and approving all the work.

This, then, was the complex deemed necessary to service the running of 181 miles (290km) of mainline railway in 1843. With Brunel's flair and concern for detail, allied to Gooch's experience of working in innovatory northern factories, the works must have been as advanced as any in the country as far as layout and machinery were concerned, if not in architectural pretension and construction. The relative meanness in the construction of the Swindon buildings, when compared with those at Derby, may simply reflect a difference in the amount of capital available. It was thus ironical that, almost as soon as the complex was completed – and despite a minor period of retrenchment by the company in 1843 – a change in strategic requirements was to cause a considerable expansion of the facilities on the site.

THE 1843 FINANCIAL REVIEW

Shortly after the works opened at the beginning of 1843 the GWR, having greatly overspent on capital works, was forced to take stock of its financial position. A company report was drawn up to consider various measures involving the 'retrenchment of Expenditure', including Brunel's future role with the GWR, rationalisation within the Locomotive Establishment and the implications of its centralisation in Swindon. The report recognised that:

> it would be impossible to secure the undivided attention and Services of Mr Brunel for any reasonable Scale of Salary, which the Company could with propriety afford to give – but if it be thoroughly

understood that he is to apply regularly and methodically about one half of his time to the Official Duties of controlling and regulating the Works in the Swindon Establishment, of watching and keeping down the Expenditure both in the Locomotive Department and in the maintenance of Way and Works and of attending the Directors to receive their Instructions in respect to those Matters ... it is the conviction of the Sub-committee that great benefit will derive from the continuance of Mr Brunel's connection with the Company, at a Salary of £1000 per Annum.[19]

As regards rationalisation in the locomotive department the report commented that the removal of 'Repairing Establishments' to Swindon and the concentration of work there, with 'good Shops and Tools', would reduce dependence on outside manufacturers and result in a reduction in overtime working. The recent lowering of wages had already resulted in a reduction in staff numbers, and it was anticipated that the introduction of piece-work, instead of day labour, would also effect a further saving.

The report appended an 'Estimate for the Locomotive Establishment for 1843' which showed a total of 423 staff. More than half of these (243) were concerned with the running of the train service – not just in Swindon but throughout the system – but most of the remaining 180 staff must have been employed at the works. Sixty were general labourers (or boys paid less than 2s per week) but the rest were skilled workers, including fifty-five fitters, erectors and millwrights, fourteen blacksmiths, fourteen strikers, ten turners, seven machinists, six carpenters and pattern-makers, four boilermakers and wheel-makers, three stationary-engine men, two spring-makers, two coppersmiths, two painters and one brass founder.

THE INTRODUCTION OF LOCOMOTIVE MANUFACTURE

Despite the cautious subcommittee review, there was to be a considerable expansion at the works over the next few years as the implications of the expanding network and traffic bore in on the GWR. From 1844, the country was gripped by 'railway mania', a period of intense speculation in railway stocks and shares. Over the next four years some 9,000 miles (14,400km) of new railway lines were sanctioned – more than four times the existing mileage. Although by no means all of these lines were built, the total mileage opened rose from just over 2,000 (3,200km) in 1844 to nearly 6,000 (9,600km) by the end of the decade. This threefold increase required a commensurate increase in rolling stock which was quite beyond the capabilities of the established locomotive manufacturers to provide. The resulting problem and response were summed up in 1850 by Dr Dionysius Lardner, a noted 19th-century pundit:

In the first instance, they [the railway proprietors] derived their supply of drawing and carrying stock from the established manufactories of engines and carriages in various parts of the country. The demand, however ... multiplied with unparalleled rapidity ... and the established manufacturers were utterly unable to meet demands so extensive ... Under these circumstances the railway companies saw themselves reduced to the alternative, either of suspending their progress, or fabricating for themselves. They, of course, adopted the latter measure, and proceeded to erect extensive Works for the manufacture of engines and carriages, at convenient points upon the principal lines.[20]

Lardner illustrated his point by reference to the London & North Western Railway Company's works at Crewe, Wolverton and Longsight (Manchester), which supplied stock for the company's own 450 miles (720km) of line and for some 220 miles (352km) of other companies' lines. He claimed that these three factories had 'absorbed a capital of nearly half a million sterling'.

At Swindon the process of self-sufficiency had begun in a small way in 1843 with the manufacture of wagons. In October of that year an order was placed 'for the construction of 18 wagons in iron to be made at Swindon in addition to those already ordered'.[21] These were evidently being made in the building originally intended as the boilermakers' shop. This situation was evidently to persist for some time, since the following November the general committee approved the invitation of tenders from 'good makers for six boilers for the six new Goods engines which are proposed to be built at Swindon', adding the rider that the 'Company's Premises are at present inadequate – while constructing the Waggons etc already ordered'.[22] The committee also approved the construction of carriage and wagon shops 'to cost £970', in addition to the already contracted gasworks and coke ovens.[23]

It is clear from the above documents that, by the end of 1844, the GWR was intent on manufacturing its own engines but did not have specialised facilities for so doing, a state of affairs that was to be rectified in 1845. First, in January of that year, the purchase of a steam hammer, from Messrs Nasmyth & Co, was authorised at a cost of £300.[24] This was accompanied by an order to Mr Napier for an 'engine traversing frame' and a 'hydraulic lifting apparatus' for the erecting shop, at a cost of some £800.[25] Napier's itemised account shows that installation of the traversing

frame started in May while the lifting apparatus was supplied in August. The work was certainly finished in September when Gooch commented favourably on its operation to Hammond.[26]

The 'Gauge Question' and the 'Great Western'

A letter written from Gooch to Hammond on 29 October is of far greater import. First, Gooch complains of the contractor's slow progress in completing the new smiths' shops, there being only three men employed on its construction instead of the thirty he thinks would be reasonable. The delay, he says, is holding up the building of forty-eight carriages, as well as retarding work on the wagons. He expresses the view that somebody else ought to be given the contract for 'the intermediate shop'. Then Gooch says that he has 'arranged with Mr Brunel to build a little engine [an ironic reference to what was, in fact, a very large locomotive] with an 8-foot [2·4⁻m] driving wheel (this I know will please you) and a 6-foot [1·8-m] fire box – the great object of building her is to have her ready to start when the Gauge Question commences in Parliament next session or on the first of April'.

Gooch goes on to say that having the 'little engine' built would be dependent on the rapid completion of the boiler-shop crane, and that he intends to see Napier about this. He acknowledges that laying rails on the walls for the overhead travelling crane would halt the wagon work going on in the boiler shop, but he says that 'the advantage of the large [ie the 'little'] engine will be thrown away if we do not get her by April'.[27] Indeed, on the same day that Gooch wrote this letter, Edward Snell, head draughtsman in the drawing office, 'commenced drawings of the Great Western', as Gooch's 'little engine' was to be named.[28]

Edward Snell

Edward Snell is an interesting character who has hitherto received only slight mention in the affairs of the Swindon railway works (principally as the author of the 1849 watercolour paintings – see Figure 19 – of the works).[29] He arrived in Swindon on 28 February 1843, at the age of twenty-two, having undergone his apprenticeship in engineering with Henry Stothert of Bath. He started work in Swindon on 1 March as a fitter at £2 per week and then, over the next two years, was successively an erector, inspector of engines and draughtsman, becoming head draughtsman in August 1845 at two guineas per week.

In April 1846 he was sent on a business trip to visit some northern manufacturers, including Joseph Whitworth & Co's factory in Manchester, Jackson's Rolling Mills in Salford and the Haigh Foundry in Wigan. Snell went via Gloucester and Birmingham on the way north, and came back via

Liverpool, Birkenhead, Chester and Crewe. On his return, at the end of the month, he immediately 'commenced drawings of the New Shops'. On 31 August 1846 he was made Superintendent of New Works at £2 15s per week and on 8 November was made 'general superintendent [sic] of the factory' – in other words, assistant to Archibald Sturrock, the works' manager.

By January 1846 further tools and machinery had been ordered, costing £2,658, and progress on the locomotive side of the building works must have been satisfactory as *Premier*, the first of the Swindon-built 0-6-0 goods engines, was completed in mid February, equipped with one of the boilers ordered from outside makers. More importantly, the *Great Western* was ready by the end of April and so outclassed her standard-gauge rivals in the trials of the following months that her performance proved a persuasive advocate for the GWR's adherence to the broad gauge. In August, Brunel was instructed 'to make arrangements with competent contractors' for the enlargement of the works as 'shown on the Plan' (ie the one drawn up in 1846, but amended in 1847), Brunel having stated that the estimate for the construction of the whole, 'including new tools and machinery ... amounts to the sum of £70000'.[30]

EXPANSION, 1845–1847

The building campaigns of 1845 through to 1847 are encapsulated in the amendments to the plan of 1846 (see Figure 20), from which it can be seen that the works were almost doubled in size during this period. The western side of the courtyard was closed to form a quadrangle by the construction of a new range, 460ft (140·2m) in length, the northern section of which consisted of a single-storey tender shop only 36ft (11m) wide. Attached to the south was an engine and boiler house for the stationary steam engine that powered the new parts of the works and provided blast to the new hearths. This was probably the 30-in (762-mm) cylinder Cornish beam engine known to have been supplied by Harveys of Hayle.[31]

To the south was a large two-storey range containing fitting and turning shops. This block seems to have been virtually identical in dimensions to the original fitting-shop block on the eastern side of the courtyard, as is shown by the comparative plans of the upper floors inset on the 1849 plan (see Figure 21). At the southern end there was a single-storey smiths' shop, 110ft (33·5m) long, containing thirteen hearths.

The traverser, outside the boiler shop, is shown in place as are the arcaded piers for the travelling overhead crane. An illustration of the boiler-makers' shop was published in *The Illustrated Exhibitor* in 1852 showing the arcading, a section of which allowed access to the traversing table in the yard. The accompanying article also shows a reheating furnace and a tyre being expanded in the adjoining tyre shop (see Figures 79 and 80).

In the north-western corner of the main courtyard, a large rectangular stores building has been added, with somewhat better office accommodation for Sturrock, now the works' manager, in its south-eastern corner. Initially this consisted of two rooms to the east of the wide-arched entrance which gave rail access to the stores, but, by 1849, a further two rooms had been provided to the west of the entrance. The change in Sturrock's title – from resident engineer to works' manager – occurred in 1843 and is significant. Originally Sturrock, whom Snell describes in his diary as 'young ... and rather swellish', had been engaged by Gooch to oversee the erection of machinery and it is apparent, from a caustic remark made by Brunel to Gooch, that the post of resident engineer was a temporary one, and not a company appointment.[32] Sturrock's translation to works' manager must have relieved Gooch of many of the onerous day-to-day tasks to do with the supervision of the works, and it explains why Gooch was able to resist pressure to move to Swindon.

The northern courtyard

A new courtyard, to the north of the main quadrangle, was created to provide the extra facilities needed to manufacture entire locomotives. To the east, a range of standard width (45 ft/13·7m) housed additional smiths' forges, while the adjacent section of the northern range housed the spring-makers. The present hipped roof over the eastern range is lightly framed by wrought-iron members. If the roof is original, as seems likely, the trusses were probably part of the consignment supplied by the well-known contractors, Fox Henderson, who were to be greatly involved in the construction of the buildings for the Great Exhibition a few years later. Charles Fox, when he was resident engineer to the London & Birmingham Railway, had built similar roofs of 40-ft (12·2-m) span over the train sheds at Euston Station in 1837, but these have long since gone.[33]

In order to accommodate the Nasmyth steam hammers, the central section of the northern side was built considerably wider. From the 1852 illustration (see Figure 79) this appears to have had a lightly framed iron roof of some 60-ft (18·3-m) span, probably also supplied by Fox Henderson. The adjoining standard-width range contained the wheelsmiths' shop, while the western range housed yet more smiths' forges.

The western courtyard

Another new courtyard, to the west of the main quadrangle, was dedicated to the manufacture and maintenance of wagons, and this seems to be

Fig 33 *A 1994 photograph of the former 1877 'K' shop (coppersmiths'), looking north. This view was taken from the southern end of the 1846–7 wagon paint shop, which was incorporated in the 1877 range. Two of the original open arches (on the left) and four of the five original Fox Henderson roof trusses of the paint shop can be seen nearest to the camera.*

the section of the works of most immediate concern to Snell. Its northern side was 305ft (93m) long, its western side 520ft (158·5m) long and the southern return 180ft (54·9m) long; all these ranges were of the standard 45-ft (13·7-m) internal width. The northern range and the northern part of the western range were occupied by smiths' shops and the remainder were truck (wagon) shops. The southern twelve bays of the western truck-shop range were open to the east, with individual rail access to each bay. The southern range had two sets of longitudinal rails, with a long inspection pit below the northern set.

Facing the open bays of the western range, and linked to them by rails, was a paint shop, 100ft by 55ft (30·5m by 16·8m), with open bays to the west

and a hipped roof. The roof framing of this block was somewhat different from that of any other on the site, probably because of the high risk of fire in the painting process. The metal trusses supported metal purlins to give them better fireproof qualities (though it is not known what material was used for covering the roof). These trusses were almost certainly supplied by Fox Henderson as part of a consignment paid for in 1847.

The paint shop was subsequently altered and extended but all five trusses have survived *in situ*, incorporated into a group of roof trusses dating from the 1870s (**Fig 33**). Although they no longer support hipped ends the outer trusses have complicated provision for the iron framing of such ends (**Fig 34**). The members in tension consist of

Fig 34 *The Fox Henderson roof truss that frames the former southern hip of the 1846–7 wagon paint shop (now part of 'K' shop).*

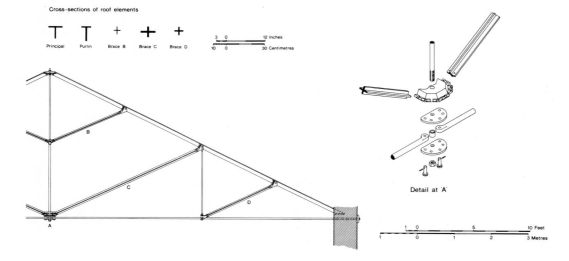

Cross-sections of roof elements

Principal Purlin Brace B Brace C Brace D

3 0   12 Inches
10 0   30 Centimetres

B

C

D

A

Detail at 'A'

1 0   5   10 Feet
1 0   1   2   3 Metres

round-section iron rods, while the two pairs of inclined struts are cruciform in cross-section. The principal rafters are larger T-section iron members, with slotted brackets for three ranks of T-section iron purlins.

By September 1847, the GWR had paid Fox Henderson the considerable sum of £11,810 for iron roofs, and the only roofs specifically mentioned in the accounts are those at Swindon. It seems likely, therefore, that most, if not all, of the western courtyard had iron roof trusses.[34] Some early iron trusses, identical to those in the northern courtyard, survive in the truncated remnants of the truck-shop ranges and these may also be original.

It has already been noted that the hipped roof of the two-storey turning and fitting shop was framed by conventional wooden queen-post trusses (**Fig 35**), but the multiple-pitched roof of the iron store was framed by king-post trusses. The latter building was greatly altered around 1889, when it was converted into prestigious offices, but the southern two bays, which housed the works' manager's office from 1847, retain their

original roof. The use of such a wide variety of roof trusses over the comparatively short period from 1841 to 1847 is revealing. The construction of traditional wooden roofs in the same building campaign as advanced iron-framed trusses indicates a willingness to experiment that is consistent with the GWR's general approach under Brunel and Gooch. The use of metal trusses for areas of high fire risk (such as the smiths' shops and paint shops), and the combination of metal and wood for buildings with exceptionally wide roof spans, also indicates an open-minded appreciation of the merits of suiting form to function (**Fig 36**).

The expansion of the Swindon works called for the provision of better services, and in September 1844 the general committee accepted three tenders for the erection of new gasworks and coke ovens to the east of the existing works. The construction of the gasworks was let in two contracts: one, worth £499 10s, went to Thomas Cooper for the buildings; the other, worth £2,525, went to Messrs Strode & Ledger for the machinery and for the mains to supply the works, the railway village and

Fig 35 *The 1846 turning and fitting shop in 1985, showing (at the far end) a different heavy-duty load-bearing floor truss from that used in the 1842 fitting shop.*

the station. A third contract was given to John Cox of Bristol for the construction of four patent coke ovens, designed to produce coke for the locomotives and purified gas for the company's gasholders.[35] The plan of 1846 shows two gasholders to the north east of the works while the plan of 1849 shows an additional holder.

FINANCIAL CRISIS

In the period 1845 to 1847 the accounts show a large number of relatively small payments to several contractors for construction work at the 'New Works', and it appears that, dissatisfied with J D & C Rigby's performance as a single large contractor (see Chapter 3), the company assumed direct control of the building campaigns over this period. Snell, writing retrospectively in 1849, claims that, in 1848, there were still 'about 200 hands employed under me building New Works, all hurry and bustle'. Later in the year, when 'the effects of the railway panic were felt at Swindon' he had to 'sack the hands and [we have] had 3 or 4 sweeping sacks through the shops since'. In fact, all major expansion came to a halt as a result of the financial crisis that began to affect the whole country from 1847, and Snell himself returned to working in the drawing office.

The trade depression which followed the financial crisis explains why the 1849 plan of the Swindon workshops shows only minor additions to the work completed in 1847 (compare Figures 20 and 21). Snell's 1849 paintings of New Swindon were probably his last work for the company and they may have been commissioned to give him something useful to do in slack times. This may also account for the production in the drawing office of a very detailed plan of the works at the same date. Snell, disillusioned at Sturrock's decision to reduce his pay from £2 15s to £2, resigned in May 1849 and emigrated to Australia later in the year.[36]

The company's financial retrenchment involved substantial wage cuts and soon led to the defection of Sturrock and of Seymour Clarke, the traffic superintendent of the London division, who both went to the Great Northern Railway in 1850. The GWR became so alarmed at these resignations that officers' salaries were restored to their former levels in June that same year. Even so, the depression of 1847–9 brought to a close Brunel's intimate involvement in the construction of the works and, with the completion of the first main building phase, it was clear that the GWR had over-extended itself in the provision of facilities at Swindon. The consequences of this will be considered in Chapter 4, but it is now time to return to the other developments that took place at New Swindon during the 1840s.

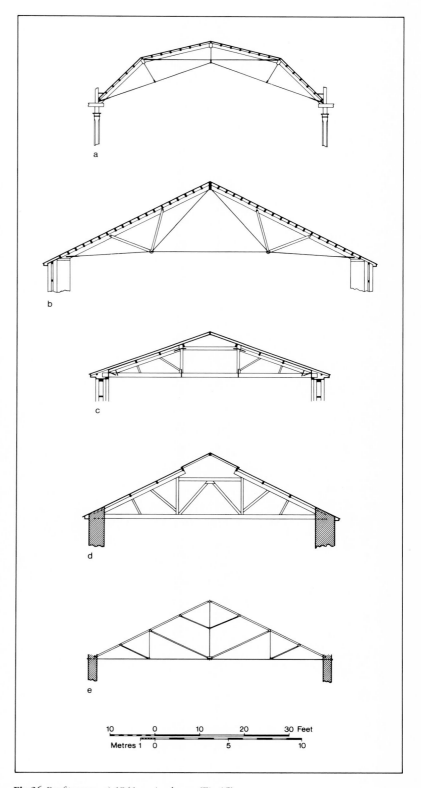

Fig 36 *Roof trusses: a) 1841 engine house (Fig 15);*
b) 1842 erecting shop (Fig 80 and Peck 1983, plate 21);
c) standard roof of 1842 (Figs 29 and 30);
d) 1842 boilermakers' shop (Figs 31 and 79);
e) 1846–7 wagon paint shop (Fig 34).

3 *The Creation of New Swindon, 1841–1849*

The massive amount of additional capital required by the Great Western Railway to complete the line (nearly twice the £3,333,333 authorised under the original Act)[1] prevented it from funding the construction of Swindon station, or the planned railway workers' village, from its own resources. Instead, on 2 February 1841, the GWR entered into an agreement with J D & C Rigby for the latter to build these vital facilities at their own expense, in return for various financial advantages (see below and p 42). The GWR provided the land for the new buildings and Brunel was personally responsible for the layout of the new settlement. He was also to design the station and the first block of cottages. The rest of the cottages in the railway village were most probably designed by his staff, though Brunel would have been involved because, as Company Engineer, he was responsible for approving all contract work carried out by Rigbys, and by other building firms.

SWINDON STATION

As part of the agreement of 2 February 1841, Rigbys were to build Swindon station at their own expense, in return for the profits derived from the refreshment rooms and hotel business to be carried out there. To sweeten the offer, the GWR agreed to stop all trains at the station for ten minutes so that passengers could take refreshments. Such facilities were considered necessary since, at that time, the journey from Paddington to Bristol lasted approximately four hours. Locomotives had to be changed at Swindon for the first few years, so the ten-minute stop also coincided with the GWR's own operational requirements. Swindon was to be the only station between Paddington and Bristol where refreshments could be obtained. Rigbys could therefore look forward to the enjoyment of a monopoly, a situation made even more attractive by the lease of the refreshment rooms for ninety-nine years at

Fig 37 *A watercolour, executed around 1841 in Brunel's office, showing the ground plan and south elevation of the northern block of Swindon station. The covered walkway between the blocks is shown in section at first-floor level.*

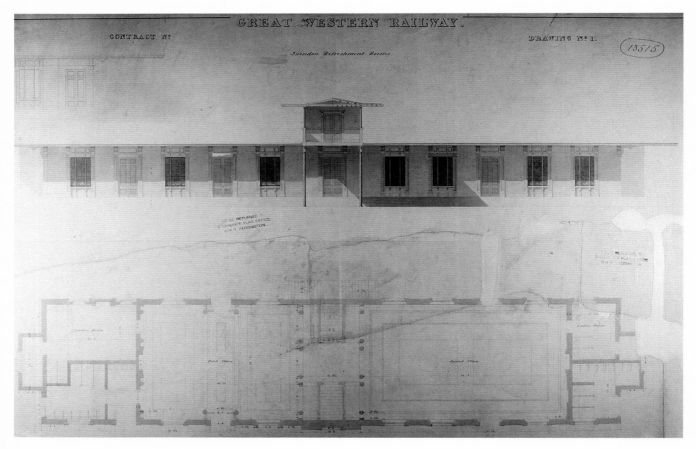

an annual rental of one penny. However, Rigbys were first required to spend about £15,000 on the construction of the building, a very substantial sum at the time, and a clear signal of the GWR's determination to provide services of the highest quality for the travelling public.

Two other London contractors – William Chadwick, the builder of the Maidenhead Viaduct, and Bailey Shaw & Smith – competed with Rigbys for the lucrative contract. No details of the respective offers are given in the directors' minutes, but it is likely that Rigbys were chosen on the strength that they were engaged in building another substantial station for the GWR at Slough, and had already built all the stations between Steventon and Corsham.[2]

The plans for Swindon station were prepared in Brunel's office (**Figs 37** and **38**). The building consisted of two separate blocks (each 170ft (51·8m) long and 37ft (11·3m) wide),[3] connected by a covered walkway at first-floor level. The walkway enabled passengers travelling between London, Bristol and Cheltenham to change trains or to obtain access to the Queens Royal Hotel from the first floor of each block (**Fig 39**). Access to the hotel could also be gained from stairs on each platform. Identical refreshment rooms were provided at ground-floor level in each building.

There were very few precedents for station refreshment rooms and hotels at that time. Brunel was probably influenced by the Wolverton station refreshment rooms of 1840 which were contained in two separate blocks, one each for the up and down platforms, although we do not know enough about the internal arrangement of the refreshment rooms there to confirm this.

The design of the station

On 10 January 1842 Brunel wrote to Francis Thompson, the North Midland Railway's architect, requesting that the latter invoice him 'for the time and trouble and expenses incurred by you on the subject of the refreshment rooms'.[4] Thompson had designed similar buildings in the past at Derby (including the Midland Hotel) and he may even have worked on the Wolverton refreshment rooms. The nature of his contribution to the design of Swindon station is undocumented, but the absence amongst the Brunel office drawings of external elevations and plans for the first floor of the building may be an indication that these were drawn by Thompson. Furthermore, Brunel's specification for the buildings makes no mention of the hotel at first-floor level. Thompson may also have given advice on the opulent interior decoration, an area in which Brunel would have had relatively little experience.

Fig 38 *The ground plans of the two station blocks, depicted around 1841. These are identical, but are orientated differently. The marble counters that were later built on either side of the central colonnade are not shown on the plans.*

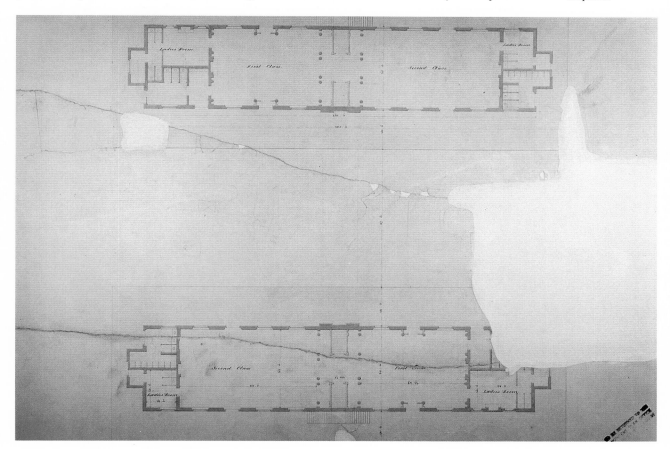

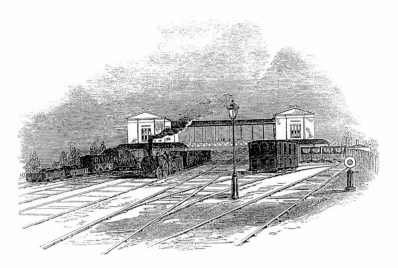

Fig 39 *Swindon station from the west in 1845.*

Fig 40 *(below) The refreshment-room kitchen in the basement of one of the station blocks, photographed around 1911 (by courtesy of the National Railway Museum, York).*

Fig 41 *(opposite above) A view looking towards the east end of the first-class refreshment room in the southern block of Swindon station. This picture dates from 1852, when Queen Victoria and Prince Albert (whose initials can be seen over the doors) stopped at Swindon en route to Scotland from the Isle of Wight. According to the description which accompanied this somewhat idealised portrayal of the station interior, 'the workmen in the employ of the company were out in great numbers, and contributed to the general display'.*

Fig 42 *(opposite) An internal elevation of the northern block of the station, showing the first-class refreshment room on the left, the second-class room on the right and a section through the two ranges. The water-colour drawing (of around 1841) is signed by Brunel and by J D & C Rigby, the contractors.*

The station buildings were loosely classical in their massing and general proportions (see Figure 39). They had a prominent cornice and pedimented end elevations containing square bays. The tripartite windows in the first-floor bays had simplified neo-classical surrounds, not unlike those used by Francis Thompson around the paired doors of the railway houses at Derby.

The buildings were constructed of Swindon stone, a calcareous sandstone obtained from the extensive quarries in old Swindon. The external walls were originally rendered, perhaps because of the difficulties associated with dressing this hard stone to the high degree of finish deemed necessary for buildings of this quality. Rendering may also have been used to disguise the irregular colouration of Swindon stone, which contains blue and grey veins.

According to Bourne, each block comprised a basement containing kitchens, cellars and accommodation for the refreshment-room attendants (**Fig 40**).[5] At ground-floor level, passengers alighting from trains were protected from the weather by a timber-framed canopy containing pendent lamps hung at intervals between the skylights. The platform floors were surfaced with 'asphalt and stone applied in an ingenious manner'.[6]

From the platforms, passengers had direct access to the first and second-class refreshment rooms. In accordance with Brunel's specification of 27 February 1841, the first-class refreshment rooms were 'to be handsomely fitted up' (**Figs 41 and 42**). The columns and pilasters were to be of scagliola (imitation marble) and a large marble chimney-piece, with handsome stove and a glass overmantel, was to be provided. The walls were richly decorated and the scheme was described in the *Devizes & Wiltshire Gazette* as follows:

> The style is that of the arabesque, following in some degree the character of the ornament in the ancient Roman baths, but partaking of more modern effects and rich contrast of colours prevailing at the Cinque de Cento period. The panels of the walls are beautifully painted in arabesque illustrating the seasons and their various attributes. The decorations of the ceilings and the richly relieved carved figures of the several compartments are in good taste.[7]

In 1842, J C Loudon, the influential landscape gardener and writer of architectural pattern-books, was much impressed with the design and decoration of the new station:

On both sides of the Swindon station, the country is flat and apparently uninteresting; but the station itself is the handsomest we have yet seen. At this station, which is considered half-way between London and Taunton, there are four large refreshment rooms, two on each side of the road, of noble proportions, and finished in the most exquisite style; with the walls paneled, Sylvester's fireplaces, and beautifully painted ceilings. Such rooms cannot fail greatly to improve the taste of every one who enters them; and, in this respect alone, the proprietors of the rail-road are entitled to the best thanks of the country. The railroad buildings on this, and indeed on every line, afford fine examples of beauty arising from no other consideration than that of fitness for the end in view.[8]

This contemporary account underlines the GWR's intention to fit the building out in the most lavish manner possible, and the *Devizes & Wiltshire Gazette* likened the interiors of the refreshment rooms to those 'of a first-rate hotel'. Much of the plate once belonged to George IV, and the china was 'of the costliest description'. In Brunel's specification, the first-class water closets were 'to be such as are used in the London Club Houses' and the furniture was to consist of 'handsome oak chairs, tables and sideboards'.

The second-class refreshment rooms were considerably plainer (see Figure 42). The dado and other woodwork were of grained oak and the walls were distempered or papered. The ceilings were coved but not painted, and the floors covered with 'oil cloth' (a precursor of linoleum) instead of carpet.

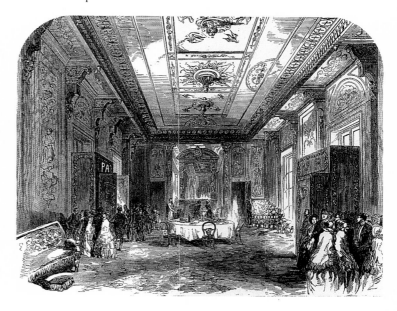

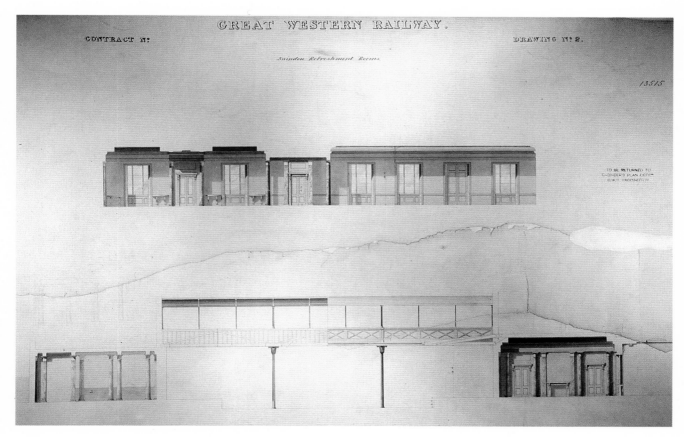

Separating the first and second-class refreshment rooms, in both blocks, was a colonnade formed of two rows of columns. Oval-shaped marble counters placed between the columns were used by the numerous attendants for serving food (most commonly sausage rolls and pork pies) and drinks (such as stout, tea and brandy). Doorways in the area enclosed by the oval counters led to the servants' staircase, giving access to the kitchens in the basement and to the hotel on the floor above.

Little is known of the arrangement or appearance of the hotel rooms themselves, except that the bedrooms were situated in the north block, while the block on the southern side of the line contained sitting-rooms and a coffee room.[9]

Poor service and overcharging

The station was opened on 14 July 1842 following an inspection of the new buildings by the Duke of Cambridge and the directors of the GWR. It seems, however, that refreshment rooms had already been operating from a temporary station building at Swindon prior to this date. These were administered by Samuel Young Griffiths, Manager of the Queen's Hotel, Cheltenham, who sublet the refreshment rooms and hotel business from Rigbys on 24 December 1841.[10] The sublease was for a term of seven years at an annual rental of £1,100 and an additional consideration of £6,000. The latter provided Rigbys with a substantial sum which could be offset against their considerable expenditure on the construction of the permanent station.

Griffiths was an absentee manager who sought to recoup his investment by charging high prices for refreshments and by skimping on the level of service provided. Bad management was to be a feature of the refreshment rooms throughout most of the 1840s, and, despite their lavish character, they soon achieved notoriety amongst rail travellers. The directors attempted to rectify the situation as early as 1 February 1842, when the business was still being carried out at the temporary station, but Rigbys and Griffiths simply ignored their demand for improvements. Typical of the complaints made to the directors was this letter, written on 1 March 1843, from a disgruntled passenger, writing under the pseudonym 'Mercator', and sent to the chairman of the GWR, Charles Russell:

> We arrived at Swindon where we disbursed seven shillings and sixpence 'in no time' for pork pies and indifferent bottled malt liquor. One of my friends had an attack of indigestion on the road, and no wonder after such a meal ... I may state that we all heartily deprecated the dictum that placed such beggarly fare before the public and said to them 'eat this or none, eat it up in less than ten minutes, and run to the train when the bell rings, as you will be left behind with nobody to sympathise with your inconveniences'...[11]

The situation became so bad that a subcommittee was established in July 1844, composed of GWR directors, with the aim of revising the charges made for refreshments and improving the management of the business; it met with little success, however. In September of the same year Griffiths wrote to the chairman offering to give up the sublease for £4,250.[12] The company seems to have looked closely at this offer, and an attempt was even made to persuade the manager of the Royal Hotel, Slough, a Mr Dotessio, to take over the running of the refreshment rooms. This, too, came to nothing, and Griffiths remained the proprietor until his sublease expired in 1848, the same year in which Rigbys sold the lease outright to John Rouse Phillips for £20,000.

The refreshment rooms under new management

Under Phillips's management, the level of service gradually improved. In 1849 the refreshment rooms at Swindon were illustrated, in cartoon form, in *Manners and Customs of Ye Englyshe*, by Richard Doyle and Percival Leigh (**Fig 43**).[13] In 1851 Phillips employed twenty-five staff, including eight refreshment-room attendants and other hotel staff.[14] A year later, George Measom, who was most impressed with the establishment, described it in considerable detail in *The Illustrated Guide to the Great Western Railway*.[15] In his glowing account he referred to the attendants as 'pretty and obliging Hebes' and to Phillips as 'that paragon of caterers'.

The company was still obliged to abide by the ten-minute refreshment stop, despite the fact that,

MANNERS·AND·CVSTOMS·OF·Yᵉ ENGLYSHE·IN·1849· Nᵒ 21.

A·RAYLWAY·STATYON· SHOWYNGE Yᵉ TRAVELLERS·REFRESHYNGE·THEMSELVES.

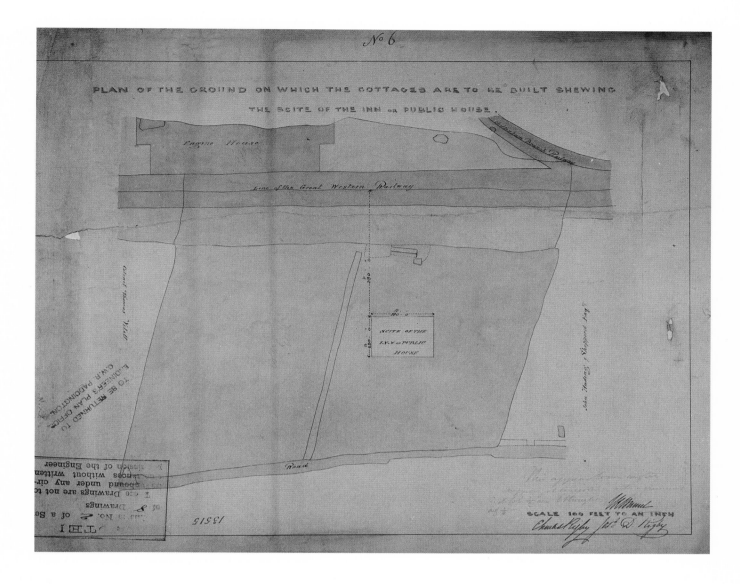

THE RAILWAY VILLAGE

Financial arrangements

The agreement of 2 February 1841 stipulated that Rigbys were required to build 300 cottages at their own expense on land owned by the company. The land had been purchased from John Harding Sheppard, a local brewer and landowner, for the considerable sum of £400 per acre (£1,000 per hectare).[17] The site lay opposite the main entrance to the proposed works, on the southern side of the main line. **Figure 44** shows a plan of the site prior to the construction of the cottages. It was drawn in late 1841 and is signed by Brunel and by both Joseph and Charles Rigby for the contractors. Sheppard retained land on the east side of the site,

by the late 1840s, a change of locomotive was no longer necessary. At first, the GWR attempted to break the monopoly guaranteed to the lease-holders by putting on express trains which did not stop at Swindon. However, Rigbys, and subsequent leaseholders, successfully took legal action to force the company to abide by the terms of the lease. The company remained saddled with the ten-minute stop until 1895, when it bought out the company managing the refreshment rooms for what was then the very substantial figure of £100,000. Despite a serious fire in the southern block in 1898, the refreshment rooms and hotel remained largely unaltered until 1972 when the southern block was demolished and the interior of the north block completely altered.[16]

Fig 44 *A GWR plan of 1841 showing the two fields earmarked for the company's cottage estate. The site of the engine house is also marked on the plan. The public house referred to was either not built or consisted of a temporary structure, demolished when the Queens Tap was erected to the south of the station in 1842–3. The two fields were purchased from the brewer, John Harding Sheppard, who also owned the land to the east. The plan is signed by Brunel and by J D & C Rigby, the contractors.*

while the land to the west was owned by another important resident of old Swindon, Colonel Thomas Vilett.

The February 1841 agreement appears to have been superseded by a revised contract made between the GWR and Rigbys dated 14 October 1841.[18] The latter stipulates that Rigbys were to expend no more than £35,000 on the construction of the 300 cottages. The estimated average cost of each cottage was therefore £116. Rigbys were to be reimbursed for this extensive initial outlay by leasing the cottages to the company for an annual rental equal to 6 per cent of their total cost. This meant that, on a total expenditure of £35,000, Rigbys could expect an annual return of £2,100. The mechanism for triggering the repayments was more complicated. For every £1,666 spent by Rigbys, the company would pay an annuity of 6 per cent. These annuities, which were payable quarterly, were not to exceed fifteen in number, and could be certified only after the works had been approved by Brunel.

The contract stipulated that the 300 cottages were to be completed by Christmas Day 1842, in time for the proposed opening of the works at the beginning of 1843. As an incentive to ensure that the cottages were completed on time, the GWR authorised Rigbys to spend more than £35,000, provided that they did so within three months of the signing of the final contract. It was therefore possible for Rigbys to increase the size of the annuities they were to receive from the company. The February agreement stated that the GWR was to lease the cottages from Rigbys for thirty years, after which they could either purchase the cottages or renew the lease. The October contract, however, stated that the cottages were to be leased for a ninety-nine-year term.

The GWR planned to pay Rigbys out of rents recovered from the employees who were to occupy the cottages. This meant that the 300 cottages were to be built at little cost to the company, since its expenditure was limited to the cost of the land, the construction of roads and footways between the cottage rows, and drainage. The company even managed to get Rigbys to agree to pay for repairs to the cottages. The contractors were to pay the annual sum of £100 to trustees for this purpose.

Delays and acrimony
On paper the Swindon contract must have seemed an attractive proposition to Rigbys. They were to receive sizeable quarterly payments for the cottages, in addition to the profits derived from the refreshment rooms and the payments due to them for building the first phase of the railway works. In fact, they over-extended themselves, and the high initial capital outlay involved in the construction of the cottages contributed to severe cashflow problems. They also had difficulty in assigning sufficient manpower to ensure the rapid and simultaneous construction of both the works and the cottages, and they had problems getting the necessary quantities of building materials to the two sites.

In the end, Rigbys built approximately 130 cottages, all of which are located on the western side of the central open space that was originally called High Street, but which was renamed Emlyn Square in 1893 (after the then GWR deputy chairman).[19] These buildings were not finished until the end of 1843, one year after the contractual deadline for the completion of all 300 cottages. Rigbys attempted to ease their financial difficulties in late 1842 by selling off to private investors eight of the nine annuities granted to them by the company. This did little to ameliorate the delays and acrimony that were a feature of the first two years of the cottage-building programme. By 1844 Rigbys had had enough and took steps to sever all involvement with the company's buildings at Swindon. However, their disputed accounts with the company were not settled until 1847. It is possible that they were close to bankruptcy at the time, a situation which may explain why they sold the lease of the refreshment rooms in the following year.

The GWR was equally to blame for the delays in building the cottages. It had been over-optimistic in expecting a single contractor to build, at its own expense, 300 cottages in little over a year. The General Committee minutes also show that the company adopted a penny-pinching approach when dealing with contractors, holding up payments for months, and sometimes even for several years. The company also sought to slow down building works deliberately during periods of recession. For all these reasons the 300 cottages were not to be completed until 1855, fourteen years after Brunel made his original sketch plan for the village.

THE WESTERN HALF OF THE VILLAGE

The sequence in which the cottages were built is shown in **Figure 45**. The earliest cottage terraces are those on the western side of Emlyn Square, and were built by Rigbys between 1842 and the end of 1843. Their design has often been attributed to Matthew Digby Wyatt, but there is no known evidence to connect him with Swindon at all, nor is there any indication that he and Brunel even knew each other at this time (they were later to meet as members of the various committees involved in the planning of the Great Exhibition and Brunel subsequently sought Wyatt's assistance in the design of Paddington station). Instead, as is clear from Brunel's own letters and reports to the GWR, he designed the first block himself, thus establishing the pattern for the second and third blocks to the south. This is entirely consistent with Brunel's overall responsibility for the design of the GWR's buildings and for the approval of all contract work, although he occasionally sought the assistance of architects, such as Francis Thompson who helped him with Swindon station. Thompson also offered to design some of the cottages at Swindon,[20] but his offer was declined by Brunel. As late as 1852, Brunel was reminded by the directors to use the services of the company's engineers and draughtsmen wherever possible, and to appoint an architect only 'if absolutely necessary'.[21]

The first block of cottages

On 19 March 1842 Brunel presented plans and drawings of the first block of cottages for the directors' approval. As a result, he was instructed 'to take the necessary steps for the building of 88 tenements in conformity with the said drawings to be arranged in two stacks of 44 each, at an expense not exceeding £100 per cottage in the entire outlay'.[22] This amounted to a block of cottages, made up of two rows of twenty-two, each cottage containing two tenements, making a total of eighty-eight dwellings in all.

Three days later Brunel wrote to Rigbys, ordering them to 'proceed immediately with one block of cottages being two rows back to back on the site originally fixed'.[23] The plans were drawn in Brunel's office in Duke Street in London from where they were collected by Rigbys. The site was staked out by Brunel prior to 31 March, and construction work on the first block started shortly afterwards.[24]

Financial constraints

The directors' stipulation that the cost of each dwelling (or pair of tenements) was not to exceed £100 caused some problems for Brunel, which he expressed in a report to the directors even before construction work began:

> In designing the cottages at Swindon I have found very great difficulties in combining a class of house sufficiently comfortable for the men & which at the same time could be let under the peculiar arrangements by which they were built at moderate rates & without loss to the company. Being anxious to ascertain how far the London & Birmingham Railway Company has succeeded in this respect I obtained through the kindness of Mr Creed [Secretary of the London & Birmingham Railway] the enclosed statement by which it appears that upon 92 cottages at Wolverton the Company are contented with 4¹/₃ & 4¹/₂ p[er] cent without allowing for contingencies of

> empty houses etc – at Camden Town something like 5 & at Tring & Blisworth under 6 p[er] cent. Now the Cottages at Swindon are to be built by a Contractor and leased to the Comp[an]y at a rental of 6 p[er] cent on the cost & to cover the loss upon empty houses, unpaid rents etc – 7 p[er] cent would not be too much to fix as the rent to the occupier so that a cottage Costing £100 must be let at 2/8 p[er] week [£6 18s 8d per annum] to repay the Company & which same cottage would let at the Wolverton works at 1/11 [£4 19s 8d per annum] as the difference is so great & economy in the first construction so essential if the principle of the Company being entirely repaid the gross rental is to be adhered to. I have prepared plans for two rows only of 22 Cottages each upon the cheapest construction I can devise & which with drainage etc will cost exactly £100 each.

> I should propose to build them as an expe[riment?] in the hopes that during their construction we may see the means of economising. I should observe the £100 does not include the cost of land – modest [–] & that rates and taxes have also to be provided for whether by the tenant or by the Company.[25]

This report shows that Brunel considered the rents paid at Wolverton to be important as a precedent in determining the likely rentals for the Swindon cottages. However, the directors' insistence on paying for the cottages entirely out of rents received from the tenants meant that the cottages at Swindon were eventually let at almost twice the weekly rental of comparable cottages at Wolverton. The rental for each cottage at Swindon was set by the directors on 6 October 1842 at 3s 6d per week, or £9 2s per annum.[26] The station superintendent was responsible for allocating cottages to employees and for ensuring that rent payments were deducted from their weekly pay.

The ratio of weekly wages to rents for lower-paid workers, such as labourers and smiths' strikers, is difficult to establish as wages varied considerably depending on the age and experience of the employee. In 1843, for example, a number of boys in the factory were paid less than 2s per week.[27] In 1849, according to company statistics, unskilled workers were earning approximately 12s per week.[28] With a two-roomed cottage costing 3s 6d per week, this meant that 29 per cent of their wages went on rent. In the vast majority of cases the senior male member of the family was the sole breadwinner since there were no employment opportunities for women, and children were generally too young to contribute to the family income. To increase the household income and thereby reduce the wages to rent ratio, workers tended to sublet space in their cottages to single male

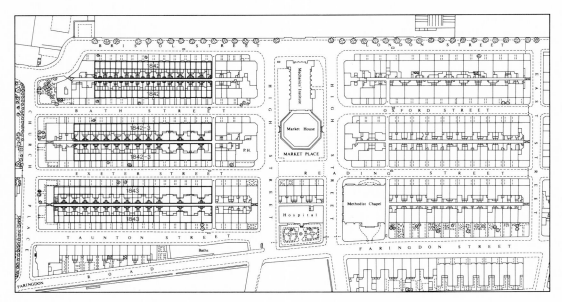

1842–3

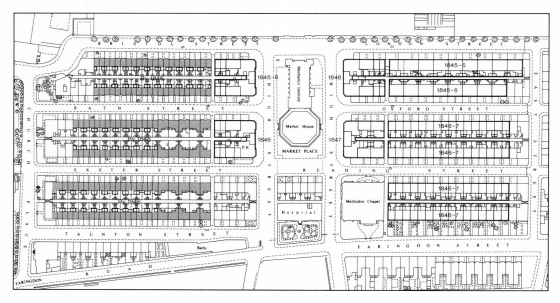

1845–7

lodgers or to other low-paid workers and their families. This led to a high number of households consisting of two or more families, and to over-crowding throughout the village.

Architectural treatment
The northernmost row of the first block faced on to Bristol Street (this, along with the other streets in the village, was named after important stations on the Great Western system). These cottages

were separated by an area of open ground from the main line and from the main entrance to the works. Because they were clearly visible from passing trains, their appearance had to impress. Accordingly, Brunel applied Elizabethan and Jacobean motifs to the stone-built façades.

In January 1842, writing to decline Francis Thompson's offer of assistance in designing the cottages, Brunel informed him that: 'I am at present only going to build a few cottages at Swindon – of

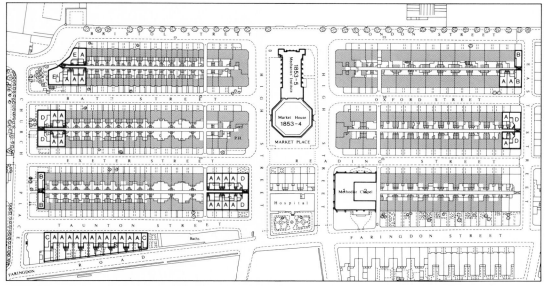

1853–5

Types A - E built 1853-4   1 Barracks, started in 1847 but mostly 1853-5   2 Courtyard

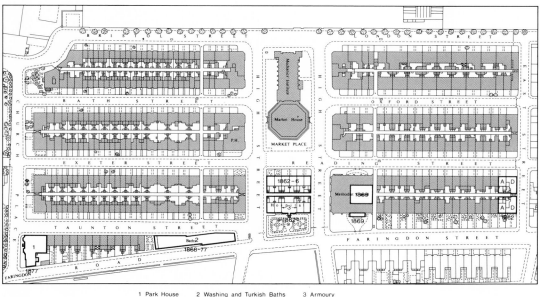

1862–77

1 Park House   2 Washing and Turkish Baths   3 Armoury

a totally unornamental character'.[29] This may simply have been an excuse for dispensing with Thompson's services, or it may be that Brunel did not consider his 'Jacobethan' cottages to be in any way ornamental. Whatever the case, the result, externally at least, was the most architecturally impressive group of railway workers' houses hitherto built in the country. The brick terraces of railway houses at Wolverton, Derby and Crewe were relatively plain and utilitarian by comparison.

The cottages in Bristol Street are arranged in pairs within the cottage row. The entrance to each pair is through a centrally placed porch, sheltered by a flat-arched canopy. The porch to every alternate pair is flanked by two-storey bay windows of shallow projection, surmounted by small gables. The window bays have Jacobean-style flush quoins. Between the bays, at first-floor level, there are largely decorative slit openings. The chamfered mullion windows originally contained

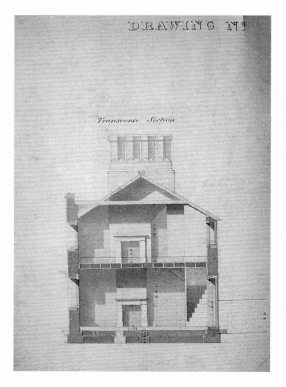

Fig 46 (above) A water-colour, produced in Brunel's office, showing the façade (north eleva-tion) of the Bristol Street terrace of cottages.

Fig 47 (right) A transverse section through one of the two-roomed or 'single' cottages. Note the absence of any internal fittings apart from the stair and fire surrounds. The tenants were expected to provide their own furni-ture.

Fig 48 (opposite above) The ground plan of the two-roomed cottages on the western side of the village. This drawing also shows the original arrangement of the rear yards and a section through one of the cesspools in the back alleys.

Fig 49 (opposite) This GWR plan was drawn in June 1846 and amended in May 1847. It shows the layout of the village at that time, the central open space (High Street, later Emlyn Square), and the villas of the works' manager and station superintendent to the north of the estate. Kitchen extensions had been added to the rear of the cottages on the western side of the village by this time. However, in his paintings of 1849 Snell exercised an element of artistic licence by omitting them altogether (see Figure 56).

lattice-paned glass. At roof level, stone chimneys, each with four diamond-set flues, delineate the cottage pairs (**Figs 46** and **47**).

The cottage layouts
The imposing external appearance of the Bristol Street cottages belied the fact that these were, in all other respects, humble workers' dwellings, offering very rudimentary accommodation. By investing so heavily in the external appearance of the cottages, Brunel was forced to economise on the interior arrangements in order to keep the unit cost to under £100. Entry to each cottage is through a door orientated at a 45° angle within the porch (**Fig 48**). There was a single room on the ground floor measuring 17ft (5·2m) by 11½ft (3·5m), containing a fireplace and an enclosed stair at the back leading to a single heated room on the first floor (see Figure 47). The front window provided the only daylight to the down-stairs room. There was no kitchen, and a back door next to the stairs led out to an enclosed yard, 21ft (6·4m) long.

At the back of the yard was a dust hole for the disposal of household dust and refuse, and a privy. Neighbouring privies were placed side by side in the yards, each pair draining into a cesspool located under the 8-ft-wide (2·4-m) alley between the two rows of cottages making up each block. The cesspools were connected by a barrel drain, of 12-in (305mm) diameter, running the length of the alley. Access to each cesspool was by means of a manhole cover in the middle of the alley. Although Brunel referred to them as such, these cottage rows were not back-to-back dwellings in the sense that they shared a common back wall; instead, the yards of each row backed on to a central alley.

These two-room cottages were intended for

multiple occupancy and must have been severely overcrowded from the day they were built. Contemporary descriptions of the cottages are rare, but Edward Snell, who arrived in Swindon shortly after the opening of the works, wrote in his diary for 1 March 1843: 'A precious place it is at present, not a knocker or a scraper in the whole place. Most of the houses very damp and containing only two rooms. Not a cupboard or a shelf ... and the unfortunate inhabitants obliged to keep the grub in the bedrooms.'[30] Where more than one family occupied a single cottage, cooking, eating and sleeping would have been carried out in a single room with little or no privacy. Life was made slightly easier by 1846, after lean-to extensions containing kitchens were built in the yards of the cottages on the west side of the village (**Fig 49**).

The second block of cottages

It took Rigbys at least six months to complete the first block of cottages between Bristol and Bath Street (later renamed Bathampton Street), a rate of progress which Brunel found infuriatingly slow. On 27 July 1842 he advised Rigbys that 'The Cottages are not going as I would have them',[31] and that he was not prepared to pay any advance 'while the works are proceeding so unsatisfactorily'. On 4 August Joseph Rigby was ordered to appear before the directors who instructed him to expedite the completion of the first block of cottages without omitting any of the details contained in the approved plans.[32] However, little progress had been made by 31 August 1842, when Brunel wrote, somewhat tersely, to Rigbys:

> With respect to ordering any more cottages as if you are six summer months in building 40 I know not what chance we have of getting the number we want built in any reasonable time. I had understood positively that the next batch if ordered should be completed by Christmas but not receiving any such written undertaking, I was about to recommend other steps being taken. If such is still your proposal you must write to me this evening.[33]

It seems that Brunel was given this undertaking, as on 1 September he was able to advise the directors that recent progress on the cottages had been satisfactory. The directors ordered Brunel to see to the completion of as many cottages as possible by Christmas 1842.

The reasons for these initial delays are unknown. To speed up the process, Rigbys had the second block of forty-four cottages between Bath (Bathampton) Street and Exeter Street built by subcontractors. By the end of October, another subcontractor had agreed to build about sixty cottages within the next few months for Rigbys.[34]

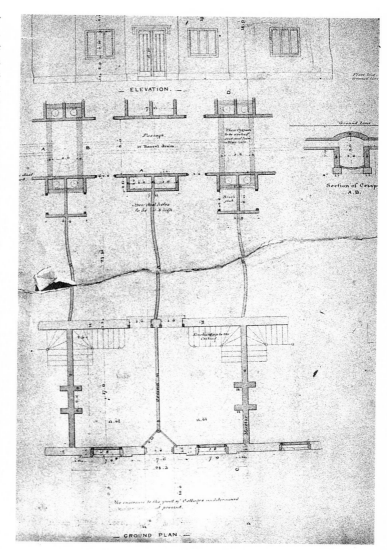

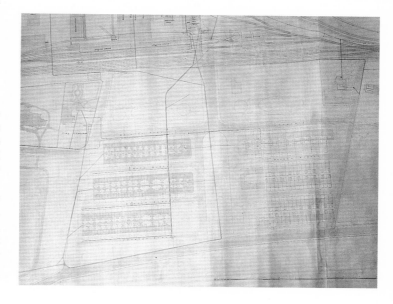

The cottages in the second block, standing on the southern side of Bath (Bathampton) Street and on the northern side of Exeter Street, are plainer than those of the original block (**Fig 50**). This may reflect the need to make more rapid progress in the construction programme, avoiding the delays associated with the first block. This time only three pairs of shallow window bays were built, at the eastern end of each row. These bays were built without the small gables which formed an attractive feature of the earlier block. In both rows, drip mouldings are employed over the entrances to the porches instead of canopies. The first two pairs of bays on the south side of Bath Street have blind slit openings over the doorways, but the row to the south has only one, on the cottage at the very eastern end of the row. The southernmost row has brick chimneys instead of the more elaborate stone ones.

It is not clear whether this economy with architectural details was authorised by the company, but it would seem reasonable for the GWR to have approved such changes in order to speed up the construction schedule. The second block was completed shortly after the opening of the works at the beginning of 1843.

Leaving aside differences in external appearance, the dimensions of the cottages in the two blocks and the building materials used were virtually identical. There were, however, five larger dwellings, known as 'double cottages' at the east end of each row of the second block (see Figure 45; **Figs 51** and **52**). These were equal in size to a pair of single cottages and could be used as tenements, or as larger houses for occupation by company officers or workshop foremen. They were each let for 7s per week or £18 4s per annum. The watercolour drawings are very detailed and similar in style to those of the first block. This suggests that they were prepared by Brunel or, at the very least, by his assistants. Less highly finished plans for the contractors also survive for the second block.

The façades of the double cottages are identical to those of the adjacent single dwellings, but there are clear differences in their rear elevations and plans. There was one large yard for each double cottage, containing a single privy and dust hole. In the centre of the back wall of each cottage is a projecting stair tower with independent access into it from the yard. The ground floor consisted of two rooms of identical dimensions to those of the single cottages, but more space was created by the removal of the internal enclosed stair and its replacement by the stair tower. The latter, which contained a winder stair, was partitioned off from the rooms on the ground and first floors.

This arrangement meant that each of the four rooms could accommodate a family without them

Fig 50 (above) Cottages on the southern side of Bathampton (Bath) Street. Compare these with the more ornate examples in the first Bristol Street block (see Figure 46).

Fig 51 (right) An elevation and ground plan, dated 12 September 1842, of one of the larger 'double cottages' in the second block, showing the projecting stair tower at the rear. The gables over the window bays were not built.

Fig 53 (opposite)This engraving from The Illustrated London News of 18 October 1845 shows the completed terraces making up the western side of the village when viewed from the south. The recently completed church and school can be seen on the left of the picture and the station is on the far right.

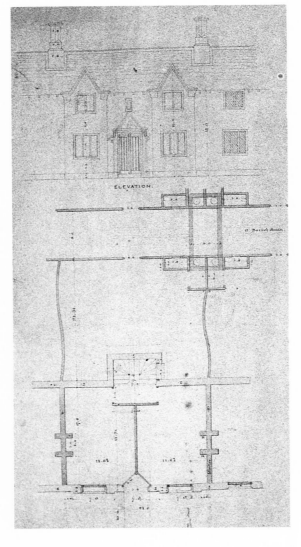

ELEVATION.

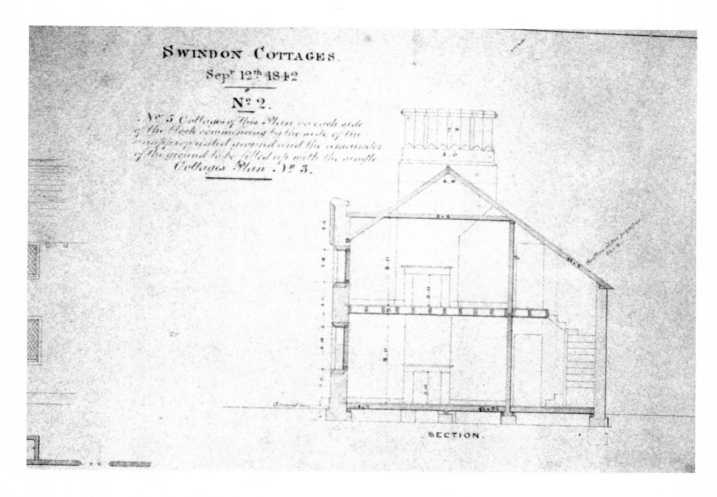

SWINDON COTTAGES

Sep.r 12.th 1842

N.o 2.

No. 5 Cottages of this Plan on each side of the block commencing by the side of the unappropriated ground and the remainder of the ground to be filled up with the single Cottages Plan No. 3.

SECTION.

having to be disturbed by the other tenants. Alternatively, the two rooms on each floor could be occupied by separate families. The family living on the first floor could reach their accommodation via the yard entrance to the stair without having to go through the downstairs rooms. In short, this plan was considerably more flexible and it allowed the tenants the choice of one, two or even four-roomed accommodation, depending on how much they could afford. Even so, all the tenants would have to use one privy, and kitchens were still not provided.

The third block of cottages

The third block of cottages, between the southern side of Exeter Street and the northern side of Taunton Street, was begun early in 1843. Approximately thirty cottages, including all of those fronting on to Taunton Street, were completed by August 1843, while another fifteen or so of those fronting Exeter Street were finished by the end of the same year (**Fig 53**). The arrangement of the cottages in this third block was identical to that of the second block between Exeter and Bath (Bathampton) Street, with ten

double cottages at the eastern end, and the remainder consisting of single cottages built to the same plan and dimensions as those to the north. The highly finished elevational drawing for these cottages (**Fig 54**) is labelled 'Rigbys'. The names

Fig 52 (above) A section through one of the 'double cottages' showing the rear stair tower.

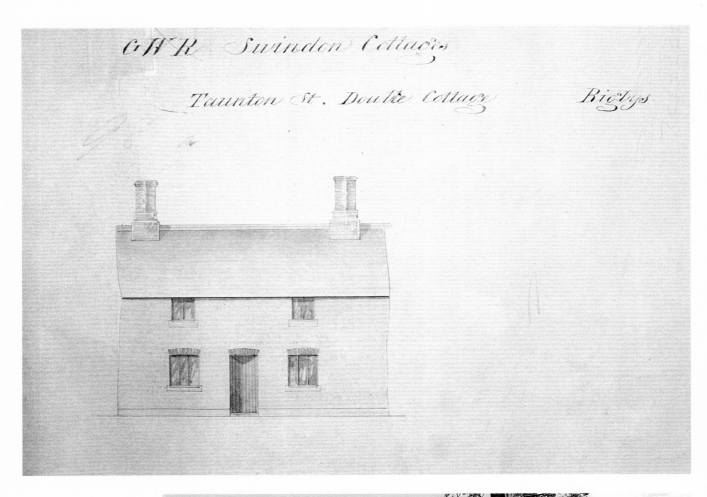

GWR Swindon Cottages

Taunton St. Double Cottage   *Rigbys*

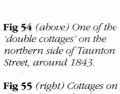

Fig 54 *(above) One of the 'double cottages' on the northern side of Taunton Street, around 1843.*

Fig 55 *(right) Cottages on the southern side of Exeter Street. These are part of the northern terrace making up the third block on the western side of the village. The absence of ornamental details and the use of coursed, squared rubble for walling gives them a more vernacular appearance than that of the two earlier blocks to the north.*

of the subcontractors, Cooper and Griffiths, are written on the bottom of plans for the double cottages. On-site supervision of the building works was carried out by R J Ward who sent fortnightly progress reports to the General Committee until September 1843.

The exterior treatment of the third block is considerably plainer than that of the first two (**Fig 55**), reflecting the need to keep construction costs to the absolute minimum. Coursed, squared rubble was used for the walls rather than dressed stone. The window and door surrounds are not chamfered and the Bath-stone lintels have been replaced by shallow-arched brick ones. The chimneys are of brick. In contrast to the more elaborate cottages in Bristol Street, these two rows have been shorn of all superfluous detail and are very much in the vernacular tradition.

Building materials

The external walls of all three blocks of cottages are made of roughly dressed Swindon stone obtained from the quarries in old Swindon. Softer, and more easily dressed, oolitic limestone from the Box and Corsham areas was used in ashlar form for the quoins, and for the window and door surrounds. The latter is creamier in colour, coarser in texture and has a greater shell content than the darker yellow Swindon sandstone.

Most previous writers on the GWR have stated that the cottages were built of stone from the Box Tunnel, the excavation of which was completed at the end of June 1841. However, the Box Tunnel was created mostly by blasting, so it is unlikely that large quantities of good-quality building stone were obtained from it. It is possible that some of the limestone used for dressings on the cottages came from the cutting to the tunnel, but it could just as easily have come from established quarries in the Box area or Corsham, brought to Swindon along the Wilts & Berks Canal. Stone from the Box area was transported by rail from Corsham to London and intermediate stations from at least as early as 3 May 1842.[35]

We know more about the source of the Swindon stone used for the cottages and parts of the railway works. On 7 October 1841, the GWR paid £70, presumably for stone, to Henry Tarrant who is listed in Pigot & Co's *Directory of Wiltshire* for 1842 as one of two stonemasons living in old Swindon.[36] This stone may have been used for the station or for the construction of the engine house or running shed at the works. In 1842 Rigbys were listed as having an office in Prospect Place, a street located close to the quarries in old Swindon.[37] Tarrant's stone yard was situated in the same street and it is just possible that he was in some form of partnership with Rigbys. Rigbys may even have taken out a lease on large sections

of the quarries from their owner, Ambrose Goddard, and employed Tarrant to quarry and dress the stone – this kind of arrangement was common enough at the time and several other contractors are known to have leased parts of the quarries from the Goddard family for building purposes in the 1870s.

The immediate problem faced by Rigbys was how to get the large quantities of stone required for the works and the cottages from the quarries, down the hill to the new settlement, over 1 mile (1·6km) to the north. The following short item of 31 March 1842 in the *Devizes & Wiltshire Gazette* explains how they overcame the problem: 'The Messrs Rigby, the able and spirited contractors for executing these great works, have just completed a tram-way at an enormous expense, labour and perseverance, for conveying stone from the Swindon quarries to the station grounds. Such a means of conveyance was absolutely necessary, from the immense quantity of stone required.' The route taken by the tramway is unknown, but it seems likely that it followed the most direct path: that is, through Eastcott and north along the public footpath, later Bridge Street, to the Wilts & Berks Canal. A temporary bridge would have been necessary to take the tramway over the canal.

THE EASTERN HALF OF THE VILLAGE

Following the completion in 1843 of the third block of cottages, on Exeter Street and Taunton Street, no further cottage rows were built until after 28 August 1845.[38] At a meeting of the General Committee of that date, J W Hammond, Brunel's assistant who was deputising for Brunel in his absence, presented tenders from five contractors (Rigbys were not included) for the construction of 'twenty double cottages at Swindon' to be built according to plans and estimates prepared by the GWR Engineer's department and approved by the directors. A tender of £6,414, for twenty cottages, was submitted by George Major (of Prospect Place, old Swindon) and accepted, on condition that he agreed to finish the cottages within five months from the date of his signing the contract (in the event, and for reasons unknown, only seventeen were built). The time limit was made necessary by the very considerable expansion of the works from mid 1845 and the consequent increase in the workforce to a peak of 1,800 in 1847. So pressing was the need for additional housing that, in November 1845, Gooch wrote to Hammond urging the rapid completion of more cottages. He stated that '10 or 12 people were living in 2 rooms, and when the night men got up the day men went to bed, and workers were leaving Swindon because they could not get a place of any kind to live'.[39]

The new block of double cottages was to be the first built on the vacant land to the east of High Street (Emlyn Square). The northernmost row was to face London Street which was an east-

erly continuation of Bristol Street, while the other row making up the block faced Oxford Street to the south. The London Street houses were built to face the villas and gardens of the works' manager and station superintendent (see Figure 49; **Figs 56** and **57**). The façades of the new cottages were therefore treated in a manner very similar to those of the very first block, in Bristol Street, with shallow window projections under small gables to either side of a single, central doorway (**Fig 58**). There the similarities end, for the London Street cottages are much larger in width, depth and height. Their greater depth meant that the rear yards and the back alley had to be smaller in order for the two rows making up each block to fit on to a strip of ground the same width as those on the western side of High Street (Emlyn Square).

The cottages each contained eight rooms and they were originally divided up to form four tenements (**Fig 59**). These were considerably more sophisticated in their planning than the earlier double cottages. The V-shaped porch has been replaced with a square lobby, 6ft (1·8m) wide, with access to the ground floor on either side of a central through passage. Beyond the lobby was a stairhall leading in turn to a back lobby and common access to the rear yard. By placing the stair in the central passage, there was no need for a projecting stair tower at the rear of the cottage. Two-room tenements stood on either side of the passage on each floor. Each tenement had a living room at the front and a bedroom at the back. All the rooms were heated from fireplaces set in the more substantial side walls. Despite the greater width of these cottages, the wide central passage took up much of the additional space. Consequently the rooms were only marginally larger than those in the earlier single and double cottages, although their greater height allowed more headroom. Kitchens and internal fittings were still not provided, and the new cottages represented only a slight improvement on their predecessors, although their larger dimensions attracted the highly skilled artisans who represented the majority of occupants in 1851.

The other cottages in this block, facing on to the north side of Oxford Street, were built to the same plan and dimensions as those facing London Street, but since their façades were not visible from the main line, or from the officers' villas, the window bays and small gables were omitted from their design, resulting in a considerably plainer appearance (**Fig 60**).

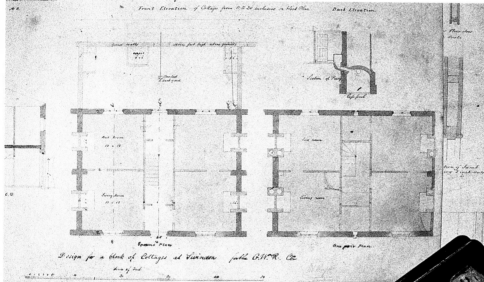

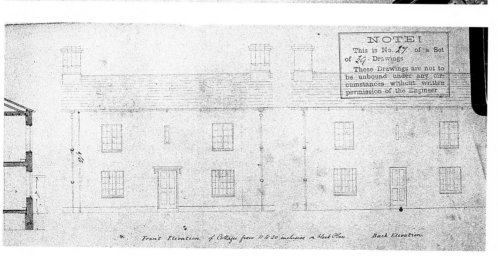

Fig 58 *(above) Eight-roomed houses in London Street in the eastern half of the village, built by George Major in 1845–6.*

Fig 59 *(above left) The ground and first-floor plans of one of the London Street houses, showing that the houses were originally subdivided into four, two-cell tenements.*

Fig 60 *(left) An elevation of an eight-roomed house on the northern side of Oxford Street. These houses were built to the same plan and proportions as the houses in London Street, but their façades do not have gabled window bays.*

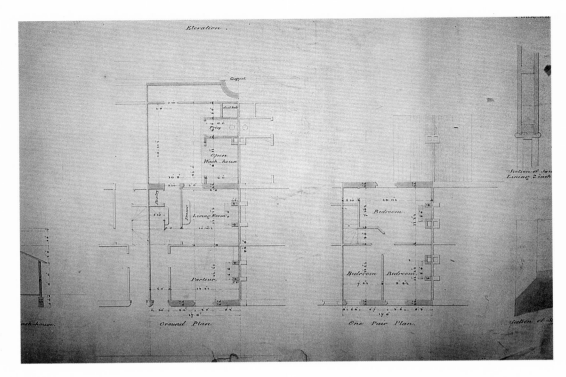

Fig 61 *The ground and first-floor plans of one of the cottages in the Oxford/Reading Street and Reading/Faringdon Street blocks of 1846–7. Note the inclusion of a wash house in the yard, and a dresser and pantry in, or near, the living-room-cum-kitchen.*

Fig 62 *The five-roomed cottages, built in 1846–7, on the northern side of Reading Street.*

Completion of the terrace blocks

On 3 August 1846 the General Committee approved the construction of two further blocks, of thirty-two cottages each, to the south of the London/Oxford Street block. These were bounded by Oxford Street, Reading Street and Faringdon Street which were aligned, respectively, with Bath (Bathampton) Street, Exeter Street and Taunton Street, so completing the grid envisaged by Brunel in 1840 (see Figure 14).

The cottages in these two later blocks were completed by the middle of 1847. They were all built to the same plan (**Fig 61**) and arranged in pairs, with their front doors placed side by side (**Fig 62**). They were also far superior to the earlier blocks, since each new cottage had five rooms. They were entered directly from the street rather than, as in the earlier terraces, through a recessed porch.

The exterior walls of the block between Oxford Street and Reading Street were built of Swindon stone, with Bath stone for the chamfered window and door surrounds. The block to the south was constructed almost entirely of Bath stone, indicating that supplies of this material were becoming more readily available at this time, and more competitive in price with Swindon stone. Four courses of Swindon stone were used above plinth level on the south side of Reading Street. The cottages in Faringdon Street are constructed in a similar manner, although here the plinth is also of Swindon stone. It seems that here the contractors for this block were making conscious use of the Swindon stone, with its higher silica content, as a natural damp-proof course, in preference to the more porous Bath limestone.

Inside the cottages, a passage leads from the front door to a stair at the back (see Figure 61). The passage continues through to the rear yard, containing a wash house, open to the sky, a privy and a dust hole. Separated from the passage by a thin partition was a heated front parlour and a small living-room-cum-kitchen, lit by a window in the back wall. As with the earlier cottages, no range was provided in the kitchen, so food would have been cooked on the open fire (**Fig 63**). This explains why both the fireplace and the hearth in the kitchen are larger than those in the parlour. This back room also contained a dresser for the storage of plates and cutlery (**Fig 64**), and a pantry was provided in the passage in the space behind the stair. Access to the three upstairs bedrooms was by means of a diamond-shaped lobby opening off the landing.

One of the cottages in Faringdon Street, now forming part of the Great Western Railway Museum, retains part of its original plan. Some of its fittings also survive (**Fig 65**), though the cottage is now furnished with items dating from around 1900. The plan indicates that the cottages were intended for the occupation of a single family, possibly in conjunction with lodgers. As such, they would have been let to better-paid workers at a higher rental. An analysis of the 1851 census shows that of the forty-eight foremen mentioned in the Fawcett List[40] of staff at the works from 1843 to 1865, eighteen of them lived in these two blocks of cottages.

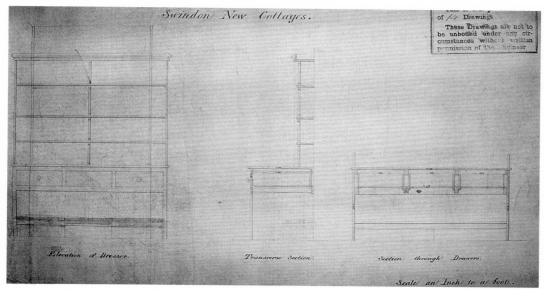

Fig 63 (*above*) *This sketch of May 1843, from Snell's diary, shows his fellow lodger, Mr Drye, cooking porridge on the open fire in one of the cottages. Cooking would have been carried out in this way throughout the village before the insertion of ranges in the fireplaces later in the century.*

Fig 64 (*above left*) *A company drawing of one of the dressers built in the living-rooms of the five-roomed cottages on the eastern side of the village.*

Fig 65 *The front parlour (far left) and the living-room (left) of the cottage at 34 Faringdon Road, re-created by the Great Western Railway Museum.*

SHOPS

The need for shops to serve the rapidly increasing population had been mentioned in the October 1841 agreement between Rigbys and the GWR, and it is clear that their provision had been part of Brunel's original plan for the village. However, the company did not decide to start building the shops until 7 November 1844, ten months after the

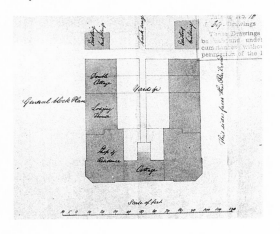

completion of the cottages making up the western half of the village. At their meeting of that date the general committee 'resolved that it is expedient to build eight shops at Swindon New Town nearly adjoining to the present cottages in order to insure a proper supply of provisions and other necessaries for the inhabitants of the Village'.[41] Before the committee put the work out to contract, it was concerned to check that it could use a builder other than Rigbys without being in breach of the 1841 agreement. Consequently it sought the opinion of the company solicitor, Charles Stevens, who advised that it would not.[42]

Six months after the general committee's resolution, Brunel had done nothing, and, on 27 March 1845, the committee instructed him 'to proceed forthwith with the shops which had been sometime ago ordered at Swindon'. On 3 July Brunel submitted plans and estimates to the committee for two blocks of shops and cottages, along with tenders from four contractors. The committee accepted a tender of £2,635 entered by William Slocombe, a Bristol contractor, who earlier that year had completed carriage sheds for the company at Bath.

Fig 66 *(right) The first shop block on the corner of Bristol Street and High Street (Emlyn Square). The three-storeyed shop residences, and the cottage between them, face on to High Street.*

Fig 67 *The 1845 contractor's plan of half of the shop block on the corner of High Street (Emlyn Square) and Bristol Street. The grey shading indicates that those rooms had stone floors.*

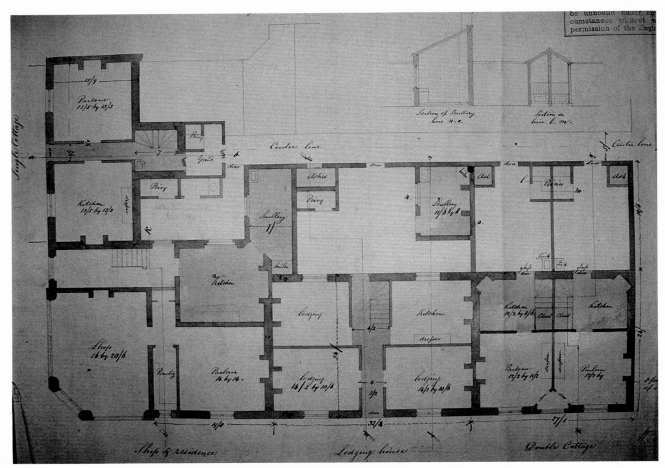

The shops were built, along with additional cottages, in blocks on the unappropriated ground to either side of High Street (Emlyn Square) (**Fig 66**). The first block to be built was located at the eastern end of the original Bristol Street/Bath (Bathampton) Street block of cottages, separated from them by an 8-ft (2·4-m) wide alley. The contractor's plans and elevations for this first block have survived, signed by William Slocombe and dated 16 July 1845 (**Figs 67** and **68**).

Each block consisted of two identical halves arranged on either side of a central alley, which was continued in line with the alley between the earlier cottage terraces. Each half terminated in a prominent three-storey block sited on the corner formed by High Street (Emlyn Square) and the principal streets running east and west from it. Each had a shop on the ground floor, with corner entry, and a shop residence on the two floors above. Between each three-storey block, fronting on to High Street, was a two-storey cottage consisting of a kitchen and parlour on the ground floor, separated by a central passage, and two bedrooms above. This superior four-roomed cottage was probably intended for occupation by

company officers or foremen. It was the first cottage in the village to be fitted with built-in furniture, having a dresser in the kitchen and closets under the stair and between the two first-floor bedrooms.

Additional two-storey dwellings were built between the three-storey sections and the existing cottage rows. The dwellings immediately adjoining the shops were eight-room lodging houses with a central entry. There was a kitchen at the back adjoining a central stair. A door led from the stairhall out into a wide yard, with the alley behind. There was a small detached scullery on one side of the yard and a privy and an ash pit on the other.

Between each lodging house and the earlier cottage rows was a pair of four-roomed cottages, together described on the plans as a 'double cottage'. Each had a parlour at the front and a kitchen at the back with a corner fireplace and stair leading to two bedrooms upstairs. These were the first of the small cottages in the village to be provided with kitchens. They were also fitted with dressers in the parlour and closets under the stair. Sinks were provided in the yards for washing clothes.

Fig 68 *An 1845 drawing showing the Bristol Street elevation of the first shop block built in the village. Note the splayed corner entry to the shop. A lodging house is shown on the right and a 'double cottage' on the extreme right (see also Figure 66).*

Design for buildings at Swindon. Elevation towards Railway N° 4 Scale 5 feet

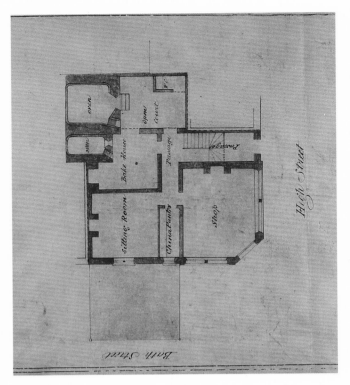

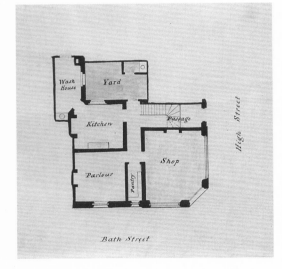

Fig 69 *The shop on the corner of Bathampton (Bath) Street and High Street (Emlyn Square) was first leased by William Perris in 1846 and operated as a bakehouse and shop (top). In 1847 the same premises (centre) were converted back to a shop residence by Richard Allnutt, who took over the lease of the company's new bakehouse in Taunton Street (bottom).*

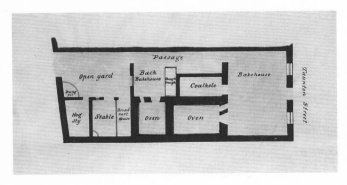

Architectural treatment

Externally the new blocks (see Figure 68) are quite elaborate when compared with the second and third blocks of cottages to the west. They were carefully designed in Brunel's characteristic 'Jacobethan' style to blend with the original Bristol Street terrace. The exterior walls are 14in thick (356mm) and made of a mixture of Swindon and Bath stone, while the dressings are entirely of Bath stone. Brunel made use of all of his favourite devices, including small gables, each featuring a blind *œil-de-bœuf* (ox-eye motif), and chamfered window and door surrounds with drip moulds above.

The arrangement of the three-storey shop blocks to either side of High Street (Emlyn Square) served to emphasise the role of this central open space as the civic and commercial heart of the village, very much as Brunel had in mind when he made his sketch plan in 1840. Thus High Street formed a central axis, continuing in a straight line to the north, passing through the centre of a large grassed area before terminating at the main line. The prominent nature of this central axis is well illustrated in Snell's paintings of the works and village (see Figure 56), and it was described as 'the grand promenade' as late as 1865.[43] In the 1840s no other railway town could rival this central avenue, or match the elegance of the tall buildings which framed it.

Leasing arrangements

Three blocks of shops and cottages, containing a total of six shops, were completed by the end of 1846. Slocombe died some time before 11 February 1847 and it is possible that other contractors were taken on to complete any unfinished works. The earliest lease probably relates to the shop on the Bristol/High Street (Emlyn Square) corner and is dated 16 May 1846.[44] The first tenants were Henry Killick and John Hawe Mason, grocers from Newbury, who rented the shop and residence from the GWR for £70 per annum. The other shop in the same block was leased two months later by William Perris, a baker from Chippenham, who converted the back part into a bakehouse containing two bread ovens (**Fig 69**, top).

Two years later the lease was taken over by Richard Allnutt, who converted the bakery back to a retail shop, following the GWR's construction of a larger bakehouse on the south side of Taunton Street (**Fig 69,** bottom). A butcher named James Copeland leased the shop on the corner of High Street and the south side of Bath (Bathampton) Street. In 1847, the GWR built a slaughterhouse on the south side of Taunton Street. The GWR bakehouse and slaughterhouse were leased to Allnutt and Copeland, respectively, for 7 per cent of their cost on 25 November of that same year.[45]

Another early tenant was Stuart Keith Rea, surgeon and brother of the Swindon works' manager, Minard Rea. Stuart leased the shop on the corner of London Street and High Street from 23 December 1846, probably for use as a surgery and dispensary. In November 1847 the GWR gave him the free use of the premises in partial payment for his services as company 'medical man' at New Swindon.

The shops were leased for fourteen or twenty-one years. The annual rent was normally £70 (though Copeland paid £85 in combined rent for his shop and the slaughterhouse). The rent was payable in quarterly instalments and the tenants were responsible for the maintenance of the buildings, being required to paint all external woodwork and ironwork 'thrice with good oil colour' every four years, and internal wood and ironwork every seven years.[46]

HOUSING FOR SENIOR EMPLOYEES

Unlike Wolverton and Crewe, little provision was made at Swindon for housing officers and foremen prior to the construction of the shop blocks of 1845–7. It is not known where Archibald Sturrock, then the works' manager, or Christopher Hill, the station superintendent, were accommodated in these early years. Foremen lived in nearby hamlets or alongside their men in the cottage rows. No precise information is available on this subject because the first detailed population analysis, the 1851 census, was not to be carried out until nine years after the construction of the village began.

At Wolverton there were six classes of house by the end of 1841, including six superior houses for clerks. The latter were 'three-storeys high and contained two kitchens, seven bedrooms, a parlour and a convenient yard, wash house, etc.'[47] At Crewe there were four classes of house provided by 1846, including villa-style lodges for senior officers, Gothic-style houses for junior officers, 'detached mansions' for engineers and 'neat cottages of four apartments' for labourers.[48]

Initially the GWR seems to have given higher priority to housing the bulk of its workforce, rather than to providing better-quality housing for senior staff. It is possible that the double cottages on the western side of the village were intended for officers and foremen, but, owing to the overall shortage of company cottages, they are more likely to have been used as tenements.

The first mention of the need for a separate dwelling for the station superintendent appears in the directors' minutes of 1 September 1842 when the company secretary, Charles Saunders, was

given permission to negotiate with Rigbys or other parties for the erection of a suitable residence.[49] No further action was taken until 21 November 1844 when plans for the superintendent's house were submitted to the General Committee for approval.

The house, described on the plans as the 'Superintendent's Villa', was completed in 1846. The building was loosely Gothic in style and rather like a parsonage in its general appearance. It was almost certainly designed in Brunel's office or in the resident engineer's office at Swindon and influenced by pattern-books of the time, such as J C Loudon's *Encyclopaedia of Cottage, Farm and Villa Architecture*, of 1833. The villa was built on an area of open ground to the north east of London Street by George Major, the contractor for the northernmost block on the eastern side of the village. The detached three-storey villa was L-shaped in plan, with a cellar containing service rooms, two parlours on the ground floor and at least four bedrooms on the first floor. There was also a brewhouse in the rear yard.

Hill, the station superintendent, had been a permanent employee of the GWR since 1842 and was therefore first in line for a separate residence. Sturrock, having originally been employed on a temporary basis to fit up the new factory, only became works' manager in January 1843.[50] The decision to build accommodation for Sturrock came on 3 August 1846 when the General Committee ordered the construction of a house for him on the corner of London Street and the northward extension of High Street (Emlyn Square). The successful tender of £1,200 was submitted by Thomas Lewis, a contractor from Bath. His name appears on the bottom of the drawing labelled 'Superintendent's Villa' indicating that Sturrock's house was probably built to the same elevation and plan as the earlier house, though the former had a bedroom on the ground floor, instead of a nursery, and a servants' bedroom in the cellar (**Fig 70**). Both villas are illustrated in a locally published lithograph of 1847, and in Edward Snell's paintings (see Figures 56 and 57). In the early 1870s, they were demolished to make way for the construction of the carriage works.

No houses were provided for Daniel Gooch or Brunel, though both were regular visitors to Swindon. Gooch had an office and bedroom at the railway works. On 19 January 1843 Brunel wrote to him: 'it is possible, although doubtless you would prefer to remain in London, that the Directors will require you to live at Swindon and take charge there yourself.'[51] In August of that same year the General Committee considered a proposal to build a house for Gooch at Swindon, but it was decided not to proceed and Gooch did not move to Swindon, in part because the appointment of Sturrock as works' manager (see p 32) relieved him of the need to oversee the works directly. The high regard in which Gooch was held, however, can be judged from the fact that his salary was raised to £1,000 in January 1846, bringing it into line with that of Brunel.[52] He was also paid a bonus of £500 in recognition of his successful establishment of the Swindon

works and his management of the first stages of the expansion programme.

Brunel had a large private office in London and his GWR responsibilities took him to all parts of the network. In a report of a committee set up in 1843 to reduce company expenditure it was stated that Brunel had to 'give frequent personal attendance at Swindon'.[53] It would have been very easy for him to stop off at Swindon on his way between

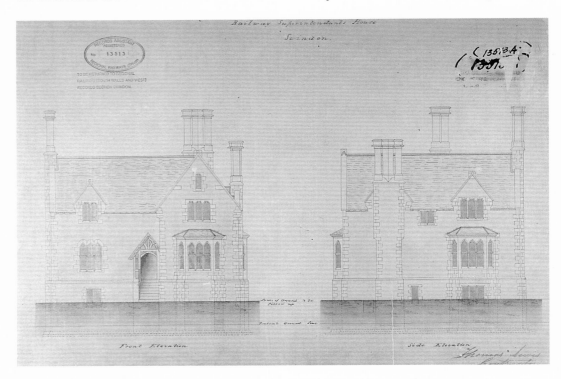

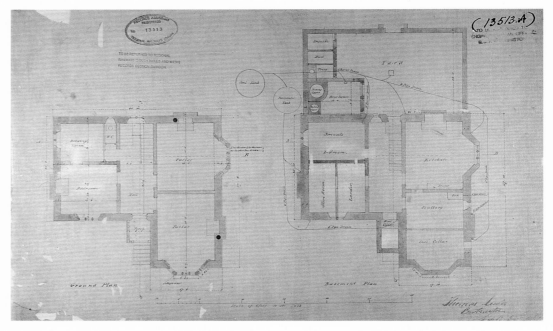

Fig 70 *Plans and elevations of the works' manager's villa, built to the north of London Street. These are dated September 1846 and signed by the contractor, Thomas Lewis.*

Paddington and Bristol, and it is known that he made regular trips to Swindon to check on the progress of the new building work (he was particularly scathing about the poor quality of the coffee served in the Swindon station refreshment rooms).

CHURCH AND SCHOOL

The spiritual needs of New Swindon were also taken into account by the company. The directors first discussed the need for a church, parsonage and school, to be funded largely by public subscriptions, in December 1842. In early 1843 a committee of directors was set up to oversee their construction,[54] and in the meantime a room in the works was provided as a temporary church. A new ecclesiastical district, based on the boundary of the Tything of Eastcott and including all of New Swindon, was also established at that time, and this became a parish in its own right in January 1846.

The committee decided that the church should accommodate 800 worshippers and be capable of future enlargement. Colonel Vilett, who owned the land to the west of New Swindon, was persuaded by the vicar of Swindon, his brother-in-law, to donate three-quarters of an acre (0·3 hectares) of land for the church. The committee sent a circular letter to several of the leading architects of the time inviting plans and estimates for the new buildings. Estimates submitted by Scott & Moffatt, and the little-known W Clephan, were chosen ahead of those from H E Goodridge and William Butterfield, whose estimates for the church were more than twice that of the two finalists.

Scott & Moffatt were eventually selected, despite the fact that their estimates had been higher than Clephan's. The committee seem to have been impressed with the plans of Holy Trinity Church in Halstead, Essex, which Scott & Moffatt had presented to them as an example of their recent work. In addition, William Gibbs, the executor for the estate of his recently deceased brother and former director of the company, George Henry Gibbs, indicated that he would give £1,000 towards the construction of the church provided that Scott & Moffatt were chosen as the architects. It is not clear whether this sum was in addition to the £500 bequeathed by the estate for this purpose in December 1842.

By 16 September 1843 subscriptions had reached £5,600. Messrs William Sissons of Hull successfully tendered for the construction of the church and parsonage, along with the school and adjoining schoolmaster's house, which were all to be designed by Scott & Moffatt. Their tender came to a total of £8,386. This left a shortfall of £2,786, which was presumably met by the GWR. In addition, the company had already paid £261 to Vilett

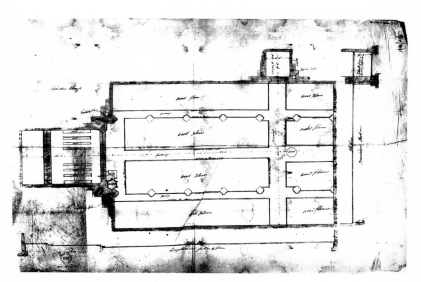

to purchase the land for building the parsonage, school and schoolhouse, and it agreed to pay the stipend of the new perpetual curate.

Construction began in late 1843. The parsonage and school were completed in 1844, and the church was consecrated with considerable fanfare by the Bishop of Gloucester and Bristol on 25 April 1845, with the directors and senior officials of the GWR in attendance. Dedicated to St Mark, the church was designed in the Decorated Gothic style with side aisles, nave and clerestory, chancel and a tower supporting a spire (**Fig 71**). The tower was a late addition by Scott, and is absent from an earlier plan (**Fig 72**). All

Fig 71 *(top) St Mark's church from the north west. The tower was built on the north side of the church to improve the view of the building from the main line.*

Fig 72 *A working plan of St Mark's church, by Scott & Moffatt, made before the tower and spire were included in the design.*

three buildings were constructed of Swindon stone with Bath-stone dressings. The interior of the church is lined with Bath stone to give a better quality finish. (See also pp 164–5, and Figures 56, 212 and 213.)

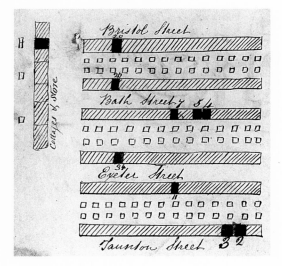

Fig 73 *This sketch, drawn by Edward Snell in his diary in 1843, shows a row of cottages and a store on the western side of the village. The black squares denote the cottages in which he lodged between 1843 and about 1846.*

LIFE IN THE RAILWAY VILLAGE

When the Swindon railway works first opened, the number of men employed was approximately 180. In addition, a large number of those running the train service also lived at Swindon. The permanent establishment, for example, made up largely of station staff, porters, and railway police, contributed another thirty-two.[55] Clearly it would not have been possible to

Fig 74 *New arrivals: a railway worker and his family, sketched by Snell on 14 March 1843, on their way from the station to the company cottages.*

accommodate all of these men, and their families, in some eighty houses, all but ten of which were small, two-room cottages. Foremen and more highly skilled workers may have been given first call on the available accommodation. James Fairbairn, for example, an engine erector and associate of Sturrock's from Dundee, lived with his family in wooden cottages at Hay Lane (Wootton Bassett Road) before moving to one of the cottages in Bristol Street upon their completion.[56] Thomas Stewart, first foreman in the smiths' shop, moved to Swindon from Paddington in December 1842, and unable to get accommodation in Swindon, took rooms in the nearby village of Stratton St Margaret.[57] Some of the cottages were occupied whilst still under construction. In May 1843 Edward Snell wrote 'rather queer lodgings mine, at present the house only 1 story high, walls of rough brick inside, and most of the rooms occupied by a barefooted Scots woman and her family'.

Those who could not find accommodation in the new cottages were put up in lodgings in old Swindon and surrounding villages, or they were housed in temporary wooden huts located close to the permanent buildings. In February 1843 Snell described the new settlement as 'a regular dull place' and referred to 'wooden houses mounted on wheels scattered about through the fields'. In August 1843 there are records referring to nine dwellings called 'Rigbys Cottages'.[58] These were not located in the existing streets, suggesting they may have been temporary dwellings provided by Rigbys elsewhere on the site to help overcome the acute housing shortage; alternatively, they could have been erected to house Rigbys' own workers during the construction of the village. It is possible that these are the structures shown on a sketch plan of the village made by Snell in 1843, showing a terrace of six cottages and a store located on the west side of the main cottage terraces (**Fig 73**). There was also a barrack room, which in April 1843 was converted for use as a temporary school.[59] This barrack may have been the 'sleeping room', which had been shifted from Hay Lane (Wootton Bassett Road) in the previous year.[60]

These temporary buildings, and the mud churned up by the contractors, must have given the new settlement all the appearance of a frontier town. Indeed, Snell described the new arrivals in Swindon as 'settlers'. He also sketched a forlorn band of immigrants, consisting of a railway worker with his wife and young family, arriving in Swindon in the pouring rain and mud (**Fig 74**). Christopher Hill, the station superintendent, wrote to Seymour Clarke, the traffic superintendent, in April 1843 to complain of the poor conditions in the new settlement. Clarke reported

Hill's comments about 'the insufficient supply of water, defective drainage, and bad state of the roads and fences, and other subjects of grievance connected with the Cottages' to the GWR's General Committee.[61] The committee instructed the company's resident engineer at Swindon, R J Ward, 'to remedy the evils complained of'. There were as yet no shops, which meant a 1-mile (1·6-km) walk up the hill to old Swindon for essential provisions.

Early population statistics

In August 1843 the company compiled a population table for the village.[62] By that time, 131 cottages had been built, including the nine temporary dwellings erected by Rigbys. There is no mention of tenements, suggesting that the multiple occupancy of some cottages in the first block was a temporary measure designed to accommodate as many employees as possible prior to the completion of the later blocks. Also rents are listed as payable for each cottage, rather than for any separate tenements within them.

The total number of occupants in the 131 cottages in August 1843 was 663, out of whom 216 were men of working age. This means an average occupancy rate of 5 persons per cottage, the majority of which had only two rooms. Four of the cottages had ten occupants each, but it is not clear whether these were single or double cottages. Of the 663 total, 114 were described as relations and lodgers. This included eighty-six males, most of whom were probably lodgers, and twenty-eight females.

The company prepared another population table for the village in January 1844, some five months later. By that time the number of cottages had risen to 149, including fourteen temporary dwellings and a public house, presumably the Queens Tap built by Rigbys to the south of the station in 1842–3 (**Fig 75**). The number of occupants had risen to 801, making an average of 5.4 persons per cottage. The 116 two-room cottages held an average of nearly 5 persons per house, while the nineteen double cottages had an average of 8 occupants per dwelling. By contrast, one two-room cottage was occupied by eleven people: a man and his wife with their five children, and four male lodgers. The village held a total of 366 children, of whom thirty-six had been born in the new settlement. There were 143 lodgers or relations, nearly 18 per cent of the population. As a single man, Snell lodged in ten different cottages in the village (see Figure 73). If his experience was typical, the mobility of lodgers as a group must have been considerable. Altogether, the village could still only accommodate just over half of the company's workforce.

Overcrowding and proposed remedies

By January 1847 there were 182 completed houses in the village, but the number accommodated had risen steeply to 1,360 persons, at an average of 7·5 persons per house.[63] In addition, there were 978 people living in the area immediately outside the village, most of whom were company employees. The recent expansion of the works meant that the population of the village and surrounding district had increased by nearly one third in 1846 alone.

The demand for accommodation continued to outstrip supply even after the completion of the terraces on the east side of the village, which took place in the middle of 1847. A document of about that time, signed by Archibald Sturrock, states that there were then 241 houses accommodating 1,735 persons, making an average of 7·2 per house. A fourth shop block was still not complete. In a desperate appeal to the company, Sturrock wrote: 'Mr Sturrock has applications for 119 houses. Mr Hill has twelve orders for houses unsupplied which gives a total of 131 applications for houses, and there are only 5 houses and 2 shops building to meet them!'[64]

The General Committee had attempted to rectify the overcrowding problem on 3 August 1846 when it instructed Brunel 'to prepare a plan for building two other blocks of cottages in front of the present Village reserving space for the residences of two officers of the Company in separate detached blocks of ground'.[65] This was followed

Fig 75 *The Queens Tap public house, immediately to the south of the station, was designed in Brunel's office and built by J D & C Rigby in 1842–3. The Queens Tap, together with the refreshment rooms and the Queens Royal Hotel, was leased to Rigbys for one penny per annum as part of the* quid pro quo *for agreeing to build 300 cottages at their own expense for the company's employees. Accordingly, the Tap was run as part of the hotel business. By 1851 a large block of stables forming the mews to the Queens Royal Hotel had been built to the rear of the Tap. These outbuildings were demolished in 1991.*

by a reference to 'one of those detached residences' being for Sturrock, the strong implication being that the proposed site for these buildings lay to the north of the existing terraces, in the area between the two villas built for Hill and Sturrock.

At the same meeting the committee authorised Brunel to obtain tenders for the construction of additional, three-storey blocks adjoining High Street (Emlyn Square). These were probably the blocks between Oxford and Reading Streets and between Exeter and Taunton Streets, on opposing sides of High Street. Plans for the latter block incorporated two superior houses for officers instead of shops.

Brunel was also 'instructed to prepare and submit a plan for building rooms, similar to a barrack, for the use of single men, with the convenience of one general sitting room, kitchen

Fig 76 *A page from one of Brunel's sketchbooks of 1847, showing the façade of a proposed town hall for New Swindon. The scheme was probably intended for the site on which the Mechanics' Institution was to be built in 1854–5, but was abandoned as a casualty of the 1847–9 recession*

etc'. Single men had previously boarded with families in the cottage terraces and in the lodging houses in the shop blocks, and the company felt that by accommodating them together they could ease the overcrowding throughout the village.

Brunel prepared plans and elevations for the new barrack building, and construction began in about mid 1847. The site chosen was on High Street (Emlyn Square) at the west end of the Reading/Faringdon Street block of cottages. The main façade (see Figure 205) was to face on to High Street, and its design was to be almost identical to that of the nearby shop blocks. It was intended as the final component in Brunel's scheme for a central axis bordered by tall buildings of homogeneous design.

In the event, all these new building proposals became immediate casualties of company

retrenchment following the onset of the post-railway-mania depression. The plans to build blocks of cottages on land to the north of the village had not been advanced and were dropped completely. The shop block between Oxford Street and Reading Street, which was referred to in Sturrock's memorandum, had been completed by this time, but the block to the south west had hardly been started. Only the ground-floor walls of the 'Barracks', as it was called, had been constructed. Snell's panorama, painted two years later, shows the building surrounded by scaffolding (see Figure 57). The three-storey block going up on the opposite side of High Street (Emlyn Square) is recorded by Snell in the later of his two paintings as virtually complete. In reality, it is unlikely to have been this far advanced since it was built anew to a completely revised plan in 1853–4. The Barracks was also completed to a revised plan at the same time, and is discussed in more detail in Chapter 8 (see pp 160–63).

A scheme for a town hall in the village did not even make it to the drawing-board, although an elevational sketch and plan of this structure, dated 9 April 1847, appears in one of Brunel's notebooks (**Fig 76**).[66] The building was to have had a seven-bay façade and a very tall central clock tower. Its intended location is unknown, but the open space in the centre of High Street (where the Mechanics' Institution was eventually built) would seem the most logical place.

The recession of 1847–1849

The impact of company retrenchment was particularly severe on the inhabitants of the village. There had been a reduction in staff numbers and wages once before, in 1843, but this was of little consequence when compared with the 1847–9 cutbacks. On 26 October 1847, Charles Saunders, the GWR's company secretary, advised Daniel Gooch that the directors intended to cut all expenditure until the financial situation improved, pointing out the necessity of 'cutting down and retrenching until better times appear'.[67] Gooch proceeded to reduce the workforce at Swindon from 1,800 to 618 within two years, discharging the men in batches of several hundred at a time.

Single men were the first to be dismissed, and by September 1849 only three were left.[68] The company probably reasoned that these men had no ties in Swindon and could more easily seek work elsewhere. This policy coincidentally resulted in the immediate removal of any requirement for a single men's barrack. Senior employees and family men were the most likely to be kept on, especially those who were both highly skilled and who had been regular recipients of bonuses for high productivity. Those who remained had to take on additional duties whilst incurring a one-quarter reduction in working hours (and hence in pay).

According to a statement issued by the company in 1842, discharged men were required to vacate their cottages within a week. It is not clear whether this policy was applied to the victims of the 1847–9 economic downturn, and it seems that those who could afford to pay rent out of their savings were allowed to stay. Those with few savings had to rely on support from colleagues remaining in work as well as picking up casual employment as agricultural labourers. Many subsequently moved with their families to cheaper rental accommodation in speculative developments being built in Westcott and around Fleet Street and Bridge Street (see pp 66–7) whilst others left the area in search of work elsewhere.

Gooch, who ruled New Swindon like a patriarch, did what he could to help the men during the depression. He seems to have been instrumental in negotiating a reduction in cottage rents in 1849, although the directors' decision was ultimately influenced by the need to stem the loss of income brought about by tenants moving out of the village to find cheaper accommodation. On 22 September 1849 Gooch advised the directors that 'we have 23 houses empty, and 17 only partially occupied by which the Company are loosing £11.3.0 per week or £580 per annum in rent and this will be considerably increased when the waggons [sic] now on hand are finished and the men on them discharged'.[69] The directors subsequently instructed Gooch to investigate a general rent reduction as a means of inducing the men to move back into the company cottages. At that time there were six classes of houses let at various weekly rents ranging from 3s 6d to 12s. Following discussion with the men Gooch recommended that rents be reduced by an average of just under one shilling. This was approved by the directors.

Health and welfare

Along with financial hardship, the inhabitants of the village had also to deal with constant ill-health caused by poor drainage and an inadequate water supply, the latter being a defect identified by Gooch in his letter of September 1840 (see p 7). In February 1843 Snell recorded in his diary that he had not been well since arriving in Swindon. He also mentioned the existence of a 'sick club' which was probably formed immediately prior to the opening of the works. Staff contributing to the club received assistance towards their medical bills. In 1844 the sick club became the GWR Locomotive and Carriage Department Sick Fund Society. Different classes of membership, offering various levels of sickness benefit, were introduced, and

membership became a condition of employment.[70] In December 1847, a separate organisation, the Great Western Railway Medical Fund Society, was formed to assist GWR employees with the payment of doctors' bills. The impetus for its establishment came from the high number of serious accidents which were occurring in the works and the consequent need to ensure an adequate salary for the company 'medical man', Stuart Rea, many of whose patients were unemployed and unable to pay for his services. Subscriptions to the Medical Fund were deducted by the company cashier from the men's wages. The Medical Fund also carried out monthly inspections of the company's cottages to ensure that they were habitable.

Water and drainage

Outbreaks of disease were commonplace in the village at the time. There were serious cases of smallpox and typhus, as well as an outbreak of cholera in 1849.[71] Many of these epidemics were caused by blocked and overflowing cesspools in the rear yards of the cottages. In August 1849 Gooch ordered Sturrock to have the drains cleaned,[72] and at the same time the company, on Gooch's recommendation, ordered that the cottages 'be cleansed and whitewashed'.[73] The company provided the lime to the inhabitants who carried out the work themselves.

An inadequate water supply was the other main cause of ill-health on the estate. From the establishment of the works until 1866 the principal water supply was from the Wilts & Berks Canal. According to a plan in the Wiltshire Record Office, dated May 1847, water from the canal was fed by means of a valve into reservoirs to the north of the station from whence it was fed by gravity to tanks adjacent to the old 'D' shop (the original fitting shop) in the works. From here it was distributed around the works and to the cottage estate, again by gravity. A map of 1846–7 (see Figure 49) shows two stopcocks on the northern side of the village (on Bristol and London Streets, near their corners with High Street). There must, however, have been a piped water supply to the village at an earlier date, since a half-plan of one of the shop blocks shows a detailed system of lead cisterns and pipes. In any event, the canal water was polluted by discharges from the works by the time it got to the village, and it was poorly filtered.

THE MECHANICS' INSTITUTION

Another welfare organisation established with the aid of the company in the 1840s was the Great Western Railway Mechanics' Institution. This was formed on 8 January 1844 'for the purpose of disseminating useful knowledge and encouraging rational amusement amongst all classes of people employed by the Great Western Railway Company at Swindon'.[74] Gooch was its first president. Members, who had to be in the employment of the company, paid a variety of subscription rates depending on their income, these being deducted out of wages.

The heart of the institution was the library which was gradually increased in size through donations from senior officers and through acquisitions funded by members' subscriptions. The members used the institution's reading-room to further their technical education and thereby improve their employment prospects within the works. Additional information was imparted through a lecture programme put on by the institution, which also organised concerts and soirées, and quickly became the focal point of New Swindon social life.

In 1845 the council of the institution took over the management of the baths provided for the workmen on the ground floor of the 1842 office and stores building on the eastern side of the courtyard at the railway works (see p 24). No baths were provided in the cottages, so these communal facilities were in heavy demand. The second annual report of the council recorded that they 'are much frequented; there being a sufficient number for about 200 persons bathing each week at a rate of 1/2d each'.[75] In November 1846 the GWR chairman, Charles Russell, wrote to Gooch for information on the baths at Swindon. In his letter he referred to 'the present mania for baths and wash-houses', indicating that the provision of baths for factory workers was a relatively recent phenomenon.[76]

The Mechanics' Institution was originally accommodated within the works, at first probably on the first floor of the wheel shop.[77] In 1846 the new 'D' (or wheel-turning) shop was used as a theatre and lecture hall by night, whilst another room in the works was made available as a reading-room and library.[78] The housing of these facilities within the works meant that members and their families had to cross the main line, thereby putting themselves at considerable risk. For this reason, the institution was allowed to hold amateur theatrical performances, from 1849, at the GWR school located to the south of the line. Lectures and adult education classes had been held there from at least as early as 1847.

The institution's presence in the works was intended to be a temporary measure; if the retrenchment of 1847–9 had not occurred, it is likely that work would have started on a permanent building in the village before the end of the decade. In September 1847 Brunel presented the General Committee with a scheme for funding a new library and reading-room at Swindon by allocating three-quarters of the profits derived from the construction of certain engines and tenders.[79] It is possible that he intended to incorporate these facilities into the town-hall building that he sketched in April of that year. In fact, construction of a permanent building for the institution was not begun until 1854 (see pp 79–81).

The company also provided its employees with a variety of recreational facilities. In 1844 it paid Colonel Vilett £1,498 for 14 acres (5·6 hectares) immediately to the west of the village for use as a park.[80] This was used as a cricket ground and, later, as a venue for fêtes and outdoor lectures. In 1848, on Gooch's recommendation, the company granted the men and their families the free use of a special train for a pleasure excursion.[81] This 'trip', as it was known, was organised by the Mechanics' Institution. It became an annual event and an important fixture in the New Swindon social calendar.

NONCONFORMIST CHAPELS

Many of the families in the settlement were nonconformists who worshipped, initially, in private houses or in chapels in old Swindon. They received no assistance from the company, unlike their brethren at Crewe, and were therefore unable to afford permanent buildings in New Swindon until the end of the decade. In 1843 Snell referred to the existence of a chapel at New Swindon. The building that housed this temporary Methodist chapel is thought to have been located next to the Golden Lion Inn.[82] Three permanent chapels were built in 1848–9. These included a Methodist chapel in Bridge Street, and a Primitive Methodist chapel in Regent Street (as the southern part of Bridge Street became known). In the same year the first Baptist chapel was built in Fleet Street, in Northern Italianate style (**Fig 77**). The first Roman Catholic church was built in 1851.

SPECULATIVE HOUSING

The 1840s witnessed a construction boom by private speculators in the area around the railway village. The most notable area of expansion was at Westcott, to the west of New Swindon, just beyond the park. In 1851, Westcott was described as a modern village,[83] and two years later there were approximately seventy cottages along the west side of Westcott Place, and along Westcott Street leading to Westcott Farm.[84] William Plummer, of Westcott Farm, had shrewdly purchased land in the area in 1843, and many of the new two-storey, brick cottages were built by him and his family from the mid 1840s.[85] Westcott Place had twelve shops in 1848, most of which were either beer retailers or shoemakers,[86] and

they formed an important adjunct to the company's shops in the village. One of the shops survives at the northern end of Westcott Place, close to the Ship Inn. The cottages, none of which remains in its original form, were generally of cheaper construction than those in the village, and they were probably let at lower rents.

The other principal areas of expansion were along Fleet Street (the main road leading to Westcott and Wootton Bassett) and Bridge Street. The latter, lying immediately east of the village, stood on the route of the main track from New Swindon through Eastcott to old Swindon. It was made into a road in 1845, paid for by public subscription. Bridge Street and Regent Street (its southward extension) were to form New Swindon's principal thoroughfare by the 1860s.

By 1851 the total population of the ecclesiastical district of St Mark, which included the village and the hamlets of Westcott and Eastcott, was 2,468, whereas that of the remainder of Swindon parish, including the old town, was 2,411.[87] In less than ten years the population of the new town had effectively outstripped that of the old. The GWR had succeeded in establishing a self-sufficient community, providing for, and controlling, virtually every aspect of its inhabitants' lives. Brunel and Gooch had presided over the construction of a railway town which – despite serious problems with drainage and water supply – was almost unparalleled in Britain at the time, and matched only by the railway town at Crewe, which possessed a similar range of buildings and included 514 company houses by 1849.

Fig 77 *A view (of around 1880) showing the Baptist chapel in New Swindon, built in 1848–9 in Fleet Street, to the east of the village. Plans for the chapel, together with a large subscription, were provided by Sir Morton Peto, MP for Bristol. The schools, added to the rear in 1868 by the Swindon architect Thomas Lansdown, have survived. The chapel has been extensively remodelled as a shop.*

The depression of 1847–9 forced the GWR to reappraise many of its existing practices and to review its facilities. The locomotive establishment, as one of the major expense-incurring departments, was subject to particular scrutiny and, as we have seen, Daniel Gooch, the superintendent of locomotive engines, was called upon to report possible economies to the directors on several occasions during the period from 1847 to 1849. By the latter half of 1849 the financial climate was such that the number of men in the locomotive department at Swindon was reduced to 618, and this figure would have included engine-drivers, firemen and others needed to operate the locomotive service. The situation was so bad that the machinery

acquired for the new fitting shop was left packed in grease in one half of the building. Gooch reported to the directors that:

> Swindon has been designed and built to employ 1800 to 2000 men and all the arrangement of tools and shops has been made to employ this number of men to the best advantage and are therefore not so well adapted for our present diminished number. The fixed charges or shop expenses are in consequence heavier than they would be in a place better proportioned to the work done. Any work that can be obtained will therefore assist to reduce these expenses, in fact we have the means at Swindon of earning at manufacturers prices at least 20,000 pounds per annum.[1]

In a later report he qualified this by claiming:

> but when we consider that our engines are now mostly 7 and 8 years old and that a great many of them have and are now receiving alterations and improvements in addition to the ordinary repairs, without any increase taking place in the cost per mile, it is proof that we are receiving some benefit from the complete shops and arrangements at Swindon.[2]

In discussion at the Committee of Consultation held at Paddington on 22 November 1849, however, some directors seemed unconvinced and claimed that there was a 'great loss to the Company by the Capital there [ie Swindon] locked up in buildings and excessive Stock of Engines'. There were '170 Engines in Stock and only 103 at work', a situation brought about partly because the GWR had overestimated the demand for 'direct working' (where GWR locomotives were used to work lines owned by other railway companies), and partly because the Bristol and Exeter lines ceased to be worked on 1 May 1849, effectively reducing the system from 312 miles (500km) to 227 miles (363km).

Swindon 'seemed now like a deserted place' and fundamental questions were asked as to the *raison d'être* for the manufacturing element of the works if the saving on manufacture was only £250 per engine. It was suggested that carriage maintenance might be contracted out and that repairs currently carried out at the 'Hospitals for Engines' at Reading and Bristol be undertaken at Swindon instead. Charles Russell, the GWR chairman, countered by explaining that the present over-capacity would be eased when the South Wales line opened and that 'the Articles manufactured at Swindon were of a very superior quality', as well

as being cheaper if capital charges were discounted.

NEW ORDERS FOR THE BELEAGUERED WORKS

The prospects for the works brightened considerably at the beginning of the second half of the 19th century, and for the next few years the GWR was to be preoccupied with more important issues than economies at the works, as the company became engaged in a bitter feud with the London & North Western Railway over the latter's penetration into the Birmingham area. Meanwhile, the broad-gauge system was developing apace. The South Wales Railway opened in June 1850, adding 75 miles (120km) to the lines worked and the Banbury extension of the Oxford line (25 miles/140km) was completed in September, whilst the Wiltshire, Somerset and Weymouth line reached as far as Frome by October. All these additions to the system required additional broad-gauge rolling stock, supplied by, and maintained at, Swindon. In August, for example, an additional eight locomotives, seventy-five coal wagons and seventy-five box wagons were ordered for the South Wales Railway at a cost of £40,000. These were welcome orders, indeed, for the beleaguered works. Nationally, preparations were under way for the Great Exhibition and a mood of cautious optimism prevailed. Mr Minard Rea was appointed to succeed Archibald Sturrock as works' manager at a salary of £350, and in June the other officers' salaries were restored to their former levels. Gradually the works returned to former levels of production.

In November 1850 Brunel asked if he could have permission to exhibit one of the large, eight-wheeled passenger engines, then being built at the works, at the 1851 exhibition. The board gave its consent on the condition that 'no alteration or addition should be made to increase to the Company the Cost of the Locomotive Engine in its Construction'. The engine exhibited was *Lord of the Isles*, which was to prove such an important advertisement for the Great Western Railway (**Fig 78**). Quite apart from this, the Great Exhibition of 1851 produced a huge increase in excursion traffic, with the consequent need for new rolling stock to be built at Swindon.

THE WORKS IN 1852

We are fortunate that, just when the enlarged works were fully operational for the first time, we have a detailed, if rather quaint, illustrated

THE GREAT WESTERN RAILWAY COMPANY'S WORKS AT SWINDON.

Figs 79 *and* **80**
Illustrations accompanying the article on the Swindon works in The Illustrated Exhibitor *of 1852.*

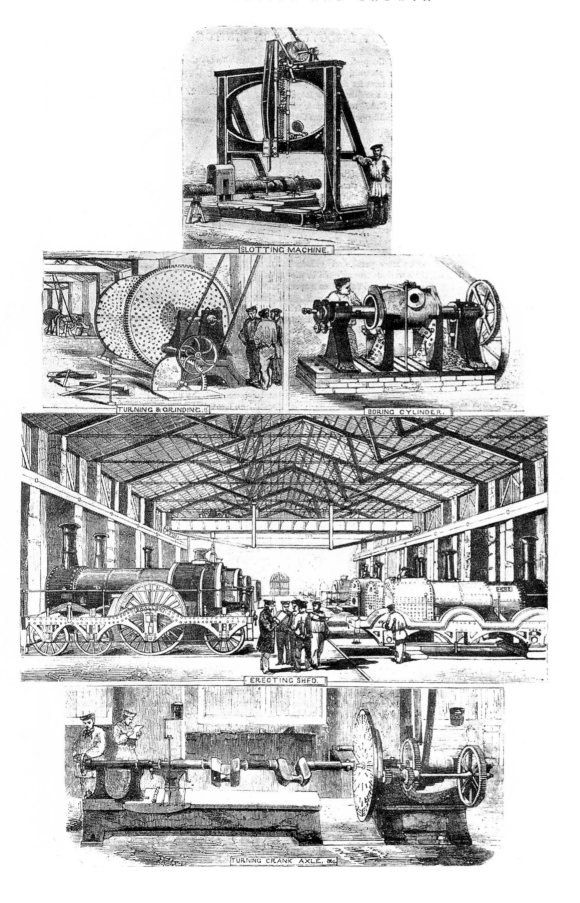

SLOTTING MACHINE.

TURNING & GRINDING.

BORING CYLINDER.

ERECTING SHED.

TURNING CRANK AXLE. &c.

account of their operation, published in *The Illustrated Exhibitor* in 1852 (**Figs 79** and **80**). Extracts from the article are here reproduced at some length, since they convey a contemporary sense of wonder that would be difficult to recapture in a more abbreviated form:

The Railway Factory at Swindon consists of two large squares, surrounded by workshops, with one or two smaller squares adjoining.

There are, moreover, two shops for the manufacture of iron-trucks and the iron-work of carriages, with which, at present, we have nothing to do. The locomotive department, to which the present remarks will be restricted, has room for no fewer than 3,000 men to work, though this number has never yet been reached.

In describing the movements of a locomotive establishment of such magnitude and extent, we begin, as is desirable, with the simplest part – the Smithery: a long range of buildings, containing the astonishing number of 176 forges, with all the appliances required for their full efficiency. Here, all the parts of a locomotive, which are of *wrought*-iron – as axles, piston-rods, connecting-rods, and the smaller pieces, which seem almost innumerable, are produced. All the various processes of a very complete smith's-shop are constantly passed through. One branch of this department is appropriated to the spring-makers, who forge and nicely temper the parts of which a spring is composed, and then fasten them together by an iron band.

From hence we proceed to observe the forging of the largest works of a locomotive. As an ordinary fire is inadequate to heat the huge masses of iron employed in their production, there are three furnaces. One of them is used in melting the scraps of iron that come from the lathes and the fitting-shops in general ... Close to the furnaces are two of Nasmyth's steam-hammers, which are invaluable in forging large masses of iron ... Our illustration shows the back of one of the furnaces, with the opening through which the men put the coal; the crane by which the iron, however huge it may be, is brought to the steam-hammer; and that vast congeries of 'sledge-hammers' itself, which works on unwearied from day to day, and from year to year. It is here represented as forging the half of a crank-axle.

The article then describes and illustrates the processes of wheel-making and tyre-fitting before moving on to the boiler shop:

The boiler-house must now be visited. The boilers are made of sheet-iron, duly prepared for this purpose. When brought to their proper size and shape, the plates have to be drilled or punched, so that holes may be made for the rivets which are to bind the various parts of the boiler together. The process for doing this may be observed in our illustration ...

The chief object observable in the engraving employed to illustrate this part of the subject is a boiler, nearly completed, and soon to leave the work shop ...

Leaving the boiler-house, we enter the foundry, the region of products in *cast*-iron – those already described being in *wrought*-iron. Here the cylinders and surrounding parts of the fabric of a locomotive are formed. Here, too, the ornamental portions, the cocks, and whistles, are cast in brass. For the foundry, however, much narrower limits suffice than for the other departments of the establishment through which we have passed. Immediately adjoining the foundry is a shop where the woodwork of the buffers of a locomotive is made; here also are the pattern-makers, the persons who make models in wood – and that with great dexterity and nicety – of whatever is intended to be cast in moist or dry sand, and that either in iron or brass. This mode is adopted in all the finer kinds of work, and it is now mentioned because, in the production of larger articles, and where a rough surface is of no consequence, the melted metal is poured into moulds of loam, when patterns are only partially, or not at all, used.

The fitting-shops now demand a visit. To supply the power necessary to put in motion the numerous machines in the factory, there are two powerful engines: one by Stothardt, with 21-inch [533-mm] cylinders; and, at the other end of the buildings, is an engine with 30-inch [762-mm] cylinders, by Harvey and Co. In the lower turning-shop, the first we enter, the axles, crank-axles, and other large parts of loco-motives, are finished.

The illustration at the top of the second page of engravings represents the slotting-machine, one of the almost invaluable machines of Messrs. Whitworth, of Manchester: the one now exhibited is, we believe, the largest they ever made ... this machine is employed to cut, from the solid metal, a hole or aperture, for the admission of the connecting-rod ... After the slotting-machine has thus acted on the crank-axle, it is removed to one of the large lathes, in which state it is shown at the bottom of the page ... At one end of the same shop is the machine for boring cylinders, of which an illustration will also be observed.

At the opposite end of the shop appears the hydraulic-press, by means of which the wheels of a locomotive, however large or weighty, are unrelentingly forced on their appointed axles. Our illustration also shows one of the large lathes for turning eight-feet [2.4-m] wheels, and also the machine for grinding steel tires, both in a fitting-shop somewhat distant from the one which has now been described. Above this shop is another, in which all the smaller and lighter parts of a locomotive are turned, in about forty-five lathes of a proportionately lighter description than are required for the heavier work. At the end of this shop is a door, leading into the brass-finishing shop, the name of which describes the processes carried on. There is yet another, called the grinding-shop, for many parts of a locomotive that were formerly finished by filing, are now ground; and adjoining this is the coppersmith's-shop, in which the feed-pipes and similar parts are made.

Finally, there is the erecting-shed, in which all the parts of a locomotive, consisting of no fewer than 5,416 pieces, are put together. To the left, in the foreground of the engraving, may be seen one of the large eight-wheeled locomotives, similar to that noble specimen of art, 'the Lord of the Isles', which many people at the Crystal Palace supposed was merely for show, not knowing that three like it are actually running on the Great-Western Railway. The Colossus that now catches the eye needs only the aid of the painter and varnisher to be fully prepared to run, in its best attire, its mighty course. To the right, on a level with this locomotive, may be observed a half-finished goods-engine, which is readily distinguished from one intended for passengers by its having the wheels of equal size. As we look towards the other end of the shed, there will be perceived a row of locomotives in different conditions, and some as mere bodies. Midway, however, between the roof and the floor, is a traversing-table, running from end to end of the building, and used for the very *light* work of lifting up engines *bodily*, to put under or take away their wheels. This stupendous result is attainted by means of a hydraulic apparatus, holding from eight to ten gallons [36 to 45 litres] of water.

The accompanying illustrations (Figs 79 and 80), though not entirely reliable since they omit some crucial detail, give valuable information about the construction of the buildings themselves. They show, for example, three different forms of roof structure over the exceptionally wide boiler, erecting and steam-hammer shops and also three different types of wall construction.

These differences in construction would seem to reflect differences in function as well as differences in date. The boiler shop has a conventional wooden queen-post roof above an arcaded track for an overhead crane which was installed in 1846 (see p 32); perhaps the arcade is of that date and therefore an addition to the original structure.

The erecting shop, on the other hand, has extra thick piers to support the track of the travelling crane and these are shown on the original drawings supplied to Joseph Whitworth & Co, suppliers of the works' machinery. The roof of this shop, though of similar width to that of the boiler shop, is framed by a more sophisticated truss which is still mostly of wood but with tension members in iron. The illustration of the

steam-hammer shop scarcely shows the roof but, from what little detail is included, it is clear that the trusses were extremely light and made entirely of metal.

THE GWR EXPANDS NORTHWARDS

The article in *The Illustrated Exhibitor* comments that the works could accommodate a still larger workforce and therefore it is not surprising that, despite a healthier order book, there was a considerable lull in the construction of new buildings throughout the 1850s.

Until 1850 the GWR had been almost exclusively broad gauge, but, as the system expanded northwards, more and more concessions had to be made to standard-gauge working (or narrow gauge as it was known by GWR traditionalists). A series of amalgamations with railways in the West Midlands expanded the GWR system to the River Mersey and brought with it an inheritance of those companies' locomotive and carriage works. To operate these new lines and works a separate northern division was created with a superintendent immediately subordinate to Daniel Gooch, the superintendent of locomotive engines. The division also required additional stocks of standard-gauge locomotives, some of which were built at Swindon, the first being completed in May 1855.

Despite this new work, the company's financial position was strained by the takeover of the northern railways, which coincided with the opening of over one hundred miles (160km) of lightly worked rural line. In September 1857 the directors decided to reduce the number of trains in overall operation on the GWR lines, leading to

Fig 81 *A marble bust of Brunel, sculpted by Edward Wyon RA, in 1862 (three years after Brunel's death) and displayed in the Mechanics' Institution. In 1863 Wyon completed a bust of New Swindon's other founding father, Daniel Gooch, to stand beside that of Brunel. A total of 1,651 employees in the locomotive department contributed to the cost of making the Gooch bust.*

less repair work at Swindon and a consequent reduction in the number of men employed there. There was to be a further reduction in the workforce the following year when the company declared an all-time low dividend of only 1·25 per cent.[3]

In the meantime, the death of Minard Rea, in 1857, resulted in a change of works' manager at Swindon. Rea was succeeded by William Gooch, who had earlier been installed as manager at the South Devon Railway's works at Newton (now Newton Abbot) by Daniel Gooch (who was William's elder brother). In September 1859 Brunel himself died, worn out by the frantic pace he had set himself, his health finally broken by the travails of his last great project, the construction of the *SS Great Eastern*, the largest ship of its time. It seems from his papers that Brunel had not been personally concerned with developments at Swindon for some time, and his death did not have the impact on the works and village that it would have had a decade earlier (**Fig 81**).

NEW ROLLING MILLS

No further significant developments took place at the works until 1860, when the directors decided to erect rolling mills 'for the working up of the worn or damaged iron ... with the aid of fresh materials ... into new rails'.[4] A sum of £20,000 was voted for the mill and machinery, to be repaid with interest over a period of fourteen years at a charge of £2,000 per annum on top of the manufacturing cost of new rails. The mills, conspicuous by their two enormous chimneys, were built in the north-western corner of the works. The occasion of the rolling of the first rail, at the end of May 1861, was reported at length in the local press:

> The new buildings are to the eye of a very simple construction and consist principally of an iron roof supported on numerous iron pillars, and covering an area of from 150 to 200 feet square [46 to 61 metres square], the four sides of the building being left quite open, with the exception of a small space on the south side, where some offices are erected.
> Thousands of pounds worth of materials, however, are hid from the eye; the floor of the building which is raised some three feet [1m] above the surrounding level, being intersected in every direction by masonry, shafting, pipes, flues, etc.[5]

Following a detailed description of the operation of the eight puddling furnaces and the rolling mills, with their reheating furnaces, the reporter comments on the immensity of the two flywheels, of 20-ft (6·1-m) diameter, belonging to the pair of horizontal high-pressure steam engines which generated 200 hp (150kW) to drive the mills; he remarks that the engines, unlike most of the other machinery in the works, were made in-house. He was obviously also impressed by the arrangement of the eight boilers which utilised waste heat from the furnaces to supply steam not only to the main engines but to 'lesser ones' and to the two steam hammers.

He also notes that the 'works have been constructed under the superintendence of Mr Ellis, a gentleman who has had much experience in the manufacture of iron' and that the workforce is notably Welsh. The production of the first rail was a momentous event: Ellis was placed in a chair and carried round the works to the accompaniment of cheers from the workforce and the blowing-off of steam. Despite Gooch having to justify the high cost of Swindon rails to the directors, the rolling mills were extended in 1862–3 to increase their production from 250 tons (254 tonnes) to 400 tons (406·4 tonnes) per week.

GOOCH RESIGNS

In 1863, the rolling mills were, however, the least of Daniel Gooch's problems, given that boardroom politics increasingly were making his personal position untenable. In 1855 Charles Russell had resigned as GWR chairman after a twenty-year reign. In the following decade, there were no fewer than six company chairmen. The same decade also witnessed several changes in the tenure and role of the company's principal engineer. Brunel had retained the title of 'Great Western Engineer' until his death on 15 September 1859, even though day-to-day operations had been undertaken for some years by his chief assistant, T H Bertram. Bertram succeeded Brunel in 1859, but retired the following year. The post was then split between Michael Lane as Principal Engineer and John Fowler as Consulting Engineer.

Meanwhile there had been great changes in the composition of the GWR board. The expansion of the GWR system had already diluted the simple distinction between London and Bristol-based directors and an Act of 1863, uniting the GWR with the South Wales and West Midland railways, brought in several new directors who had little allegiance to the broad gauge, or to the existing GWR officers. That same year, one of the new directors – William Potter, a former GWR director and critic of past management – was elected chairman, while Charles Saunders, the company secretary since the GWR's inception, resigned at the age of sixty-six due to ill health. Saunders had been a staunch ally of Gooch, and his departure left Gooch even more vulnerable.

The new board appointed a committee to oversee the running of the locomotive division, which had, until then, been Daniel Gooch's direct responsibility. The committee's chairman, C R M Talbot, had formerly been chairman of the South Wales Railway and had already clashed with Gooch in the past over the latter's working of that railway under contract. The atmosphere deteriorated to the extent that Gooch walked out of two of the three meetings of the committee, and it is a testimony to the regard in which he was generally held that he avoided dismissal.

In the end, Gooch himself decided to resign, having amassed a considerable fortune by this time, and having developed a great many other business interests outside the GWR. First, however, he sought to secure the succession of his brother William (the works' manager), or of Joseph Armstrong, to his post of superintendent of locomotive engines. Determined to prevent this, Potter approached Charles Sacré of the Manchester, Sheffield & Lincolnshire Railway, and asked him to fill the post. Potter was foiled only by Gooch's strenuous lobbying of the other directors, who settled on Joseph Armstrong as Gooch's replacement. When John Gibson, the carriage and wagon superintendent, resigned later that year, Armstrong was given that additional responsibility and William Gooch had little choice other than to leave, along with his brother Daniel, in April 1864.

NEW SWINDON AND ITS INHABITANTS

According to the 1851 census, the first to cover New Swindon, the population of the railway village at that time was 1,454 and the average occupancy rate was just over 6 people per cottage. This was higher than in 1849, but not quite as bad as the occupation density of 7·5 persons per cottage reached at the height of the railway mania in 1847. In 1851, the predominantly two-roomed cottages making up the western half of the village contained an average of 5·2 persons, whilst the larger cottages on the east side housed an average of 7 persons. Company employees at that time preferred to reside in the village, close to the work, rather than in nearby hamlets such as Westcott. Of the 104 workers living in Westcott, 39 per cent were employed by the GWR and the average occupancy rate of 4·5 persons per cottage was lower than that in the village. Only twenty-two railway employees resided in old Swindon in 1851, an indication of the separation between the old market town and New Swindon which existed until the end of the century.

Predictably, the smaller cottages making up the western half were occupied mainly by semi-skilled and unskilled workers, including 65 per cent of all the labourers living in the village.

These cottages were generally too small to accommodate lodgers, which explains why there were only twenty-five lodgers here, compared with sixty-two in the eastern half. Even so, there was a degree of overcrowding, and three of the two-roomed cottages each housed ten people.

COTTAGE SIZE AND STATUS

Occupancy rates on the more affluent eastern side of the village were closely related to the size and status of the different cottage types. The higher rents charged on this side of High Street (Emlyn Square) meant that there were eight cottages unoccupied in 1851, whereas all the cottages on the western side were occupied.

The large eight-roomed cottages on London Street housed highly skilled artisans or professional employees, many of whom came from heavy industrial areas in the north of England. Number 7 London Street, for example, was occupied by Peter Appleton, a forty-two-year-old engine-driller from Haslingden, Lancashire, his wife and two nieces. Lodging with them were three civil engineers in their twenties, including F A Bucknall, who was to become works' manager for a short time from 1864, and John Fraser, the then assistant works' manager.

Six of the eleven houses in London Street were occupied by just one family whilst four houses were shared by two families; the last, Number 5, contained four families, each presumably living in two-cell tenements. By contrast, Number 12 London Street, housed just three people: the company surgeon (Charles W Hind), his assistant and his housekeeper.

In the case of No 11 London Street, we know a little of the short life of one of the lodgers. Edward Lane, son of the lithographer to Queen Victoria, was apprenticed to the drawing office in 1847, at the age of seventeen. Though he died of typhus in January 1850, shortly before his twentieth birthday, he left a fine collection of drawings and sketches of locomotives and machinery – now a prized possession of the National Museum of Science and Industry, Science Museum Library.[6]

The plainer, eight-roomed houses on the northern side of Oxford Street were tenanted by a mixture of skilled, semi-skilled and unskilled employees at a much greater occupation density than the cottages to the north. The average occupancy rate for these houses was 11·3 persons compared with 6·8 in the London Street houses. All but two of the double houses in Oxford Street contained tenements. Two of the houses each contained eighteen persons housed in four tenements, whilst others were divided into either two or three tenements.

The five-roomed cottages on the southern side of Oxford Street and in Reading and Faringdon Streets housed an average of 7 people. These cottages were each designed to accommodate one family, but by 1851 some contained two. In Reading Street, nine of the thirty-three cottages were occupied by two families. The tenants here were mostly skilled workers such as engine-fitters, erectors and boilermakers. **Figure 82** gives a breakdown of the major occupational groups represented in the village.

THE ORIGINS OF THE WORKFORCE

One of the cottages in Faringdon Street was occupied by William Laverick, an iron forgeman from Bedlington, Northumberland, the town in which Daniel Gooch was born and raised. Laverick was sufficiently well paid to be able to afford a servant. According to the Fawcett List (see Chapter 3, note 40), he was the 'first contractor' for steam-hammer work at the factory. He was a typical member of the élite group of workshop foremen who, by virtue of their position, exerted considerable influence over the men in the factory. Most of the foremen were highly skilled workers, in their thirties or forties, deriving from the north-east of England or Scotland who had been recruited by Daniel Gooch or Archibald Sturrock when the works were first established.

Not all of the foremen lived in the railway village. In 1851 William Nicholson, the first foreman of the fitting and turning shop and one of the most senior employees at the works, lived with his family in Westcott Place. His monthly pay

in 1849 was £7 4s 6d. By comparison, labourers were paid up to £3 12s 7d per month, the precise amount depending on their experience and ability.[7]

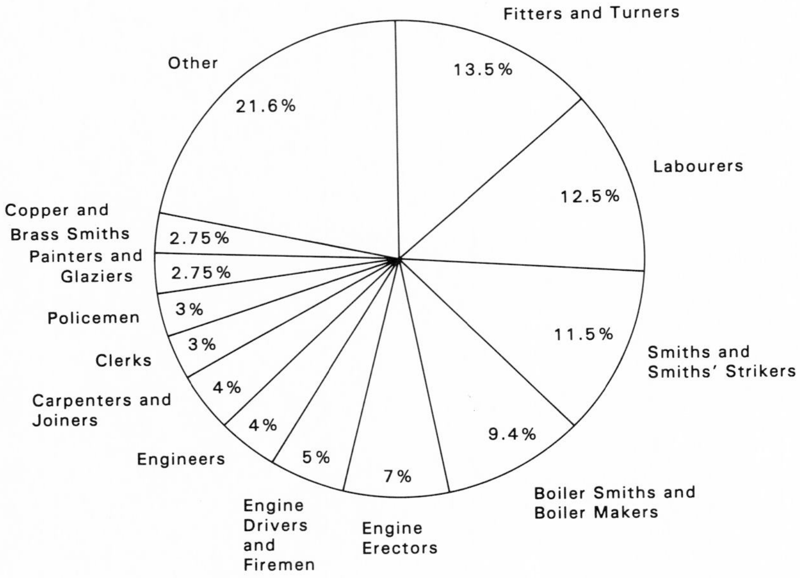

The birthplaces of the men residing in the village in 1851 are shown in **Figure 83**. Men from the north of England and Scotland made up 31 per cent of the village workforce. This group probably would have represented a larger proportion of the population in 1843, but by 1851 some had moved away, to be replaced by local men who had served their apprenticeships in the works over the preceding eight years. Nevertheless, in 1851 only 8 per cent of men in the village had been born in Wiltshire and most of this group consisted of unskilled employees. The vast majority of the workforce (ie 92 per cent) was imported. Other important catchment areas for labour were the industrial areas of Bristol, and Gloucestershire.

The workforce was a young one, the average age being thirty-two. A few boys, such as twelve-year-old Thomas Keefe of Bath Street, were employed as junior clerks or messengers, whilst older boys of fifteen or more were employed as apprentices, often in the same trades as their fathers. There were virtually no employment opportunities for the women of the village. The few who worked were mostly widows of GWR employees, or young women working from home as laundresses or dressmakers.

WELFARE IN THE VILLAGE

From 1850 the population of the village began to increase as a result of the new jobs created by the gradual improvement in the company's financial position. Consequently, the shortage of shops began to be felt again. One of the six shops in the village was vacant. In response to this situation, a group of Swindon mechanics petitioned the directors in February 1851, requesting that they be allowed to rent the shop for use as a general store; their proposal was accepted in return for a rent of £70 per annum.[8] In the same year a co-operative bakery was established in New Swindon, only seven years after the first co-operative shop was opened in Rochdale.

The population increase also exerted pressure on the already inadequate drainage facilities, and this, coupled with growing overcrowding in the village, threatened the health of the inhabitants. In 1849, residents representing 10 per cent of the rated population of Swindon parish petitioned the General Board of Health to apply the Public Health Act of 1848 to the whole parish including New Swindon. This would have involved the establishment of a local board of health with responsibility for the provision of adequate

Fig 82 *The occupations of GWR employees residing in the village in 1851. The category 'other' includes a wide range of specialised occupations, such as engine-buffer makers, iron planers, millwrights and tin-plate workers.*

Other 21.6%

Fitters and Turners 13.5%

Labourers 12.5%

Smiths and Smiths' Strikers 11.5%

Boiler Smiths and Boiler Makers 9.4%

Engine Erectors 7%

Engine Drivers and Firemen 5%

Engineers 4%

Carpenters and Joiners 4%

Clerks 3%

Policemen 3%

Copper and Brass Smiths 2.75%

Painters and Glaziers 2.75%

drainage and drinking water. The petition was initiated by residents of old Swindon, but opposed by GWR directors who were worried that the introduction of the Act would involve them in considerable expenditure.[9]

The inspector appointed by the General Board of Health to investigate the matter recommended that a local board be established for old Swindon in the first instance, and that a separate board be set up for New Swindon at a later stage. Further inquiries were held to determine the boundaries of the proposed board, but it was not until 1864 that separate boards of health were established for old and New Swindon. Prior to that, churchwardens and parochial overseers had been responsible for the affairs of the parish, and the GWR had been able to act as an unofficial local authority in New Swindon, exerting close control over its own properties and influencing the development of adjoining districts through the partial funding of new roads.

Improvements and repairs
In an effort to avoid the establishment of a local board for New Swindon the company began taking belated steps to improve conditions for its tenants. In February 1851 it employed Edward Streeter, a contractor from Bath, to carry out repairs to its newer cottages in Oxford, Reading and Faringdon Streets. The older cottages on the west side of the village were in need of more extensive repairs and on 1 March 1852 the company contracted Streeter to keep all the cottages in good order for a seven-year period.[10] The company's specification was exceptionally detailed. It stipulated that roads, drainage gutters, fences, footpaths, lamp-posts, and water-pipes were to be kept in good repair. Rubbish and ashes were to be cleared from the dust holes in the cottage yards on a regular basis and privies and drains were to be routinely flushed out.

The 243 cottages in the village and the bakehouse and slaughterhouse to the south were to have their external woodwork painted twice during the seven-year term. The cottage interiors had to be whitewashed, colour-painted or papered, and the kitchens, wash houses and privies were to be whitewashed or limewashed. All fixtures and fittings had to be kept in good repair. Footpaths in Reading and Faringdon Streets were to be laid with asphalt 2½in [63mm] thick, to match a similar footpath in Bristol Street, and the yards and wash houses were to be paved. Streeter was to be paid £380 per annum over the seven-year term, with an additional 10 per cent payable upon satisfactory completion of the contract.

The company also sought to encourage its tenants to keep their properties in good order by offering prizes for the cleanest dwellings, and for the neatest and most productive front gardens.[11] By so doing it hoped to avoid costly repairs and reduce the threat of disease.

Disease and sanitation
The GWR's attempts to improve conditions met with little success: in September 1853 the company surgeon at Swindon, Charles Hind, informed the directors of a serious outbreak of typhoid, typhus fever and related diseases in the village. Fourteen people in the village died of these diseases during 1852 alone, and a total of 400 cases was reported.[12] Hind asked the directors to take immediate steps to clean and improve the drains 'for the purpose of preventing any increase of fever and of averting the dreaded approach of cholera'.[13] There was a severe outbreak of cholera that same month in Newcastle upon Tyne. The directors attributed the outbreak of disease at Swindon to Streeter's neglect of his contractual obligations and they ordered the resident engineer, Michael Lane, to ensure that the necessary works were undertaken.

The principal cause of the disease was the stagnant, polluted water which overflowed from blocked cesspools. In a written statement of December 1853 to the General Board of Health Inspector, William Lee, Hind remarked that 'the surface drainage has been defective, arising from an insufficient dip in the yards and back courts or alleys to carry the surface water to the deep drains'.[14] The clay pan, 60ft (18·3m) in depth, that underlies much of New Swindon also prevented water from soaking away. Dr R H Goolden, giving evidence on behalf of the company at Lee's

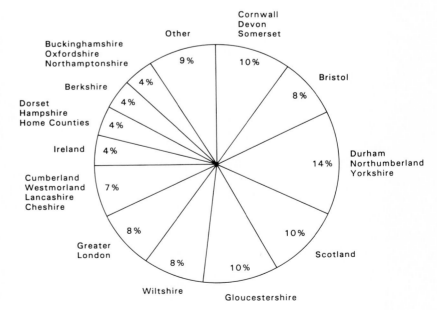

Fig 83 *The birthplaces of the working men living in Swindon village in 1851 expressed as percentages of the total number of GWR employees in the village.*

Inquiry, stated that the wet clay subsoil was the main cause of disease, a contention dismissed by the inspector who blamed the inadequate sanitary arrangements in the village. In October 1853 the company decided to pave all the backyards and alleys in the village at a cost of about £2,000. This was reported 'to be indispensable for the preservation of the health and lives of the inhabitants'.[15] Pennant stone, 2½–3in (63–76mm) thick, was used for paving.

The water supply

By 1853 tap water was being supplied to every house, but the supply still came from the impure waters of the Wilts & Berks Canal. The company partly boiled and evaporated the water before filtering it through sand and charcoal, but the inspector still considered it unfit for drinking, and cited this as a significant contributor to ill-health in the village. The formation of a new company to supply fresh water to old and New Swindon was considered by the GWR in 1854, but the proposal attracted little initial support in New Swindon. The GWR seems to have taken the issue more seriously, and the company went so far as to have plans for a new supply drawn up by Brunel and a contract let to Roland Brotherhood for £6,500 before withdrawing from the scheme, possibly because of a lack of funds.[16]

In 1858 the company sank a well between two of the reservoirs to the north of the station, but, despite initial optimism, the water was found to be brackish and unfit for human consumption. A fresh water supply was finally provided by the Swindon Water Company in 1866. The GWR bought nearly half of its shares and was the company's biggest client.

THE FINAL BUILDING PHASE

Overcrowding remained a pressing problem for the GWR in the early 1850s. No additional dwellings were built in the railway village, and the population increased from 1,454 in 1851 to 1,965 in 1853. In his evidence to Lee's Inquiry in late 1853, Michael Lane, the resident engineer, stated that 'within the last two years, but especially within the last 18 months, there has been a large increase in the number of persons employed upon the company's works ... There was not accommodation for so large a population, and the houses have been very much crowded.'[17] Many GWR employees looked beyond the confines of the village for their accommodation. In 1851 the population of the ecclesiastical district of St Mark (which included outlying hamlets) was 2,468. By the end of 1853, Charles Hind, the company surgeon, estimated that the population had reached 5,700 without any commensurate

increase in new cottages (the figure of 5,700 was probably an overestimate – the actual population may well have been nearer 4,000). Of the new speculative developments that did go up, few had adequate sanitary arrangements, an outcome which the application of the 1848 Public Health Act to New Swindon was supposed to prevent.

The directors took their first steps to ease the overcrowding in the village on 31 March 1853 when they considered Daniel Gooch's suggestion that the Barracks and the block of cottages opposite it on High Street (Emlyn Square), begun in 1847, should be completed, and revised plans for both were approved.[18]

Two-storey end blocks in Bath stone were also approved for the eastern and western sides of the village. The company obtained sites for these blocks by realigning the obliquely angled Church Place and East Street, which until then still followed the line of the original field boundaries (see Figure 44), to form terraces of equal length on both sides of High Street (Emlyn Square) (see Figure 45). The end blocks were faced with ashlar and were of the same high-quality construction as the three-storey blocks in High Street. The new buildings were intended to close off the exposed cottage yards on each side of the village and to form ornamental entrance ways to the back alleys (**Fig 84**). Their design is very similar to the three-storey blocks and they can therefore be viewed as being entirely consistent with Brunel's original scheme (see pp 14–15 and Figure 14).

Five classes of cottage

The company also intended to build a terrace of fourteen cottages on the segment of land forming the south side of Taunton Street. These, together with the cottages in the end blocks, and those in the block on the south-western corner of High Street (Emlyn Square), amounted to a total of fifty new dwellings, bringing the number of cottages in the village close to the 300 originally envisaged. The fifty new cottages were designed according to five different plan types, referred to on company drawings as classes 'A' to 'E'. The distribution of the different classes of cottages within the new blocks is shown in Figure 45c. Each of the five classes is described in Chapter 8 (see p 155 onwards).

In July 1853 the company advertised for tenders for the construction of the fifty cottages and the Barracks.[19] One of the successful contractors was Edward Streeter, who was to build the class 'B' and 'D' cottages, while another Bath contractor, May & Son, was given classes 'A', 'C' and 'E' and the Barracks. Their combined tenders totalled £13,900, although this was later increased to £14,796. Streeter seems to have withdrawn at an early stage, presumably because he was

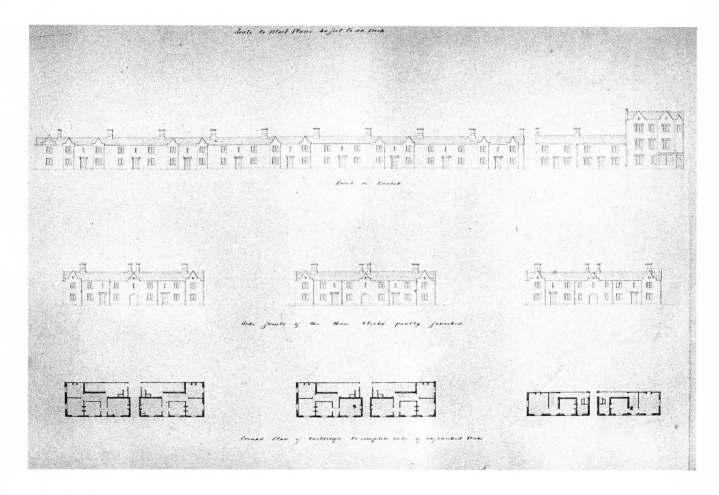

already fully engaged on the cottage-repair contract. He also tendered successfully for the new Mechanics' Institution building (see below). His contracts for the class 'B' and 'D' cottages were then taken over by May & Son who, like J D & C Rigby a decade earlier, soon encountered financial difficulties.

In October 1853 May & Son wrote to Brunel asking for an increased payment on account of an altered time-scale for the building programme and an increase in the cost of materials. The contractor was instructed to proceed to the completion of the buildings, at which time the company would investigate his claims. However May & Son were in no position to carry on and a week later they again wrote to Brunel declaring themselves 'incompetent to proceed from want of funds'. Brunel recommended that May & Son be granted an additional payment 'to prevent the works from being stopped which from the present crowded state of the village would be very injurious'. Building works continued into 1854 and by March of that year they were two-thirds complete. The company paid May & Son a total of nearly £18,000, including payments to help offset the

increases in the cost of materials and inaccuracies in their tenders. Even so, they seem to have run out of money before they could start work on the block of four cottages at the eastern end of Reading and Faringdon Streets, which was not to be built until 1862. The construction of the Barracks dragged on into 1855. The original tender for the revised design (see p 160) was £4,000, but this figure was later inflated by substantial cost overruns; in 1869 it was said to have cost the company about £10,000.[20]

THE MECHANICS' INSTITUTION

With the works working to full capacity again, the space occupied by the Mechanics' Institution (see p 66) was reclaimed by the company. On 1 September 1853 Daniel Gooch delivered a prospectus to the directors outlining a scheme for the formation of the New Swindon Improvement Company, to fund the construction of a new building for the Mechanics' Institution, along with a covered market to augment the inadequate retail facilities in the village. The driving force behind the scheme was the works' manager,

Fig 84 *Elevations and ground plans (of around 1853) for the blocks to be built on to the East Street ends of the terraces on the eastern side of the village. The drawing at the top shows the façades of the London Street houses.*

NEW SWINDON INSTITUTION AND MARKET.——Mr. E. ROBERTS, ARCHITECT.

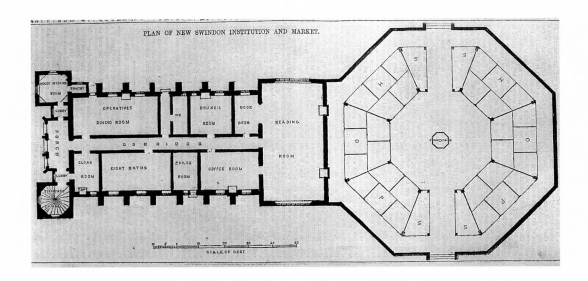

PLAN OF NEW SWINDON INSTITUTION AND MARKET.

SCALE OF FEET

Fig 85 *(top) A view from the north west of the proposed Mechanics' Institution building and attached covered market. (bottom) A ground plan of the two buildings.*

Minard Rea. Shares in the new company were sold to raise the estimated £3,000 required for the construction of the complex.[21]

As a site for the new buildings, the GWR leased the vacant land in the northern half of the square known as High Street to the New Swindon Improvement Company in return for a nominal annual rental of 5s. The GWR also contributed £100 per annum to the new company on condition that it provided a range of communal facilities, such as a library, reading-room and baths. Brunel drew up a plan of the proposed site for the GWR. This was to mark the first stage of the infilling of his grand promenade, and it is possible that the site had been reserved by him from an early date for some such purpose. The placing of these buildings at the very heart of the village symbolised the GWR's dominant role in the lives of the residents and its interest in their welfare and educational advancement.

The foundation stone was laid by Lord Methuen, on 24 May 1854, in the presence of about 10,000 people. He was assisted by Daniel Gooch, Minard Rea and the architect for the building, Edward Roberts of London. The *Swindon Advertiser*, newly founded that year, reported that 'a new building designed for the mental, moral and social advancement of the new town was commenced under the most favourable auspices'.[22] In its view the institution 'had the effect of diverting the minds of the younger portion of the inhabitants into a channel pregnant with good things, and throwing a genial influence around the neighbourhood'. The part of the new building containing the Institution was opened on 1 May 1855 six months after the completion of the covered market.

The design for the Mechanics' Institution (**Fig 85**) can best be described as a robust version of Perpendicular Gothic; as such it differed some-what from Brunel's more usual 'Jacobethan' style. Some conformity with the rest of the village was achieved by the use of Swindon stone for walling and Bath stone for dressings. The principal entrance was formed by a porch set between castellated towers at the northern end of the building (see pp 153–4 for further details). The covered market (see Figure 197) was octagonal in shape and attached to the southern end.

SPECULATORS AND BUILDING SOCIETIES

The fifty cottages erected by the company from 1853 to 1854 were far from sufficient to meet the demand for housing in New Swindon. Additional private accommodation was provided by specula-tors such as John Harding Sheppard, who owned a large block of land immediately to the east of the village. The site was surveyed by Sampson Sage, an architect from old Swindon, and the indi-vidual building plots making up the estate were put on the market in 1855.[23] Buyers were able to take a mortgage with the developers and complete the purchase at a later date. The plots were probably priced at a premium because of their close proximity to the village and the works, and they sold rather slowly as a consequence. At the end of 1855 the developers offered an extra incentive to prospective purchasers by redeeming land tax on each plot. This measure seems to have had little effect, since many of the sections remained unsold by 1870.[24]

The first building society to become active in New Swindon was The Wilts Equitable Property Society and Savings Fund, founded in Trowbridge in 1846 and made permanent in 1849. By 1855 it had an office in Swindon, where it advertised flexible mortgage terms for prospective builders and purchasers. Virtually nothing is known about the types of house funded by the society; in 1857 as part of its expansion into Swindon, it was involved in the creation of an estate in New Swindon (the precise whereabouts are not known), but otherwise it seems to have operated on a relatively small scale.[25]

Some builders, such as Frederick Key of Wood Street, in old Swindon, attempted to undercut the opposition by offering to draw low-cost plans. His advertisement in the *Swindon Advertiser* of 4 June 1855 states (albeit in rather ambiguous terms) that 'the advertiser having devoted a considerable part of his time to cottage building with regard to economy, can supply a lot of plans neatly got up ... with a specification and cost price, to save 20%, on any style required for £1 0s 6d, what is usually charged from £5 0s 0d to £7 0s 0d'.

BUILDING MATERIALS

Most of the new cottages were built of brick supplied by several small brickworks operating in the Swindon area, a few of which were probably established in the 18th century.[26] The Kimmeridge-clay pan underlying the area was ideal for brick-making, and the use of this mate-rial increased following the removal of brick tax in 1850. In 1861 C A Wheeler put his 2-acre (0·8-hectare) brickworks, located on the Stratton St Margaret Road, on to the market. The site had a brick field, drain-tile works, kiln and drying sheds. Citing the GWR's plan to build rolling mills at Swindon as a selling point, he stated in his adver-tisement that 'the great demand for dwelling-houses consequent on the recent decision as to vastly increasing the Locomotive Works, cannot fail to create a thriving brick trade'.[27]

Building materials for both the village and the works were brought in by barge and landed at nearby canal wharves, such as the newly estab-lished wharf adjoining the Golden Lion Bridge on the Wilts & Berks Canal.[28] The wharves served as focal points for suppliers of building materials: next to the Golden Lion Wharf, for example, was a brickyard bought by William Tarrant, a builder from old Swindon, in 1860.

Not all private developments were humble brick cottages, however. Falcon Terrace (**Fig 86**), on the eastern side of Westcott Place, was a supe-rior Swindon and Bath-stone terrace of about 1849 which incorporated cottages arranged to either side of a central, pedimented public house.[29]

Fig 86 *Falcon Terrace, built of Swindon and Bath stone, on the east side of Westcott Place, around 1849. A terrace of brick-built houses was subsequently added at the northern end of the block.*

Fig 87 *A plan and section of the XI Wiltshire Volunteer Rifle Corps armoury, built to the south of the covered market, in High Street (Emlyn Square), in 1862. The building was converted to the GWR accident hospital in 1871–2. It then became the Village Community Centre in the mid 1970s.*

railway in England presents such magnificent rooms'.[30]

Plans for a new road to connect the village with the station, which had been drawn up by Sheppard in late 1846, were again resurrected and approved by the company in 1852. The GWR paid for the new road and bridge across the North Wilts Canal, whilst local landowners appear to have provided subscriptions of £300 towards its construction.[31] The company did little to keep its own roads in good repair and in 1856 the workmen petitioned the directors to improve the streets in the village. Gooch estimated that the repairs would cost as much as £1,200. The Expenditure Committee was only prepared to sanction a payment of £300 for this work in the first instance.

THE STATION

The population explosion in New Swindon was accompanied by increased usage of the local passenger trains and a greater volume of freight traffic. This placed increased pressure on the facilities at Swindon station, and plans to lengthen the platforms and construct a new carriage shed were approved in 1855. Earlier, in 1850, cast-iron columns had been erected on the edges of the platforms to help support the wide, cantilevered canopies. The refreshment rooms underwent extensive renovation in early 1856 when the proprietor, John Rouse Phillips, had the ceilings of the first-class rooms painted in oils 'by first-rate artists'. The local press reported that 'upwards of twenty artists, besides painters', were engaged on the work and that 'no other

RECESSION, AND THE DEATH OF MINARD REA

The lay-offs of 1857 (see p 73) echoed those of exactly ten years earlier, although in this case the cutbacks, resulting from company policy rather than a general economic malaise, were less severe. The impact of this second period of retrenchment on the lives of workmen and their families must have been considerable, although the company did not feel it necessary to take any extraordinary steps to ease their suffering. The workmen had also been dealt a blow in 1857 when the widely respected works' manager, Minard Rea, died of consumption at the age of thirty-five. The *Swindon Advertiser*, which covered his death in considerable detail, wrote that 'he had felt ... strongly his grave responsibilities as leader and director of the

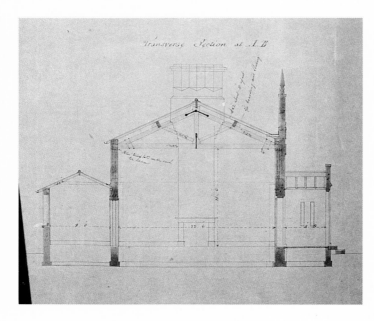

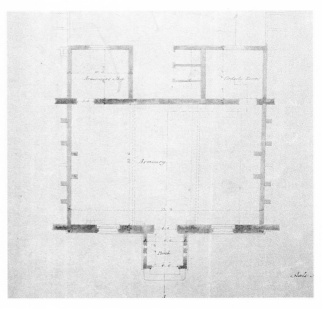

Fig 88 *A view of New Swindon from the south west in the early 1860s. The parsonage, church, and schools are visible on the left, and the completed western half of the village is on the right. The works are shown in the distance. The Wilts & Berks Canal and towpath can be seen in the foreground.*

moral and social well-being of all those under him, and the consequence was, he was looked upon rather as a friend than as a master'.[32] Rea had effectively been the head of the community and his funeral provided an opportunity for an unprecedented outpouring of grief by the workforce. The works and the shops in the town were closed and his coffin was carried by works' foremen from his villa to St Mark's church. The cortège was formed by 870 workmen all dressed in black. Daniel and William Gooch were among the mourners.

THE 1861 CENSUS

From 1859 the company's financial position began to improve, and by the time of the 1861 census the population of New Swindon had risen to 4,167 persons, an increase of 68·8 per cent on the 1851 figure of 2,468. The combined population of Swindon parish including both the old and new towns, was now 6,856. The principal areas of expansion had been along Bridge Street (where forty-eight cottages were erected by 1861), Fleet Street and around the hamlets of Eastcott and Westcott. The number of company employees living in these hamlets and in old Swindon had increased as a result of the shortage of new housing in areas close to the works. The demand for housing in New Swindon became even more acute after the opening of the rolling mills in May 1861 and the arrival of Welsh iron-workers to operate them. Initially they were accommodated with their families in the Barracks which was converted into a series of two or three-room tenements

following its failure as a single men's hostel (see pp 160–61).

THE ARMOURY AND DRILL HALL

At the beginning of 1860 about 150 company employees formed themselves into the XI Wiltshire Volunteer Rifle Corps, in response to a feared invasion by the French army under Napoleon III. Other railway towns, such as Crewe, reacted in a similarly patriotic manner to this threat. The new Swindon corps was placed under the command of William Gooch, who was given the rank of senior captain whilst other works' officials were also made officers. The volunteers drilled on the open ground in High Street (Emlyn Square) to the south of the covered market until, in 1862, the company approved the construction of an armoury and drill hall on the same site (see Figure 45d; **Fig 87**). The armoury was flanked by adjoining cottages constructed of squared Swindon stone. It was given an ashlar façade of Bath stone and a pedimented central section over a porch. Its style was loosely Jacobean to match the surrounding buildings (see Figure 134).

By the time these buildings were completed virtually all available sites in the village had been built on (**Fig 88**). The company's cottage-building plans were complete, all except for a terrace of six cottages which was built, probably by the GWR's own workforce, just to the north of the armoury and completed in 1866. Although the company continued to build facilities for the Medical Fund, from the mid 1860s onwards its policy was to rely entirely on private developers and building societies to provide new housing.

5 *The Armstrong Era, 1864–1877*

oseph Armstrong's arrival at the Swindon
works in 1864 was to usher in a new era,
unfettered by personal and sentimental devo-
tion either to the broad gauge or to Brunel's
very individual building style. Armstrong came
from the GWR's northern division, with its standard-gauge tradition, but he had been schooled
for over ten years in the working practices of the
GWR, and so can scarcely be considered an
outsider. Born in 1816 in Cumberland, he was
brought up and educated on Tyneside where he
came into close contact with many of the
pioneers of locomotive construction. Before
taking up the post of assistant locomotive superintendent with the Shrewsbury & Chester Railway in
1847, he had worked on railways in Durham,
Lancashire, Yorkshire and the south east. He
succeeded to the post of locomotive superintendent in 1852 and when, in 1854, the GWR
absorbed the Shrewsbury & Chester and the
Shrewsbury & Birmingham railways he became
superintendent of the northern division, immediately subordinate to Daniel Gooch. At the Stafford
Road Works, in Wolverhampton, he had been
constructing standard-gauge locomotives to his
own designs since 1859. He was able to bring this
wealth of experience to his new post of locomotive, carriage and wagon superintendent of the
GWR (**Fig 89**).

ARMSTRONG'S NEW REGIME

Even before Daniel Gooch left in June 1864,
William Potter, the GWR chairman, had requested
Armstrong 'to draw up a programme of arrangements in the Locomotive and Carriage
Establishments of the Company on the under-
standing that Mr William Gooch and Mr Gibson,
the respective incumbent managers, would not
remain in the service of the Company'.[1]
Armstrong's reply, written from Wolverhampton
and dated 19 May, displays a strong grasp of
priorities across the entire GWR system and, as his
recommendations were to set the agenda for
many years to come, it is worth quoting from
them at length:

> In compliance with your request that I should furnish
> you with a programme of the arrangement which I
> may have to recommend in the re-organisation of the
> staff of your various Locomotive, Carriage and Wagon

Establishments, I beg respectfully to lay the following
suggestions before you, which will be all that I think
it necessary to make at the present time.

In the first place it will be necessary to consolidate the repairs of the Narrow Gauge Locomotive
Stock at the Stafford Road Works, as soon as the new
buildings which have been already applied for, can
be got ready for the same, and I would strongly
recommend that this work be pushed forward with
the utmost possible dispatch. This would leave the
Shops at Worcester, which are central for such a
purpose, available for such of the repairs of the
Narrow Gauge Carriage and Wagon Stock as are at
present carried on not only at Worcester but at
Hereford and other places. I propose that Mr Stewart
the present Foreman, shall remain in charge of the
same for the time being.

As regards the superintendence of the Narrow
Gauge Establishments, I propose that it be placed in
the hands of Mr George Armstrong, who shall reside
at Wolverhampton as Manager of the Works there
and District Superintendent of the Narrow Gauge
system generally, together with some portion of the
Broad Gauge, and that his salary commence at £400
per annum.

That he shall have as his Assistant Mr William
Dean, whose duties will comprise the rendering of all
necessary assistance in the Shops at Stafford Road, as
well as the general supervision of the Offices which
he holds at present at £170 a year, for the extra duties
I propose to advance his salary to £200 per annum.

I propose to concentrate the whole of the
Accounts of the Locomotive and Carriage departments at Swindon Offices, the general supervision of
the same to be placed under Mr R L White now the
accountant there and who formerly for several years
was my Chief Clerk on the Northern Division. Mr
White would also act as my Chief Clerk under the
new arrangement, and I propose that his salary be
advanced from £250 to £350 per annum. I have no
doubt that in a short time we shall be able by this
method of concentration greatly to reduce the
number of Clerks employed at the various
Establishments.

As I am myself about to reside at Swindon for
the present, I propose to appoint as Manager of the
factory there, the Assistant to Mr W F Gooch viz
Mr F A Bucknall at a salary of £400 per annum which
I should wish to advance to £500 in the course of
two years, provided that the work is carried out to
my satisfaction during that time.

The Gentleman I propose to place in charge of the Carriage and Wagon Department is Mr Fraser, and as he will have to reside in London, that his salary be £400 per annum, this is to be increased on the same conditions and to a similar amount to Mr Bucknall's. There will be of course numerous minor alterations to be at once commenced upon and to proceed as circumstances may suggest, but with these I presume I need not trouble you on this occasion.

I am Sir

Yours obediently

Joseph Armstrong

These recommended appointments were implemented and only that of Bucknall was to be short-lived. Within a year, the post of works' manager had passed to Samuel Carlton, a foreman from the Stafford Road Works who was to hold the position for thirty-two years.

EXPANSION AND MODERNISATION

Armstrong took up his post in increasingly troubled times for the company (about which see more below). Nevertheless, he immediately embarked on a cautious programme of expansion and modernisation at the Swindon works. In July, the locomotive committee referred to the chairman a report from Armstrong proposing that the workshops should be altered at a cost of about £12,000, and that £10,000-worth of new machinery should be provided. Some of this money appears to have been allocated to extensions to the steam-hammer shop, created by

Fig 89 *Joseph Armstrong (locomotive, carriage and wagon superintendent at the works from 1864 to 1877).*

Fig 90 *A design drawing of 1864 depicting a cross-section of the engine house and showing Armstrong's alterations to Brunel's original structure.*

infilling the western half of the northern court-yard. Armstrong was also able to expand the main repairing facilities, for example, by equipping the engine house with heavy-duty overhead cranes (**Fig 90**).

At the end of April 1865, a long article in the *Swindon Advertiser,* reprinted from *Railway News,*

reported that about 1,700 officers, artisans and workmen were employed at the works and that Armstrong had erected a 'new Engine Shop' (**Fig 91**) in the courtyard to the west of the original engine house, 'but it is not yet filled with the tools and machines ordered for it.' The new shop shared the western wall of the earlier building and 'this fine room has an area of 3,694 yards [3,088m²] the roof part of which is glass, being in three spans of about 45ft [13·5m] each, supported on iron columns'.

Two ranks of those cast-iron columns, bearing the cast inscription 'CLARIDGE NORTH & CO ENGINEERS BRISTOL', have survived, along with the 1842 wall to the east, but the western wall (apart from the stub ends) was replaced by a rank of columns in 1873. These latter columns, bearing the cast inscription 'GWR WOLVERHAMPTON' and dated 'DECR 1872' and 'JANY 1873', were inserted when the last remaining 28ft [8·5m] of courtyard was roofed over (**Fig 92**).

The reporter went on to comment that a 'self-acting travelling gib crane, worked by a rope' traversed the entire length of the shop and that a

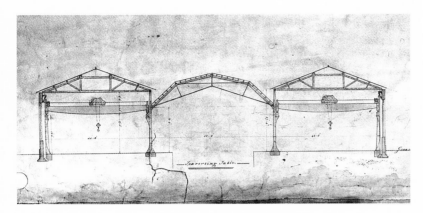

Fig 90 *A design drawing of 1864 depicting a cross-section of the engine house and showing Armstrong's alterations to Brunel's original structure.*

Traversing Table

drilling machine, supplied by Beyer, Peacock & Co, was capable of taking six engine frames at once. *Astill's Directory*, a few years later, reported that 'R' shop, as this was called, contained 'the magnificent and costly plant used in the construction of the Company's giant Engines' and that 'the engine employed to drive this large collection of machinery is equal to 153 horse power [114kW], worked at a pressure of 120 pounds to the square inch [8·27 bar] and making 120 strokes to the minute'. In April 1865 the directors voted £2,385 for an extension to the steam-hammer shed and in August a further £3,240 was allocated for machinery 'as the present stock ... is inadequate to carry on all the repairs and works'.

THE RETURN OF GOOCH

The *Railway News* article of 1865 had also noted the construction of locomotives, tenders and coke trucks, but perceptively remarked that there 'are no symptoms of passenger carriages or goods waggons'.[2] In fact, broad-gauge carriages were ordered from outside suppliers and maintained at Paddington, while standard-gauge stock was manufactured at the recently acquired works at both Saltney and Worcester. The latter works had suffered a serious fire in November 1864 and the GWR, led by William Potter, considered centralising all carriage production on a 22-acre (9-hectare) site at Oxford, this being the meeting-point of its two operating divisions, which were divided, principally, by the gauge difference. Potter's departure in September 1865, after a failed boardroom gamble to increase his personal power as chairman, put any such plans into abeyance and left something of a power vacuum. It also opened the way for Daniel Gooch's return as none of the remaining directors was willing to accept the post of chairman. Gooch, of course, was eminently qualified for the post, being a successful businessman with an intimate knowledge of the company, but he was reluctant to return so soon after leaving in such unpleasant circumstances. Finally, persuaded by former colleagues as well as the directors, he agreed to take the post in a part-time capacity and was elected chairman in November 1865.

Fig 91 (opposite below) The 'new Engine Shop' (or 'R' shop) of 1865, as it appeared in 1882.

Fig 92 The 1873 extension to 'R' shop, photographed in 1882.

The financial review that Gooch then instigated revealed that the company was seriously over-extended, and even projects in progress were curtailed. The crisis in the banking world the following year seriously embarrassed the GWR. The company had debenture and loan obligations of over £14 million, and servicing the interest was proving to be a major drain on the company's liquid capital. The GWR sought to raise new loan funds to cover these commitments, but was unable to do so because of the banking crisis and the lack of confidence in railways as a good investment. Gooch had just become Conservative member of parliament for the Cricklade constituency (which included Swindon) and it took all his financial acumen and personal influence to save the company from outright bankruptcy.

THE NEW CARRIAGE WORKS

The company's position gradually improved under Gooch's strict financial regime so that, by late 1867, the issue of a carriage works could again be considered. With Potter gone and Gooch in control it is not surprising that Swindon emerged as the chosen location, especially as the company already owned the requisite land. The board approved an initial sum of £26,000 for the carriage works in March 1868 and, on Armstrong's recommendation, appointed Thomas Clayton as carriage and wagon works' superintendent. The site of the first buildings of new carriage works is shown on Edward Snell's painting (see Figure 56) as an open space lying between the railway and the village and to the east of the school. The first two phases were to fit around the two officers' houses to the east but these were subsequently demolished (see p 108).

Work progressed rapidly on the construction of the westernmost of the buildings, which was to house the sawmills. By March 1869 these were in partial use, as is recorded by the report of a 'frightful accident'. A sixteen-year-old boy, wandering about the shop while his sawing machine was stopped, went into the cellar where the drive shafts were being erected, got caught up on one of the shafts and was killed instantly. The coroner's jury remarked that 'the machinery in these shops is fixed on a much better principle

Fig 93 *The 1872 carriage shop, photographed in 1882.*

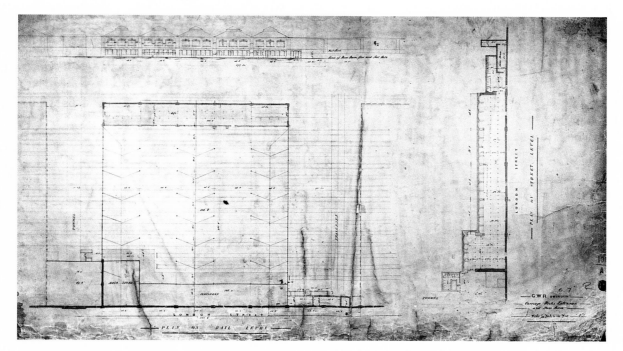

than in other places, as all the shafting is under the floors to avoid accidents of this kind'.[3]

The carriage works were a very significant development for New Swindon. In February 1871, the *Swindon Advertiser* reported that despite being 'as yet very incomplete and ... only partially erected', they already employed some 1,100 men – 800 in coach building and 300 in manufacturing the ironwork for carriages.[4] The same article forecast that this number would grow considerably and it gave a description of the one shop (**Fig 93**) that was then complete. This stretched as far as the Mechanics' Institution and its outside appearance was described as:

> dead, heavy, and substantial; the walls, which are of immense thickness, are built of blue lias stone, with Bath stone quoins and string courses ... the floor of the shop (there is only one floor) which is two acres and three quarters [1·1 hectares] in extent, is covered by a succession of wide roofs, partly of slate and glass, supported on rows of huge iron columns, which being hollow are made to serve as channels for carrying off the water from the gutters formed between the roofs.

The engine house was located in a basement, formed by the need to raise the ground floor to the level of the railway. It contained a 250-hp (186-kW) horizontal engine with a 17-in (432-mm) cylinder and 2-ft (610-mm) stroke working at 130psi (8·96 bar) and a tube boiler to raise the necessary steam. Waste steam was used to heat the workshops by means of steam pipes. It appears from the article that, notwithstanding the incompleteness of some of the buildings, all the carriage manufacturing processes were in operation and finished carriages were being turned out. The article reported that, in the separate 'painters' shop', which occupied a 'very large area of ground', a first-class carriage would receive no less than fifteen coats of paint and three coats of varnish. Also reported was a rumour to the effect that an order had been issued for 100 new standard-gauge engines, 1,000 trucks and several hundred carriages, the work divided between Swindon, Wolverhampton and Saltney, with Swindon getting the lion's share.

Construction work, under the energetic, if somewhat abrasive, management of Thomas Clayton, proceeded steadily eastwards and its progress and phasing can be followed by the dates on the tall cast-iron columns. A timber shed and carpenters' shop, for example, were built in 1870 only to be incorporated into larger blocks in 1872. Thus columns inscribed 'GWR WOLVERHAMPTON MAY 1870' appear amongst columns dated 'FEB^Y 1872' and 'MARCH 1872' and the sequence ends with columns dated 'DEC^R 1875' at the extreme eastern limit of the development.

The fall of the ground towards the east of the carriage-works' site allowed for a lower ground floor at street level from the subway entrance eastwards. For much of its length this floor was only three bays deep, with two ranks of cast-iron columns supporting a jack-arched brick floor, but towards the subway it widened to five bays (**Fig 94**). This level was initially used as a canteen for up to 500 workers – the first time such a facility had been provided (**Fig 95**). It was later

Fig 94 *The London Street elevation, and plans at both levels, of the central carriage shop, in a drawing dated 18 December 1876.*

expanded to accommodate nearly 1,000 workers. Structurally the carriage works were rather unexceptional, as their main function was to provide an extensive covered working area with limited power requirements but with multiple rail access via traversers.

The *Swindon Advertiser* article on the carriage works ran over three issues and concluded by noting that:

> For some months past, workmen have been employed putting up a queer looking erection at the southwest corner of the carriage shed, and which said erection bids fair to rival the neighbouring church tower and steeple both as to height and prominence in distant view. It consists of several tiers of large long iron columns standing on each other, and banded together into a compact framework, about twenty-five feet square [7·6m] by seventy-five

feet [22·9m] high. On top of this framework there will be a water-tank.

The working capacity of this tank (**Fig 96**), at 6ft (1·8m) deep, was 41,000 gallons (186,386 litres) of water, enough to provide a high-pressure supply throughout the carriage works for fire-fighting purposes (**Fig 97**).[5]

Thomas Clayton did not see the development through to its conclusion as he left Swindon in 1873 to take up a similar, but better-paid, post with the Midland Railway. He was replaced by James Holden, manager of the GWR carriage works at Saltney.

THE GENERAL OFFICES

By the early 1870s, the works at Swindon thus comprised three separate elements, or

Fig 95 *The canteen below the carriage shop, photographed in 1882.*

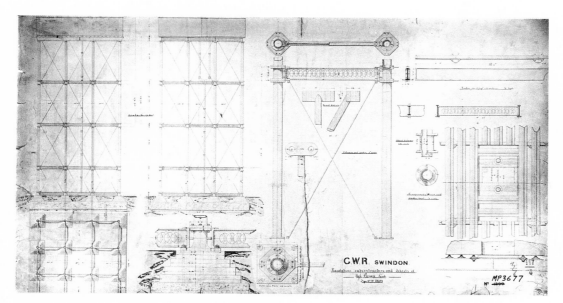

C.W.R. SWINDON.

MP3677

Fig 96 *(left) A drawing, dated 22 June 1870, showing constructional details of the 1872 water tower at the western end of the carriage works, built to provide water at high pressure for fire-fighting purposes. The total height of the structure is almost 75ft (22·9m).*

Fig 97 *The 1872 water tower, photographed before the removal of the original tank.*

'Establishments', with the rail mills (the rolling mills and their associated puddling furnaces) having a separate identity from the locomotive works and the carriage manufacturing department. Though each had its own manager, they were under one general management system, housed in the 'extensive range of handsome and well-appointed offices set apart for the Officers of the Company, and their large staff of Clerks'.[6] This range was a two-storey, twelve-bay extension that Armstrong had had built in 1869 against the eastern elevation of the southern pavilion of the original office wing. The ground floor of this range has two ranks of cast-iron columns dated NOV^R AND DEC^R 1868. The general offices, as it was to become known, was connected to the town by a subway below the main railway line and the newly installed carriage works' traverser. The subway issued opposite the Mechanics' Institution and provided a much safer main entrance to the works than the level crossings hitherto used.

EMPLOYEE NUMBERS AND OUTPUT

By this time the number of 'officers, artizans etc' employed at the works had risen to 3,900 – including, for the first time, a number of women employed in the trimming shop. A sewing shop, also to be worked by the 'sterner sex', was shortly to be added – 'an important step, as it will afford occupation for a goodly number of the unemployed wives and daughters of Mechanics and others in the Town'.

In 1872, the works turned out some seventy new standard-gauge engines, over 2,000 wagons and nearly 200 passenger coaches, in addition to all the routine repair and maintenance work. The cumulative effect of all these developments can

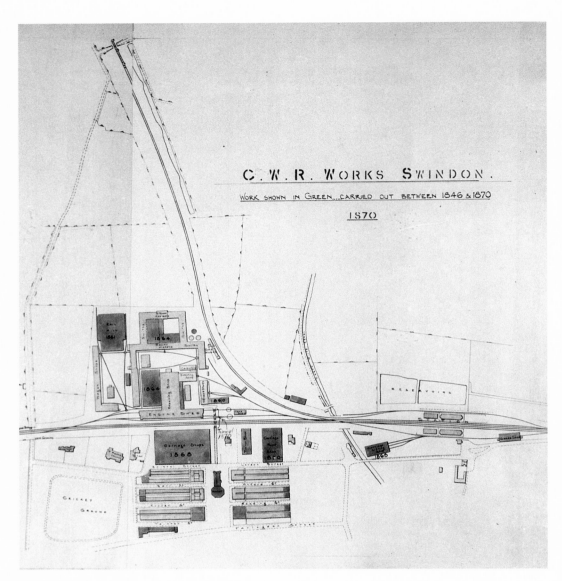

C.W.R. WORKS SWINDON.

WORK SHOWN IN GREEN...CARRIED OUT BETWEEN 1846 & 1870

1870

Fig 98 *The railway works in 1870, one of a series of plans first produced retrospectively in the drawing office in Churchward's time and then revised each decade until the 1950s.*

be seen in the first of a series of plans (known as the Hawksworth plans) produced retrospectively in the drawing office in Churchward's time, then revised each decade until the 1950s (**Fig 98**).

CONTEMPORARY ACCOUNTS OF THE WORKS

There was considerable public interest in the works at this time and, as we have already seen, they provided a great deal of copy for the local press. In addition to the three-instalment article on the carriage works published in 1871, the *Swindon Advertiser* had already run a two-part article on 'A Night Visit to the New Swindon Puddling Furnaces and Rail Mills' in 1869, and, in 1871 it was to run a further series of fifteen articles under the heading 'Notes of Visits to the New Swindon Workshops'.

The article on the rolling mills marvelled at the noise, infernal prospect and scale of the undertaking which, in 1868, consumed no less than 21,000 tons (21,336 tonnes) of pig iron, old rails and scrap, and 20,000 tons (20,320 tonnes) of coal, while 169,000 fire bricks were used to repair the furnaces. Unlike the rest of the works, the mills worked day and night, and, in the one year, sent out 17,180 tons (17,455 tonnes) of rails – 'a sufficient quantity, if placed in one connected line, to reach from London to Lands End, with some twenty-five miles [40km] to spare' – a graphic illustration of the wear and tear to which the wrought-iron rails were subject.

The 1871 articles display the insatiable fascination the Victorians had with all things mechanical. Most of the texts consist of long and detailed accounts, couched in quaint 'layman's terms', of the operation of steam hammers (of which the works had ten) and the reverberatory furnaces, of the forging of wheels and the fitting of tyres, of the construction of boilers and fire-boxes, and of everything from the simple manufacture of rivets, nuts and bolts to the skilled manufacture of springs.

The new fitting and turning shop, designated 'R' shop, was an obvious delight, with three instalments devoted to its wonders, including the works' 'hooter' mounted on the roof of 'R' shop's engine house. This hooter, the article claimed, 'has many times been heard up and down the Vale of White Horse at points from thirty to forty miles [48 to 64km] distant from each other'. Indeed, a row with a local titled landowner over the hooter occasioned a sixteen-verse ditty in the *Swindon Advertiser* that year.

The articles also extolled the benefits of producing standardised parts as a great economy in the manufacture of new engines and an even greater convenience in the replacement of parts. They concluded by reviewing the changes that had come about in the manufacture of locomotives since the pioneer days of George Stephenson, when there would have been insufficient 'mechanics and machinery in the whole world' to match the current output of the Swindon works alone.

The GWR was itself undergoing a fundamental change at this time, as the standard gauge was progressively displacing the broad gauge. A substantial part of 'the great backbone and artery' of the broad-gauge system – the London to Swindon section of the Bristol line – was being altered to take standard-gauge traffic. This was to provide a standard-gauge connection, via Gloucester, to South Wales. A large new engine shed (**Fig 99**) was constructed, in readiness for the change, between the South Wales line and the old Wilts & Berks Canal, while a new carriage-storing shed was built to the north of the station.

THE WESTWARD EXPANSION OF THE WORKS

In 1872 plans were prepared for an extension to the works that would radically alter the arrangement of work on the site – a development larger in scale than any hitherto undertaken at Swindon. An agreement to purchase all the land between the works and Rodbourne Lane, to the west, was drawn up with Mr W V Rolleston on 1 March 1872, although the sale was not finalised until late 1873, when a cheque for £11,514 was paid to Messrs Young & Co, solicitors.[7]

The plans provided for what was, in effect, a new locomotive manufacturing factory to be built to the west of the works, with only minor conversions to some of the existing buildings, thus freeing most of the original core for the repair of locomotives. The main elements of the new extension were a boiler shop, erecting shop, tender shop, machine shops, iron foundry, brass foundry and engine-painting shop, with the

Fig 99 *The standard-gauge engine shed of 1871, photographed in 1882.*

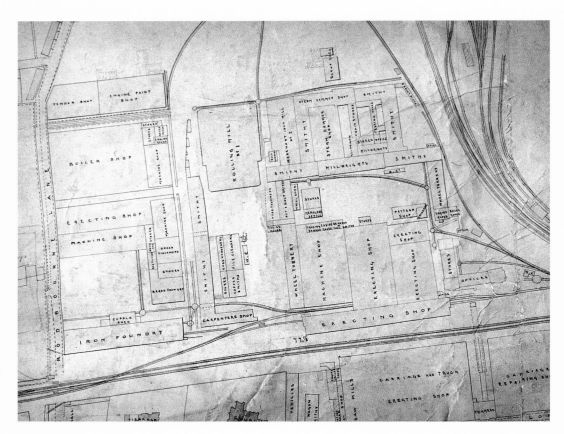

Fig 100 *(right) A GWR plan of July 1885 showing the full extent of Armstrong's building campaign on the locomotive works' site.*

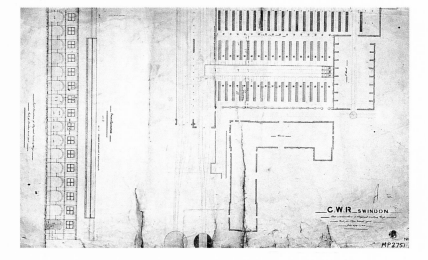

Fig 101 *A GWR drawing of July 1874 showing Armstrong's extension of 'B' shop to the east of Brunel's engine house. It also shows Armstrong's 1870 extensions to the 1842 office and stores building.*

appropriate stores, finishing shops and a power house for both steam and hydraulic power. By 1880 these were to total more than 225,000 sq ft (20,902m²) in area (**Fig 100**).

At the same time, the engine-repair facilities were greatly enlarged by the construction of a large shed ('B' shop) on the site of the original copper and brass foundries, incorporating Brunel's original engine house (**Fig 101**). This, along with the original erecting shop, comprised

an engine-repairing facility of 'upwards of 100,000 sq ft [9,290m²]' in area (**Fig 102**). Several facilities appear to have been shared. These included 'R' shop, which was used for general machining and fitting, plus the wheelsmiths', wheelwrights', millwrights', carpenters' and pattern-makers' shops, as well as a new chain-testing house. This chain-testing house (**Fig 103**) was built in 1874 as a narrow range bisecting the remaining piece of open courtyard in the northern quadrangle. The entire building was, in effect, a very sophisticated machine, with wrought-iron roof trusses incorporating lifting pulleys and a central channel accommodating the test bed for the hydraulically operated, 130-ton-load Ransome Chain Testing Machine (**Fig 104**).

Architectural treatment

This generation of buildings was the first on the site to be built mostly of brick and to make major use of iron technology for the internal construction. In these respects, they were the first Swindon buildings to resemble railway workshops elsewhere, both in construction and architectural detail. The 1874 extension of the original engine house, for example, was achieved by replacing Brunel's wooden columns with cast-iron columns, the wood-framed roofs over the pit bays with light metal-framed roofs and the masonry

pier-and-panel east wall by a rank of columns, thus allowing for the enlargement of the covered area by a further 140ft (42·7m) to the east, where it was enclosed by a masonry wall with blind arcading and clerestory windows. This wall, which has survived the demolition of much of the rest of 'B' shop, is quite unlike its neighbours in detail and massing. The earlier masonry buildings relied upon pier-and-panel construction for architectural effect, but this wall, with its brick-dressed blind arcading and window openings, and brick corbels to the cornice, would not, apart from the use of stone, be out of place in contemporary railway works at Crewe, Derby or Ashford.

The GWR seems to have been aware of the distinctiveness of its earlier buildings and especially of the predominant use of stone rather than brick. As a matter of policy, the buildings which fronted on to the GWR's railway lines were always given masonry façades, and, where existing stone

Fig 102 'B' shop in 1895, showing the steam-operated traversing table. The original Brunel roof survives above replacement columns.

Fig 103 (below left) The chain-testing house of 1874, showing the chain pit with pulley trusses above (photographed in 1987).

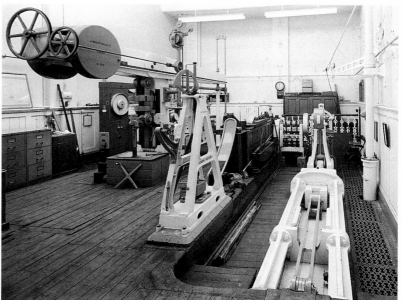

Fig 104 The chain-testing house of 1874, showing the Ransome Chain Testing Machine (photographed in 1987).

Fig 105 *The Rodbourne Road wall from the south west. In the middle distance are the six gables of Armstrong's 'V' shop, with the 1880s' extensions nearer to the camera. The arched brick coursing above the tunnel under the road is visible in the southernmost bays of the original 'V' shop. The tunnel was constructed in the early 20th century, with hydraulic lifts installed at either end. These allowed boilers to be taken from 'V' shop to be tested in the steaming shed to the west of Rodbourne Road.*

buildings were extended, the extensions were also built of stone, albeit not always of the same provenance. The impressive new boundary wall fronting Rodbourne Road departed from this principle, however: built about two years later than 'B' shop, it echoes the latter's blind arcading, corbels and cornicing. For a substantial part of its length, the boundary wall also served to form the western elevation of the new engineering workshops (**Fig 105**). Rodbourne Road itself was changing in character, from an agricultural lane to an important highway serving as a link between New Swindon and the expanding dormitory settlements to the north of the works, though at this time the main line still ran across it, by means of a level crossing.

The new locomotive factory
The new locomotive factory was truly immense: the main workshops were T-shaped with a fifty-bay eastern frontage, some 653ft (199m) long and 86ft (26·2m) deep, and a broad central stem, 256ft (78m) in width, stretching a further 312ft (95·1m) back to Rodbourne Road (**Fig 106**). The foundry formed the southern boundary of the development with a 400ft (121·9m) frontage to the railway. Its main hall was 80ft (24·4m) wide with a central block of four furnaces to the rear flanked by a smaller range of pattern stores, coke stoves and associated stores (**Figs 107** and **108**). The plans for this development are variously dated from 1872 to 1875, though construction would not have started before the land was legally acquired in 1873 and the columns in the front ranges of the main workshops are inscribed

'GWR WOLVERHAMPTON' and dated 'AUG 1874' and 'SEPT 1874'.

The boiler shop and erecting shop, which together formed the stem of the T, consisted of a hall, six structural aisles wide and twenty-four bays long, with ranks of two-tier cast-iron columns supporting light iron-framed roofs. An entrance, 37ft (11·3m) wide, was located in the eastern frontage; occupying bays thirty to thirty-three, this accommodated a traverser in the third aisle serving the erecting shop to the south and the boiler shop to the north (**Figs 109** and **110**).

Though the eastern range, making up the top bar of the T, formed a single architectural composition, it was nevertheless subdivided into blocks of different functions and depth. At the southern end, the brass foundry and associated finishing workshop occupied eleven bays, and, in addition to the two main 40ft-wide (12·2m) structural ranges, it had a third range, 25ft (7·6m) wide, to the west. The brass furnaces were located in this range and were worked from the main range via an arcade of arches supported on squat cast-iron columns (**Fig 111**). The blocks flanking the traverser entrance were used as machine shops, with the northern machine shop originally open to the boiler shop to the west (**Fig 112**).

The northern end of the main range was occupied by the power house which contained steam engines and hydraulic plant. The hydraulic accumulator was housed in a tower attached to the northern end of the range.

Despite being structurally and functionally interconnected, the front range and the stem seem to have been built separately, and possibly by

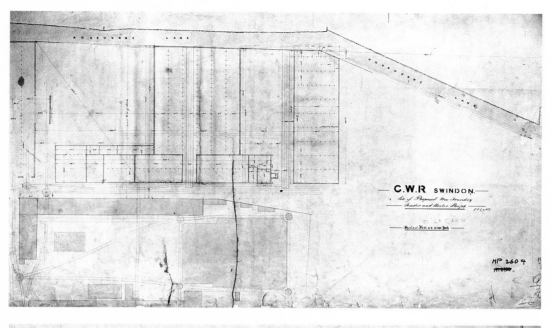

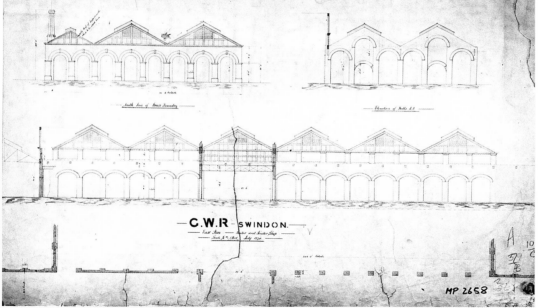

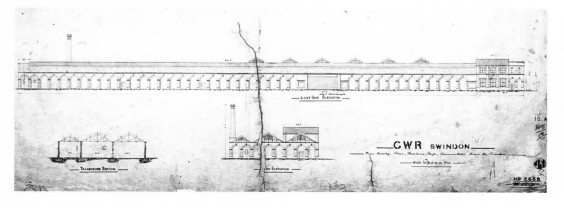

Fig 106 *Armstrong's loco-motive factory. (top) 'Site of Proposed New Foundry Tender and Boiler Shops'; (centre) 'East Face – Boiler and Tender Shop'; (bottom) 'Brass Foundry, Stores, Machine Shops, Accumulator House etc; Swindon'.*

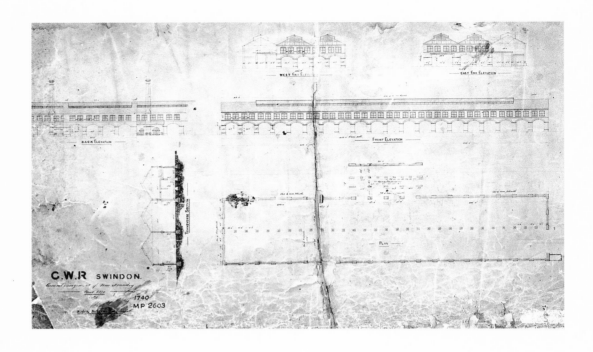

Fig 107 *A GWR drawing, of April 1874, entitled 'General arrangement of New Foundry'.*

Fig 108 *(right) The north aisle of the 1874 foundry in 1882.*

Fig 109 *(opposite top) Armstrong's new erecting shop of 1874, photographed in 1882. This shop occupied the southern aisles of the original 'V' shop.*

Fig 110 *(opposite) The new boiler shop of 1874, photo-graphed in 1882. This shop occupied the northern aisles of the original 'V' shop.*

different contractors. There are surprising differences in architectural detail between the two elements, and there seems to be no GWR-inscribed ironwork in the stem, which is altogether more massive in its construction (**Fig 113**).

The final major element in the first phase of this development was a northern range containing the tender shop and, to its east, a paint shop (**Figs 114** and **115**). This block was arranged in nine structural aisles, running northwards, the tender-shop bays having overhead cranes (see Figure 189). Of the twenty-eight bays in its southern elevation, twenty-six were open, having double-leaved doors and rail access, provided by a traverser in the yard. The building plans for this range are dated September 1876, the money for its construction having been voted in January of that year.[8] To the north of the tender shop was a brickyard with three kilns supplying the works with at least some of the bricks required for these new works.[9]

The rest of the development incorporated the 1847 western range and paint shop of the former wagon works. The southern section of the western range was converted to the brass shop and a smiths' shop, and the northern section to an angle-iron smiths' shop, while the former paint shop was

Fig 111 *(above) The casting-floor of the brass foundry. The arcade of cast-iron columns allowed ease of movement from the furnaces behind to the casting-floor in the foreground.*

Fig 112 *(right) The 1874 machine shop, in 1882.*

greatly extended to provide a coppersmiths' shop (**Fig 116**). This work was carried out in 1877, so the initial phase of the new factory appears to have been completed by the end of that year. However, Joseph Armstrong did not live to see the fruits of his endeavours: he was taken ill early in 1877 and died on 5 June in Matlock Bath.

EXPANSION OF THE SETTLEMENT

Cambria Place

Returning to developments in and around the village, the company's reluctance to build any further cottages after 1862 meant that the Welsh workers and their families, who were brought to Swindon in 1861 to operate the rolling mills, had to put up with cramped and unsanitary conditions in the Barracks. Recognising an opportunity, the manager of the rolling mills, Thomas Ellis, is said to have formed a private company in late 1863 to build a cottage estate for his workmen,[10] located on a field known as Kingsdown Close. The site was owned by Ambrose Lethbridge Goddard and was located immediately to the south of the GWR cricket ground.

The estate consisted of two rows of cottages, each containing two terraces. The northernmost

Fig 113 *A view showing the junction between the two principal structural elements of the new locomotive factory. Despite the obvious differences in architectural detail between the walls on either side of the central opening, the structure was built all in one go. The deep, arched recesses visible on the far side of the opening were originally open, giving access from the machine shop to the erecting areas.*

Fig 114 *(below) The 1876 paint shop, in 1882.*

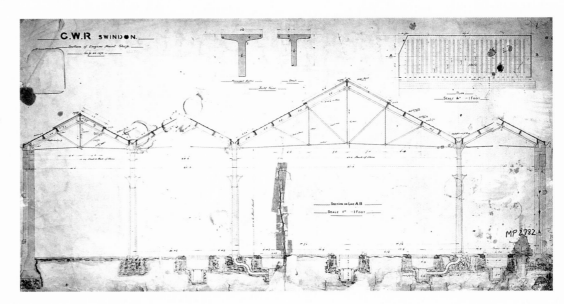

Fig 115 *(right) A GWR drawing, of 1870, entitled 'Section of Engine Paint Shop'. The roof truss is typical of those used in the building campaigns of the 1870s.*

Fig 116 *(below) A plan of the coppersmiths' and brass shops of 1877. Later alterations are also shown, together with those proposed in 1908.*

Fig 117 *(bottom) An 1864 plan of the Cambria Place estate built to accommodate Welsh iron-workers and their families, brought to New Swindon to operate the new rolling mills in 1861.*

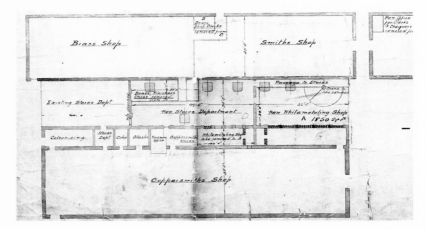

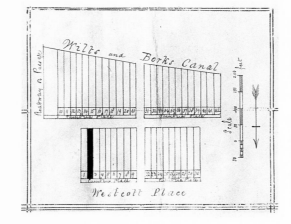

Fig 118 *(opposite top left) A view along the Faringdon Road façades of the cottages making up the north-eastern terrace of the Cambria Place Estate. Some of the cottages at the eastern end of this terrace have been disfigured by the insertion of modern shopfronts.*

Fig 119 *(opposite top right) The plans for 143 Faringdon Road, one of the best-preserved cottages on the Cambria Place estate. A modern, two-storeyed extension replaces the original rear annexes. Upstairs, the front bedroom has been subdivided into two rooms.*

row faced north, on to Faringdon Road, whilst the façades of the southern row faced towards the Wilts & Berks Canal, which then formed the southern boundary of the estate (**Fig 117**). A narrow back road, now known as Cambria Place, ran in an east–west direction between the gardens of the northern row and the backs of the southern one. The back road was bisected by a second street, orientated north–south, which divided the development into four terraces. Each terrace origi-nally consisted of eight to twelve cottages, but additional cottages had been added to the southern row by 1876.[11] Long thin gardens behind each cottage were used for growing vegetables and for keeping pigs.[12]

Virtually nothing is known of Ellis's building company, although it is quite possible that the estate was built by the same men who had already built the GWR rolling mills. John Williams, the occupant of the cottage originally numbered 2 Cambria Place, was a mason by trade, and it seems likely that he, too, was closely involved in the construction work. The development may even have been a joint venture between Ellis and Goddard. Goddard appears to have supplied most of the capital, as well as the land, since a deed in the Wiltshire Record Office shows that he took out a mortgage of £1,600 to build the cottages.[13] Some of the cottages were finished by March 1864 and let at 2s 6d a week. Work continued until 1869 when the leases of thirteen cottages, described as 'newly-erected and substantially built Dwelling Houses with garden plots' were put up for auction.[14] Weekly rents for most of the cottages had risen to 5s by that time. The tenants may also have been granted the right to buy the cottages, as

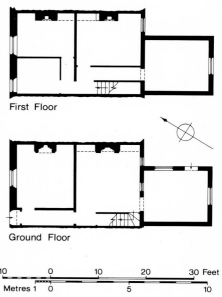

First Floor

Ground Floor

```
10        0        10       20      30 Feet
Metres 1  0                5              10
```

Williams purchased the freehold outright from Goddard for £57 in 1876.

The façades of the cottage terraces were built of snecked Swindon stone extracted from Goddard's quarries in old Swindon, whilst the dressings were, once again, of Bath stone (**Fig 118**). The rear elevations, of red brick, were largely hidden from public view. The cottages were similar in plan to the later cottages in the village and contained four principal rooms (**Fig 119**). On the ground floor there was a front parlour and a back kitchen with an enclosed staircase (**Fig 120**) leading up to two heated bedrooms on the floor above (**Fig 121**). The back yard probably contained a wash house and privy. Two cottages added in 1876 each had a pantry measuring 4ft (1·2m) by 6ft (1·8m) attached to the rear wall of the kitchen. The kitchen fireplaces in these cottages were originally fitted with ovens, and both of these features may have been incorporated into the earlier cottages as well.

Cambria Place was very much a Welsh enclave. Services in the Baptist chapel built at the centre of

Fig 120 (below left) The enclosed staircase to the first floor in 143 Faringdon Road.

Fig 121 (below) An original fire surround and grate in one of the bedrooms of 143 Faringdon Road.

the estate in 1866 were conducted in Welsh and English and, on a GWR map of 1882, Cambria Place is described simply as 'Welsh Buildings'.[15]

According to the 1871 census the forty-four cottages that had been built by that time accommodated approximately 300 people at an average of 7 people per dwelling. Of the workmen living here, 66 per cent listed their birthplace as Wales, whilst another 8 per cent were Englishmen with Welsh wives. Most of the men had previously worked in the South-Wales iron industry. Daniel Gooch himself had worked with a Thomas Ellis at the Tredegar Ironworks in his youth and it seems likely that the Thomas Ellis who came to Swindon in 1861 to establish the rolling mills was the latter's grandson.[16]

THE BOARD OF HEALTH

The year 1864 was an important one for New Swindon. Along with the departure of Daniel Gooch as locomotive superintendent, and his replacement by Joseph Armstrong, it was also the year in which democratic local government was established for the first time, in the shape of the New Swindon Local Board of Health. From the outset, however, the board was dominated by company employees. Six of the twelve members first elected to the board were company men, and they included William Gooch and Thomas Ellis. The non-GWR men were traders, contractors and farmers who were largely dependent upon the GWR for their livelihoods. The role of the local board was to approve plans for new buildings, to ensure that adequate provision was made for drainage and the disposal of sewage, and to take on responsibility for the repair of adopted roads and for keeping them clean. It was also the principal supporter of the Swindon Water Company which, by the beginning of 1868, had installed water pipes along the roads within the local board district.

In spite of strong GWR representation, the local board was not afraid to confront the company when its activities threatened the health of the inhabitants. In 1866 the board took legal proceedings against the GWR in an attempt to force the company to repair the Barracks after the building had been condemned by the board's inspector.[17] The outcome of the board's legal moves is unknown, though the company did carry out minor repairs to the building before selling it to the Wesleyan Chapel Trustees in 1867 (see p 161). The election to the local board of senior company officials such as Joseph Armstrong, who served as board chairman from December 1867, had the effect of forcing the GWR to abide by local by-laws. However, the board had no jurisdiction over the roads in the village, which were

owned by the company. In 1867, anxious to avoid interference by the board in its own property, the company's Expenditure Committee ordered 'steps to be taken for the preservation of the Company's rights in respect to the roads generally at Swindon'.[18]

Relations between old and New Swindon

Old Swindon had its own local board and for the most part remained aloof from the mushrooming new town to the north. A journalist writing for the *Railway News* in 1865 described the two towns as 'curious representatives of age and youth – of the jog-trot past and the go-ahead present'.[19] Nevertheless, traders in old Swindon and in the villages surrounding the new settlement benefited considerably from the expansion of the works. The spending power of company artisans and labourers living on the outskirts of New Swindon was markedly greater than that of agricultural workers and this had a knock-on effect on the economy of the rural hinterland.

The residents of old Swindon were keenly aware of the advantages of having the GWR works on their doorstep and, following the decision in 1864 to transfer the carriage works to Oxford, it was the gentry, traders and builders of old Swindon who sent a 'memorial' to the GWR in mid 1865 asking that the works be built at New Swindon instead. The memorial was signed by 172 people, including Ambrose Lethbridge Goddard and Mrs Rolleston, the daughter of Colonel Thomas Vilett, whose names were at the top of the list. The memorialists argued that it would make sound economic sense to have the locomotive and carriage works in the same locality and that provision had been made for 'a numerous population' at New Swindon. They also stated that there was a plentiful amount of land available at reasonable cost for expansion and 'that cottages and accommodation for the work people would be amply provided'.[20] Twelve other towns and cities, including Bristol, Gloucester, Worcester and Reading, lobbied the company to the same end, but, as has already been shown, it was New Swindon which was given the carriage works in 1867.

THE SWINDON PERMANENT BENEFIT BUILDING AND INVESTMENT SOCIETY

The construction of the carriage works resulted in a large influx of railway workers into the town and created a huge demand for new housing. Unlike earlier boom periods such as 1862, when the demand for new houses seemed to catch it unawares, the company took immediate steps to provide houses for the anticipated influx. This time, though, its approach was completely different. Rather than fund the construction of large numbers of houses itself, something which it could not hope to do in the prevailing economic climate, the company decided to act as a facilitator by supporting the establishment of the Swindon Permanent Benefit Building and Investment Society (later known as the Swindon Permanent Building Society) in 1868.

The aims of the society were explained at a public meeting held in the hall of the Mechanics' Institution on 27 August 1868. The meeting was chaired by Sir Daniel Gooch (Gooch was created a baronet in 1866 for his work in overseeing the laying of the telegraphic cable across the Atlantic) and attended by, amongst others, Joseph Armstrong, R L White, Samuel Carlton, William Ellis and James Haydon, all of whom were directors or trustees of the new society. Through the society, the GWR effectively placed the onus on its employees to provide their own housing, through savings and investments. The GWR may have felt that it had some kind of moral obligation

to check the tendency of the men to spend their wages as quickly as they earned them. Certainly this was the prevailing view of the time, as expressed by Richard Jefferies, the polemical local author and journalist, who considered it 'a grave defect in his [the workman's] character'.[21] In other respects Jefferies felt that the majority of the men were intelligent 'and not a few ... well educated and thoughtful'.

The society's estate

The society aimed to persuade the workmen to buy shares as a form of investment which could be used as a deposit on a new house. As an incentive to do this, the GWR sold the 17-acre (6·8-hectare) Great Culvery field, located to the south of the railway station, to the society for the relatively low price of £250 per acre (£625 per hectare) for subdivision into 180 building plots (**Fig 122**).[22]

The GWR's reasons for subsidising this development, and the approach of the society's directors,

Fig 122 *An 1869 plan of the Swindon Permanent Benefit Building and Investment Society estate, laid out to the south of Swindon station.*

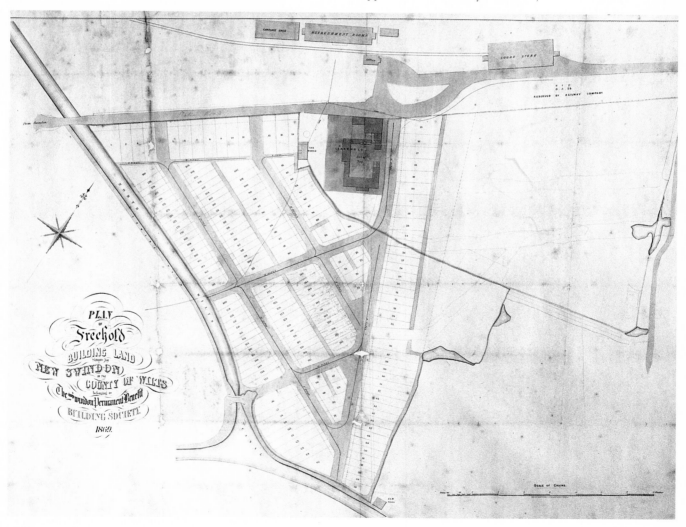

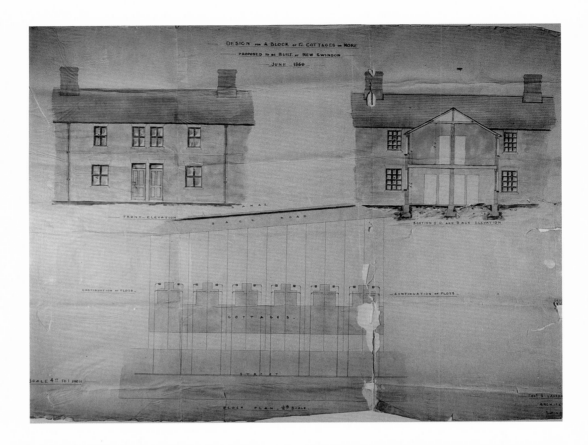

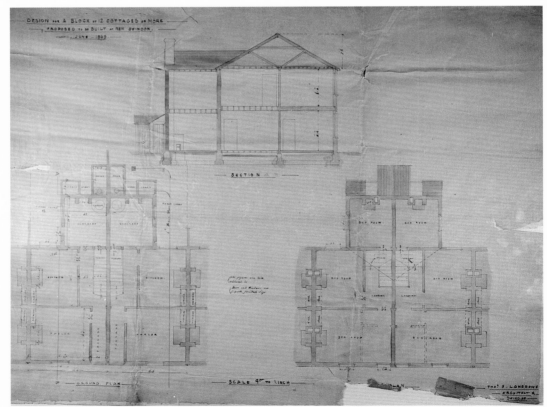

Fig 123 *Plans, section and elevations by Thomas Lansdown (dated August 1869) for a terrace of twelve cottages in Cheltenham Street on the Swindon Permanent Benefit Building and Investment Society estate.*

were outlined in the following statement to the public meeting by one of the trustees, Mr R Strange:

The only drawback to building in Swindon had been the extreme price of land. Their worthy chairman [Sir Daniel Gooch] had noticed the fact that there would be great advantage in placing the men nearer the works than had been the case hitherto. The same fact had enabled Sir Daniel Gooch to induce the Directors of the Great Western Railway to place at the disposal of this society a large portion of freehold land, which they intended offering to the artisans of Swindon at a very moderate price – much lower than would otherwise be the case. The society would induce men to cultivate the habit of saving their money, as they could now invest it at a profitable rate of interest. If they had no large amount to begin with they could enter as investing members, and soon save sufficient to pay their first deposit on the house, and then whilst paying off the remainder a man would pay considerably less than his rent, and would soon have the house his own.[23]

The society received strong support from the workmen, and, by the time the public meeting was held in August 1868, £4,000 had already been invested with the society's secretary, William Hall, a senior clerk at the works. The society undertook to build 100 houses by mid 1869;[24] indeed, by 1871, 200 buildings, mostly terraced houses, had been built on the estate.[25] A piped water supply was provided for the estate by early 1869, when a sewage system was laid down.[26]

Dwellings and shops

The houses on the estate were built of local red brick and most contained two or three bedrooms. A terrace of twelve houses, which appears to have been built by the society to provide model dwellings, was designed by Thomas Smith Lansdown, the architect of old Swindon, and approved by the local board in 1869 (**Fig 123**).[27] The houses in the terrace were arranged in pairs with their front doors placed next to each other. A front parlour and, behind it, a rear kitchen opened off a passage which was made wider at the back of the house to accommodate the stairs; these led up to three bedrooms, one of which was positioned over the scullery. The scullery, containing a copper for washing clothes, led off the passage at the back of the house. Behind the scullery was a paved courtyard with a privy and separate bins alongside for coal and ashes.

The estate also had shops and a public house, originally called the Great Western Hotel (now the Flag & Whistle – **Figs 124** and **125**). This was erected on society land on the opposite side of

Wellington Street from the Queens Tap.[28] The pub was designed by Lansdown and built in 1869–70 for Messrs Arkell & Son, a local brewer. The building had a large circular bar opening off a ground-floor vestibule and, at the rear, a yard with stables and coach house. It was ideally situated to accommodate travellers alighting at the station. Apart from the Flag & Whistle virtually all of the buildings on the estate have since been demolished to make way for modern office buildings.

SMALLER ESTATES

From 1869 two smaller estates were laid out to the east of this development. One of these was promoted by the Oxford Building and Investment Company Limited and laid out from 1870 on a field known as Briary Close, using the local firm

Fig 124 An 1869 elevation and section by Thomas Lansdown for the Great Western Hotel (now the Flag & Whistle public house) built for a local brewer, Messrs Arkell & Son, located just to the south of Swindon station on the Swindon Permanent Benefit Building and Investment Society estate.

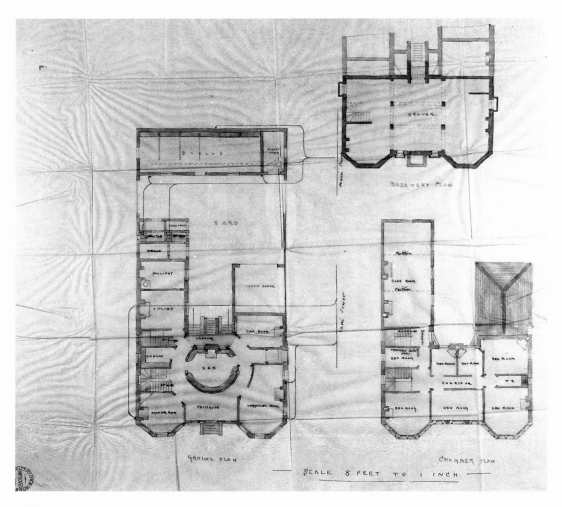

SCALE. 8 FEET TO 1 INCH.

Fig 125 *Plans of Lansdown's Great Western Hotel.*

of Lansdown and Shopland as architects and surveyors (**Fig 126**). They laid out 108 building plots ranged along four principal streets named after Oxford colleges or streets. The brick-built terrace houses and shops here were similar to those on the Swindon Permanent Building and Investment Society estate, although some houses on Merton Street were larger, with six rooms and canted bay windows at the front. Another smaller estate, centred on Mill Street and Haydon Street, was laid out to the north of the Oxford Building Company development by Merrin & King from late 1870.[29]

Two other estates were laid out just to the south of the old hamlet of Upper Eastcott. These were the Merrin & King development, based on Byron and Wellington Streets, and Gilberts Hill, begun in 1869 by a private speculator, R Bowley, and later taken over and extended to 268 plots by the United Land Company Limited of London. Plots on the latter estate may well have been overpriced because approximately 150 remained unsold by 1878.[30] By the mid 1870s the accommodation provided by these new developments

exceeded that in the railway village, though this, by virtue of its close proximity to the works, market and Mechanics' Institution, remained the nucleus of New Swindon.

OFFICERS' HOUSES

The villas of the works' manager and the station superintendent, on the south side of the line, were demolished to make way for new parts of the carriage works. The villas were replaced by two detached houses built to the north of the station reservoir, along with a pair of substantial, semi-detached houses demolished in the 1940s.[31] The detached villas, which were themselves demolished during World War I, were remarkably similar in design to the original 1840s houses and were probably built with stone salvaged from them (**Fig 127**). A large house for Joseph Armstrong, named Newburn House (after Newburn-on-Tyne where he was raised), was completed by 1873; this was located adjacent to the main line and well to the west of the cricket ground (**Fig 128**).

'MORE BRICKS AND MORTAR'

Contemporary writers viewed the rapidly expanding industrial town, set as it was in the heart of rural north Wiltshire, with a sense of wonderment. Jefferies thought it a kind of modern miracle and wrote of it, in 1875: 'in the Eastern tales of magicians one reads of a town being founded one day where there was nothing the day before. Here the fable is fact and the potent magician is Steam.'[32] Yet, despite all this building activity, there was still a strong demand for housing, partly as a result of the expansion of the works towards Rodbourne Road from 1873; this, with the carriage works, had created something of a double boom. Jefferies noted that: 'notwithstanding all the building that has been going on, despite the rush of building societies and private speculators, the cry is still "More bricks and mortar", for there exists an enormous amount of overcrowding'.[33]

The housing shortage seems to have been at its most acute in 1870. At a dinner for the men employed in the carriage works in March 1871, the carriage and wagon works' manager, Thomas Clayton, 'spoke of the want of house accommodation in Swindon as one of the difficulties to be contended against, and showed

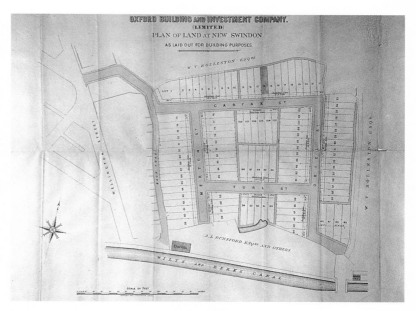

Fig 126 *A plan of the Oxford Building and Investment Company Limited's estate, laid out in 1870 to the east of the estate of the Swindon Permanent Benefit Building and Investment Society.*

Fig 127 *(below left) One of the managers' houses built in the early 1870s to the north of Swindon station reservoir. They replaced the villas of 1846 (see Figure 70), which were demolished to make way for the carriage works.*

Fig 128 *(below right) Newburn House, the substantial brick villa (now demolished) erected for Joseph Armstrong to the west of the GWR cricket ground in 1873.*

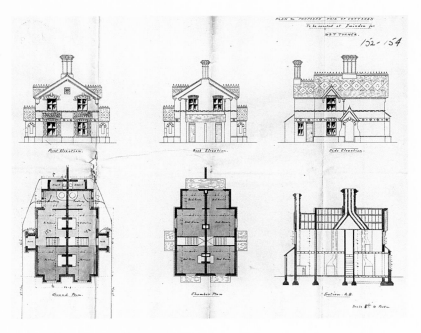

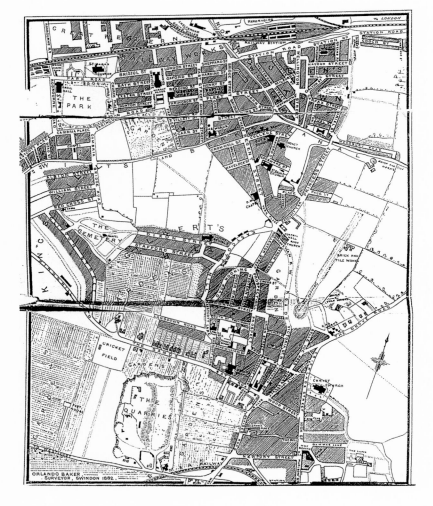

that, through the exertions of building and other societies and private enterprise, we were much better off in that respect than we were twelve months ago'.[34]

In 1871 the *Swindon Advertiser* reported on the expansion of the town in the following terms:

> the long talked of Carriage Works are brought to Swindon also, and as a consequence another town or colony has sprung up to the East of what are known as the 'Company Cottages', and until recent years constituted the bulk of New Swindon, so that the place now is, and is likely for a few years to remain, in a state of unusual activity and bustle, and the sharp clear ring of the mason's trowel mingling with the 'clank' of machinery and the 'rumble' of passing trains, will yet be heard for many a long day, whilst amongst the inhabitants there will be found the owner of the mortar-bedaubed clothes as well as of the smoke and smut-begrimed face.[35]

In the same year, the population of New Swindon reached 7,628, an 83 per cent increase since 1861. By contrast, old Swindon now had a population of 4,092. The shortage of housing led to a noticeable increase in rents, which Jefferies commented upon in 1875, describing the high rents as 'almost prohibitory, and those who take houses underlet them and sublet them till in six rooms three families may be living'.[36]

BUILDING MATERIALS

With the housing boom came an insatiable demand for building materials. Thomas Turner's Swindon and Stratton Tile and Pottery Works, in Cricklade Road, underwent extensive enlargement to meet the demand for bricks. In 1871 Turner built a pair of semi-detached houses at the front of his property to advertise his various clay products (**Fig 129**).

An even larger company, the Swindon Brick and Tile Company, was established on the south bank of the Wilts & Berks Canal in the early 1870s (**Fig 130**). It was then the largest brickworks in Wiltshire, and its circular Hoffman kiln was capable of producing 25,000 bricks a day. In 1877, the company's advertisement stated that 'the character of the clay and its method of working has enabled the Company to produce a very hard and durable article, the demand for which is very considerable and is daily increasing'.[37] Lime was also in great demand: in 1872, for example, 300 tons (305 tonnes) of 'best lime' were delivered to Swindon station.[38]

Swindon stone continued to be used, primarily for foundations. A number of contractors working for building companies took out leases on parts of the quarries in old Swindon. In 1871, an

Oxford builder, James Stroud, leased 40 perches (1,000 cubic feet, or 28·3 cubic metres) of the quarry from Ambrose Lethbridge Goddard in order to supply stone to the estate being built on the Oxford Building Company land.[39] The quarries could not supply all of the stone required, however, and 29,425 tons (29,896 tonnes) of stone had to be imported from quarries in west Wiltshire between 1864 and 1878.[40]

Large quantities of building timber were transported to New Swindon and offloaded either at the canal wharves (**Fig 131**) or alongside the railway line. In 1871 it was reported that 'there began to accumulate on nearly every vacant spot along the line immense stacks of timber; huge English-grown trees, and ponderous logs of foreign wood, with stacks of deals "piled" to an alarming height'.[41] Softwoods, slates and other building materials were sold at auction yards adjacent to the Wilts & Berks Canal and occasionally transported by barge, at no extra cost, as part of the conditions of sale. In 1877 Swindon Wharf had a powerful crane, warehouses, sheds, and two timber yards with saw pits and sheds.[42] Despite this building boom, the canal companies were unable to compete with rail transport, a factor which led to the disputed and protracted sale of the Wilts & Berks Canal Company between 1874 and 1877.

SWINDON STATION

Rail-passenger traffic using Swindon station increased considerably during the decade 1870–80. In 1872–3 a two-storey booking office (**Fig 132**) was erected to the south of the original station, built of stone and carefully designed to match the earlier buildings. This new booking office quickly proved inadequate and a large brick extension was added to its eastern end by 1880. Both buildings were demolished, along with Brunel's southern station block, in 1972.

HEALTH AND WELFARE

The rapid increase in population associated with the establishment of the carriage works placed great strain on the Medical Fund's welfare institutions. Because of the demand for additional space in the Mechanics' Institution building, the Medical Fund established new washing baths in the yard between the rear wings of the Barracks in 1864. Earlier, in 1860, the directors had allowed the workmen to build Turkish baths in the Barracks' yard. When the Barracks was converted to a Wesleyan chapel in 1868, the Medical Fund erected a new building, containing washing and Turkish baths, on the triangular piece of land between Taunton Street and

Fig 129 *(opposite top) A pair of display houses, at 152–4 Drove Road, built by Thomas Turner, the Swindon brick manufacturer, in 1871.*

Fig 130 *(opposite) A map of old and New Swindon in 1882 by Orlando Baker. At this time there was still a marked separation between the two towns. The circular Hoffman kiln of the Swindon Brick and Tile Company can be seen to the south of Medgbury Road on the right of the map.*

Fig 131 *(above) Webb's timber wharf on the Wilts & Berks Canal, south of Cambria Place, 1873.*

Fig 132 *A GWR publicity photograph of 1927 showing the booking office to the south of Swindon station. This ashlar building, erected in 1872–3, stood on the site of an earlier booking office and is similar in appearance to the earlier station blocks. The brick extension on the right of the photograph was completed by 1880 (compare Figures 98 and 138). The building was demolished in 1972.*

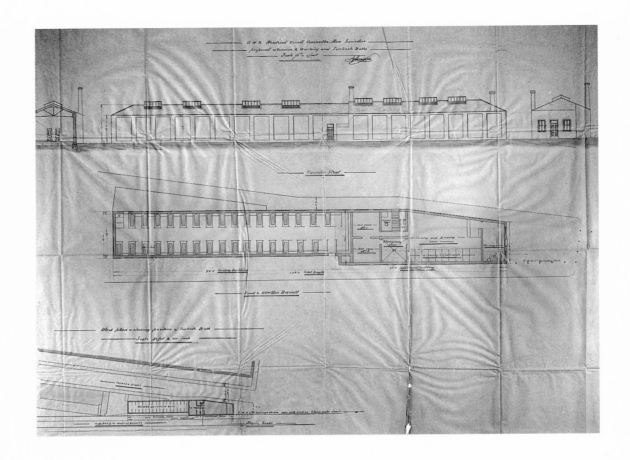

Fig 133 (top) Plan and elevations of the GWR Medical Fund washing and Turkish baths, built on the triangular plot between Faringdon Road and Taunton Street in 1868 and extended in 1876–7. The building was demolished in 1970.

Fig 134 An early 20th-century view of the front of the GWR accident hospital (formerly the armoury), showing the formal garden beds and perimeter railings. The central section of the façade is little altered from its original appearance (see Figure 87).

Faringdon Road (**Fig 133**; and see Figure 45d). The site was owned by the GWR and was probably leased to the Medical Fund at a nominal rate. In the same year the GWR provided land next to the Gloucester branch line, within the works' site, for an indoor swimming bath; this was managed by a private operator who leased it from the Medical Fund.

The high number of serious accidents suffered by GWR workmen in the late 1860s led to calls for an accident hospital in New Swindon. Three fatalities occurred in the space of a month in 1869 when workmen were hit by trains whilst attempting to cross the main line. The victims were usually carried by stretcher to nearby inns and manhandled upstairs to an empty bedroom to await the attention of the company medical officer. The GWR was criticised in the local press for failing to prevent these accidents, and, in March 1869, Frederick Cadogan (the Liberal Member of Parliament for Cricklade) raised the issue in the House of Commons.

New Swindon's hospital

As the company was developing the carriage works at this time it took the opportunity to build a tunnel under the line in 1870. This helped reduce the number of serious accidents, but the requirement for a hospital for New Swindon remained, and on 28 February 1871, Armstrong wrote to the directors:

> The want of some provision for the reception of accident cases has long been felt at Swindon and the recent increase in the number of men and quantity of machinery employed, in consequence of the opening of the new carriage shops, has made the necessity for this more urgent than ever. There is a strong desire on the part of the Company's workmen that something should be done.[43]

His suggestion was that the XI Wiltshire Volunteer Rifle Corps armoury should be converted to a hospital and that one of the adjoining cottages be made into a nurse's residence. The estimated cost of the conversion, which Armstrong felt should be borne by the GWR, was £130. The cost of furniture and internal fittings was to be met through workers' subscriptions and fundraising. The proposal was approved and the hospital was ready to receive its first patient in December 1871.

The new building was operated as a cottage hospital. Originally, it had a front garden with flower beds, gravel paths and iron railings forming a pleasant outlook for the patients (**Fig 134**), though in 1927 the garden was covered over when a temporary extension was built on it. The hospital's one ward measured 34ft (10·4m) by 22ft (6·7m), and originally contained five beds.[44] To the north of the ward were the reception area and operating-room, both entered from an alley at the back. A room for carrying out post-mortems was located on one side of the operating-room, with a bathroom on the other. The nurse's cottage to the east had an interconnecting door with the ward. The hospital was endowed with a donation of £1,000 from Sir Daniel Gooch, a sum matched by a rise in the Medical Fund members' weekly contributions.

The cottage adjoining the hospital on the west side was converted to a dispensary and consulting-room, with a sitting-room and bedroom for the resident dispenser on the floor above. This was necessary because an earlier dispensary, located in a small room in the company surgeon's house, had been unable to cope with an average of over 700 visitors per day in the winter months.

In 1876, following a report from Armstrong, the directors also agreed to build a new house and surgery for the company's chief medical officer and his family, at an estimated cost of £1,500. This substantial house, of yellow brick, was built at the east end of a terrace of cottages (now demolished) situated on the south side of Taunton Street. The house itself, now known as Park House, has survived, facing on to the Park (**Fig 135** and see p 158).

Company improvements

With the provision of fresh drinking water by the Swindon Water Company from 1868, a sewage-disposal system (in 1872) and good hospital facilities, the health of New Swindon inhabitants began to improve in the early 1870s, following a severe outbreak of smallpox in the town in 1871. Epidemics of scarlatina and typhoid fever occurred

Fig 135 *Park House, built in 1876–7, on the south-western corner of the railway village, as a residence and surgery for the company's chief medical officer. The building was later used as a medical examination centre for men seeking employment in the works and as GWR footplate staff.*

not infrequently after that, and the Medical Fund attempted to alleviate the effects by supplying free disinfectant in the form of carbolic acid to its members. Lime, for whitewashing cottages, was also distributed to members from a limehouse at the west end of the Faringdon Road Baths.

Conditions of employment also improved – the Nine Hours Movement, a campaign to reduce working hours begun by workers in the North of England, led to the introduction of a fifty-four-hour week at the beginning of 1872, and there was a return to weekly (from fortnightly) pay.[45] Employment opportunities for women were boosted in 1876 when a large London clothier, J Compton & Sons, built a sewing factory on a site to the east of the carriage works. Designed by a New Swindon architect, J J Smith, the factory initially employed 300 women. Additional school accommodation was provided by the GWR in 1873 when a large school for girls and infants was constructed in College Street, on the southern bank of the Wilts & Berks Canal (**Fig 136**).

Many of these improvements were initiated or supported by Joseph Armstrong who exhibited a strong empathy with his employees. Armstrong was probably behind the landscaping of the cricket ground in 1871–2, when an entrance lodge was built on the eastern side of The Park and gardens laid out around it (**Fig 137**). A substantial new pavilion was also erected by company workmen at the western end of The Park. A new drill hall for the Rifle Corps was built at the north-eastern corner of The Park in 1871, following the armoury's conversion into the accident hospital.

New thoroughfares

The westwards expansion of the works to Rodbourne Road, from 1873, led to a considerable amount of house building in that part of New Swindon. Within a few years the hamlet of Even Swindon, to the east and north of the works, had been joined to New Swindon. Some of the new streets were laid out by private speculators, such as W E Morris, whilst others were constructed by land societies, such as the Oxford Building and Investment Company Limited. Building plots on these developments, which lay outside the local board's jurisdiction, proved popular because of their close proximity to the new Rodbourne Road works' entrance. Another area to be developed from the mid 1870s was Gorse Hill, a tiny settlement to the north east of the town. The impetus for its growth was the construction of the wagon works to the east of the junction between the main line and the Gloucester branch.

A new cast-iron bridge, built over the Wilts & Berks Canal in 1870, helped to establish Bridge and Regent Streets as the principal thoroughfare in New Swindon. Many of the cottages along this route were converted into shops, and in 1877 a large part of Regent Street was paved with Bristol Blue stone.[46]

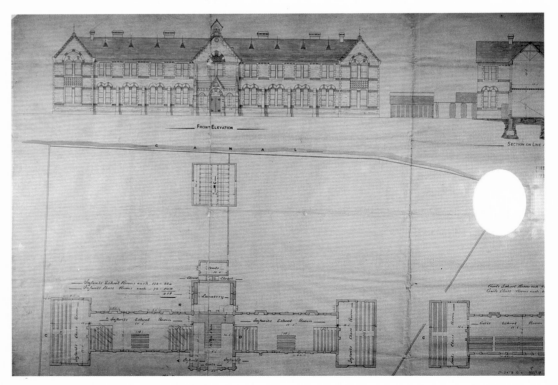

Fig 136 *The GWR girls' and infants' schools in College Street, built by the company in 1873 on the southern bank of the Wilts & Berks Canal. The girls' school was on the first floor. The schools were adopted by the new Swindon School Board in 1879 and demolished in 1961.*

THE END OF AN ERA

Armstrong's sudden death in 1877, like that of Minard Rea twenty years earlier, plunged the town into mourning. Armstrong had been extremely popular and, according to *Astill's Original Swindon Almanack* of 1878, his death 'cast a gloom over the entire community'. His funeral was attended by thousands, and special trains were laid on from London and Wolverhampton to bring some of the mourners to Swindon.[47] The trains pulled up at a temporary platform, erected for the occasion, alongside Armstrong's villa, Newburn House. During his term as locomotive superintendent he had overseen virtually every aspect of New Swindon life, and had made a very considerable personal contribution to the development of what was now no longer a village, but rather a burgeoning town.

Fig 137 *The park-keeper's lodge, greenhouses and formal gardens on the eastern side of The Park, photographed in 1893.*

Joseph Armstrong's death at the age of sixty may have been unexpected but the GWR was not left without an obvious successor. William Dean had followed Armstrong from Wolverhampton in 1868 as chief assistant and now, some nine years later, was able to take up the reins at Swindon as locomotive, carriage and wagon superintendent. Dean was born in London in 1840 and had been apprenticed to Armstrong at the Stafford Road Works, Wolverhampton, in 1855, finishing his education at the Wolverhampton Working Men's College. In 1864, Armstrong recommended him to be works' manager at Stafford Road, working under George Armstrong, the divisional superintendent, when he was only twenty-four-years old. Now, at the age of thirty-seven, he was to continue the programme of centralisation and expansion at Swindon that his mentor, Joseph Armstrong, had introduced. Somewhat later, he was to preside over the final demise of the broad gauge.

ARMSTRONG'S LEGACY

The GWR was a very different railway in 1877 from the one that existed when Armstrong came to Swindon in 1864. All lines south of the Paddington–Bristol line had been narrowed by the end of 1874, with some 208 miles (333km) being converted in the month of June 1874 alone. The GWR had absorbed the Bristol & Exeter Railway in 1876 and the entire route to Penzance was soon to come under its direct control with the acquisition of the South Devon and West Cornwall railways. These lines, totalling some 440 miles (704km), were mostly operated by broad-gauge locomotives and thus the stock of these engines, maintained by the GWR with all heavy repairs carried out at Swindon, was to reach its peak at this time. In 1872 the company had also embarked on its most ambitious project so far: the construction of the Severn Tunnel, which would greatly shorten the route to South Wales. Though the tunnel was not to be completed for another fourteen years, the fact that the GWR could begin construction work demonstrated that the company had fully recovered its confidence after the financial crises of the late 1860s. Once the tunnel was completed the maintenance of its three pumping stations was to become the responsibility of the locomotive works' manager at Swindon.

The acquisition of so many neighbouring lines in the south west meant that, by the time of Armstrong's death, the GWR had grown to be the largest railway in the country, owning more than 2,000 miles (3,200km) of line. The GWR was also unusual in concentrating not just the majority of its locomotive, carriage and wagon manufacturing and repair facilities under a central management on a single site, but also so much of its issuing stores and general administration. Thus, while the London & North Western Railway's locomotive works at Crewe may have rivalled the Swindon locomotive works in size, no other railway town could match the range of manufacturing processes and skills and company employment opportunities that Swindon had developed.

THE WORKS IN 1878

Astill's Original Swindon Almanack for 1878 devoted more space than usual to the works in its routine description of New Swindon. Lamenting Armstrong's death, it greeted Dean's appointment in typically overwrought prose:

> in acknowledgment of his known zeal and ability as the coadjutor of Mr Armstrong [Dean] received the highest encomiums from the Chairman and Directors of the Company – the appointment being also popularly received by officers and men alike connected with the Works.

Its 'descriptive sketch' of the works took the form of a guided tour and its incidental comments are of value to the historian because they make mention of minor features and details that would otherwise escape attention, or which have long since disappeared, leaving little in the way of physical evidence. Thus we learn that there was an iron turnstile and enquiry office at the entrance to the 1870 subway and, in the offices at the other end, a 'Time-office through which the men have to pass to reach their respective workshops'. There was also a telegraph-office for 'the use of the Establishment whereby instant communication may be had with any Station or Depot of the Company's system'.

The 'R' shop received its usual fulsome description and we are told that, in the boiler and tender-making shops (opened in 1875), not only were boilers made for locomotives but also for 'the Marine Engines used in the Company's extensive

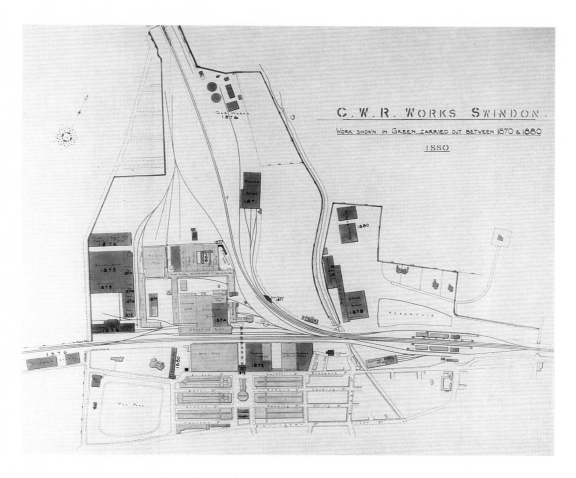

shipping service'. We also learn that these shops contained a steam traverser, fitted with a powerful crane, several overhead cranes and a hydraulic riveting plant 'which formed an interesting feature at the American Centenary Exhibition at Philadelphia in 1876'.

In the 'D' and 'N' shops, fitters and turners worked on wheels for all three departments, as did the wheelwrights in 'S' shop. 'K' shop, housing the coppersmiths, had recently been enlarged while the carpenters and pattern-makers in 'H' shop supplied all the works' joinery. The steam-hammer shop now contained thirteen large hammers and the rolling mills were worked day and night from Monday morning to Saturday noon under the supervision of Mr W Ellis.

The developments to the north of the station were also noted, with the site of the reservoir (formerly used for storing water fed to the works from the Wilts & Berks Canal) now 'being covered with extensive erections destined for the repair of wagons'. New Swindon had also become the depot for the company's chief stores department and the 90-acre (36-hectare) works now employed some 5,000 staff.

CHANGES IN THE LATE 1870S

Britain entered a period of deep economic depression in the second half of the 1870s that was to last until the early 1890s, but the Swindon works continued to expand for a few more years to service the company's new commitments. In the recently built locomotive works, a small extension had already been added to the west of the power house but in 1879 most of the northern wall of the works was replaced by a rank of columns and a further two 40ft (12·2m) aisles and a lower 24ft (7·3m) aisle were built to the north, thus creating a huge open hall, 350ft by 310ft (106·7m by 94·5m), with its northern wall flush with the end of the front range (**Fig 138**).

Minor additions were also made to the general offices and to the (now largely infilled) northern quadrangle. The site occupied by the original gasholders, alongside the spring shop, was converted to a plate-layers' yard when a new gasworks was built in 1878 in Rodbourne Cheney, to the north of the new engine shed. This gasworks was large enough to meet the greatly increased demand from all the new developments

Fig 138 *The railway works in 1880.*

Fig 139 *Smiths' hearths in the eastern wagon works in 1882.*

in both the works and New Swindon. Local directories record that it was fully operational by 1879 and also that the GWR brickworks, to the north of the works, 'had been for several years' producing bricks for the company's own use.

The end of the decade witnessed the works' first major casualty to technological obsolescence. The rail mills, once much-vaunted, could only produce wrought-iron rails and were closed because of competition from cheaper, and more effective, steel rails manufactured by outside suppliers. The rolling mills and furnaces survived, however, as they played a vital role in recycling the scrap metal produced in large quantities by the other processes in the works. It appears that few men were discharged, so some of the workforce may have been redeployed in the new wagon works, which were then being built on land immediately to the east of the North Wilts Canal.

These wagon works, like the carriage works, principally consisted of covered working areas of no very great sophistication in terms of building construction, but they also required facilities such as smiths' forges, steam hammers and stores (**Fig 139**). Over the next two decades, first under the management of James Holden and then, on his departure in 1885, under George Jackson Churchward, the wagon works developed in size and independence. Wheel, tyre and brake shops were added and local drawing-office facilities were provided. None of the buildings of the

carriage and wagon works on this northern site survived the redevelopment of the area that took place in the 1990s. Though they were not glamorous enough to attract the same attention as other parts of the works, early photographs record their appearance and many facets of their operation have been immortalised in Alfred Williams' *Life in a Railway Factory*, published in 1915 but recording working conditions some twenty years earlier.

STAGNATION IN THE 1880S

By 1880 the depression of the previous few years had at last begun to bite at Swindon and short-time working was introduced, only to be lifted the following year. Not surprisingly, there was little further development on the wagon works' site apart from the provision of a chair foundry in the yard to the north of the main foundry, and there were comparatively few significant additions to the works throughout the 1880s. The Hawksworth plan for 1890 shows that almost all the development in the previous decade was focused on the area to the east of the Gloucester line.

By the mid 1880s much of the impetus that, in earlier times, had driven Brunel, Gooch and Armstrong to develop one of the premier railways in the country had ground to a halt. The broad gauge was dwindling away but its conversion was a steady drain on the company's finances, tying up funds that might have been more profitably employed elsewhere. Even so, conversion of the gauge was an important achievement, and the final conversion of the main line from Penzance to Paddington over a single weekend in May 1892 was a feat of heroic proportions (see below).

The torpor that otherwise seemed to afflict the railway stemmed from other causes. Sir Daniel Gooch (**Fig 140**) was still chairman of the GWR, but he was preoccupied by his many other business and political interests, and by major problems with the Severn Tunnel. Most of the other senior GWR staff were growing old (though William Dean was only in his late forties) and the railway management was becoming more conservative. The directors were inclined to make austerity measures, once so necessary for the survival of the company, a virtue in their own right, and the timetables reflected those of an earlier era. The traffic superintendent, G N Tyrell, for example, was seventy-two years of age when he retired in 1888, having held his post since 1864, and in later years he appears to have been loath to make any allowance for the fact that the speed of locomotives had increased.

THE DEMISE OF THE BROAD GAUGE

The GWR was no longer even in the forefront of locomotive design, though Dean himself was keen on experimentation and the goods engines which he designed were to operate long into the following century. It is symptomatic of the corporate mood that in Dean's period in office no new broad-gauge express engines were designed, or thought necessary, even though the gauge was to persist for much of his reign. For some time new broad-gauge engines had been built as 'convertibles' while locomotives dating back to Sir Daniel Gooch's superintendency were 'rebuilt' several times. Thus the GWR did not capitalise on the advantages of the wider gauge, which had been so dearly won, and the opportunity to impress the world, with what could have been a matchless series of express trains, was never taken. Gooch himself had long recognised the inevitability of the demise of the broad gauge, even conceding as much as early as October 1874.[1] His death in October 1889, at the age of seventy-three, removed the last sentimental obstacle to its extinction.

Conversion arrangements

Once the date of May 1892 had been chosen for the conversion of the final lengths of broad-gauge line, arrangements had to be made at Swindon for the reception of thousands of pieces of rolling stock which either had to be converted or scrapped. The stock consisted mainly of wagons

and carriages, but the GWR still had nearly 200 broad-gauge locomotives at the end of 1891, most of which would end up in sidings at Swindon.

The logistics of this exercise have already been covered in detail by other historians, and only the salient facts need be repeated here.[2] The company had already (in 1884) purchased 25 acres (10 hectares) of land to the north of the station and, in 1888, it bought two further lots of 20 acres (8 hectares) each, one to the north of the new wagon works and the other, significantly, to the west of Rodbourne Road. In 1891 several further land purchases consolidated these acquisitions into an overall holding sufficient to provide up to 16 miles (25·6km) of sidings. These had to accommodate 150 locomotives and 500 carriages at 36ft (11m) each and 3,000 wagons at 18ft (5·5m) each, making a minimum requirement of 14·7 miles (23·6km).

In preparation for the final track conversion, scheduled to take place over the weekend of 20–22 May 1892, considerable landworks had to be undertaken, especially to the west of the works, and second-hand rail was gathered from all over the system. In the event, the final conversion of the line went remarkably smoothly, with all the redundant rolling stock marshalled at Swindon. The resultant work of conversion and scrapping was to tide the works over the remaining years of the depression until, in 1894, a nationwide resurgence in trade allowed the full benefits of the Severn Tunnel to be realised.

In 1892, A H Malan, writing in an illustrated description of the works, described the actual methods by which carriages were converted from broad to standard gauge. Those already built to

Fig 140 *Sir Daniel Gooch in later years, as chairman of the GWR, a post he was to hold until his death in October 1889.*

standard-gauge dimensions, but carried on broad-gauge bogies, could be changed 'within the space of half-an-hour!' This was accomplished in the changing shed where the floor at the 'parts where the wheels rest' was capable of 'rising and falling'. The carriage bodies were raised clear of their bogies by hydraulic power, propped up while their bogies were lowered beneath the floor and run out of the shed, whereupon narrow bogies were substituted by a reversal of the process. This procedure, 'the clever invention of some of the heads at Swindon', illustrated not only the capabilities of hydraulic power but served 'also to show the ability of the staff to grapple with great undertakings'.[3]

THE WORKS IN 1892

In the same year that Malan wrote this description, the GWR published a booklet (possibly as part of the publicity material to accompany the *Lord of the Isles* to the 1893 Columbian Exhibition in Chicago) entitled *The Town and Works of Swindon*, twelve pages of which were devoted to a description of the works. This claimed that the works were 'the largest establishment in the world for the manufacture and repair of Railway engines, carriages and wagons, about 10,000 men being employed under one management'. The locomotive factory accounted for half this total, the rolling mills and running sheds for 300 men each, the carriage works and sawmill for 1,800 and 400 men respectively, and the wagon works for 1,600. There were some 300 office staff and a further 350 shared amongst

Fig 141 *The imposing hydraulic crane in 'V' shop, photographed in 1882.*

the stores department, plate-layers, etc. It was also stated that some 1,500 locomotives, 5,000 carriages and 30,000 goods vehicles had been built since manufacturing commenced at Swindon in 1846.

The bulk of the description took the form of a tour of the works, beginning in the iron foundry, 'a magnificent shop, 400 feet [121·9m] long by 80 feet [24·4m] wide' where castings of all descriptions were produced including columns and pipes cast vertically in a deep excavation close to the cupola furnaces. The chair foundry, brass foundry and stores were briefly noted on the way to the boiler shop, where an 'immense Hydraulic Crane capable of lifting a weight of 30 tons [30·5 tonnes]' (**Fig 141**) and the hydraulic flanging press were of particular note.

The adjoining engine house, with its steam engine for driving the machinery and steam pump for the hydraulic system, came in for some attention. The latter was connected to an accumulator which gave a pressure of 750psi (51·7 bar) to power machines in every part of the shop. The rolling mills and smiths' shops were passed on the way to the repairing shops and 'R' shop, which still contained much of the original machinery supplied by Joseph Whitworth & Co. The carriage works were next on the itinerary, with a lengthy description of the sawmill, where underfloor, fan-exhausted culverts conveyed large quantities of sawdust, cuttings and shavings to be burnt in the steam engine's boilers.

The trimming shop attracted mention as the only department of the works where women were engaged. About 100 women were employed in various carriage-trimming tasks, such as french polishing, sewing and net-making, and the 'arrangements for the comfort of the women appear to be carefully studied. They are provided with a separate entrance and leave at somewhat different hours from the men.'[4]

EXPANSION IN THE 1890S

The GWR was now to enter what many regard as its 'golden age', with Swindon at the heart of its operation.[5] Several circumstances conspired to shake the company from its torpor. In 1895 came the appointment of Viscount Emlyn, later Lord Cawdor, the new and energetic young GWR chairman, and in October of that year the GWR at long last (and at huge cost) rid itself of the ten-minute refreshment stop imposed on all trains passing through Swindon. The following year saw the appointment of a new general manager, J L Wilkinson, who was intent on returning the GWR to its position as the country's premier railway.

The works, having rested for more than fifteen years on the fruits of the expansion programme of the 1870s, were ready by the mid 1890s to take advantage of this change in regime. They were soon to experience another surge in development comparable in magnitude to that of the 1870s. Progress was initially fitful following the death (in March 1896) of Samuel Carlton, who had been works' manager since Joseph Armstrong's reorganisation in 1864. Carlton was to be succeeded by George Churchward, who moved across from the carriage and wagon works where he had just embarked on a programme of expansion. As the original carriage works site, south of the main line, was now fully developed, further large buildings had to be sited to the north of the new wagon works. Beginning with a carriage-lifting shop in 1894, there followed a stamping shop in 1897 and a carriage-stock shed in 1899.

On the locomotive works' site there was little immediate building development, apart from minor accretions to the tender shop and the coppersmiths' shop, a points and crossings shed (**Fig 142**), built in 1896 to the north of the rolling mills, and a new iron store, built in 1897. Following Churchward's transfer, however, there was a major programme of retooling across the entire works. This involved the erection (in 1899) of a large iron-framed machinery store on made-up land at the extreme northern edge of the site (**Fig 143**).

The provision of a new iron store, with improved rail access, had been an urgent necessity since the conversion of the former iron store, in the main yard, to provide a substantial extension to the office of the locomotive works' manager. This conversion, for which drawings existed as early as 1887, predated Churchward's

Fig 142 *(above) A crossing layout being assembled in 'X' shop in 1944. The precise formation under construction is not known for certain, but it is possibly a standard-gauge turnout crossed by one rail of a large travelling crane track of unknown gauge. It may have been for use in a naval dockyard.*

Fig 143 *(left) The 1899 machinery store photographed in 1985, before being dismantled for re-erection on the preserved West Somerset Railway (formerly the GWR Minehead Branch).*

Fig 144 *The works' manager's office, viewed from the north west in 1985. The two southern-most bays (at the end on the right) contained the manager's office of the late 1840s. They are separately roofed and constructed from quite different stonework.*

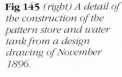

Fig 145 *(right) A detail of the construction of the pattern store and water tank from a design drawing of November 1896.*

Fig 146 *(below) The pattern store in 1985, with the foundry ('J1' shop) beyond.*

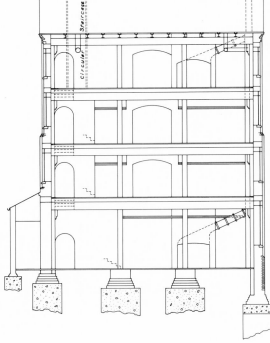

appointment as manager by a few years, and was carried out in some style. The new offices (**Fig 144**) had a central atrium with a fine iron staircase (see Figure 180) while the floor was supported by tall cast-iron columns with acanthus-leaf capitals – a far cry from Sturrock's original cubicle squeezed under a stair landing. At the same time the general offices seem to have expanded into the stores section of the original office range, following the construction of a large new general-stores building on the far side of the Gloucester line, designed to serve the needs of the locomotive department.

A somewhat more significant portent of things to come was the appearance in 1897 of the first permanent building to be constructed to the west of Rodbourne Road, on the land originally acquired for stockpiling redundant broad-gauge

rolling stock. This was the massively constructed, four-storey, fireproof pattern store which, surmounted by its huge compartmentalised water tank capable of holding 230,000 gallons (1·1 million litres), still dominates the Rodbourne Road bridge and the main railway line (**Figs 145** and **146**). The pattern-makers themselves continued to be housed on the main site, in the former machine and fitting shop of the original works, but the location of this store, as we will

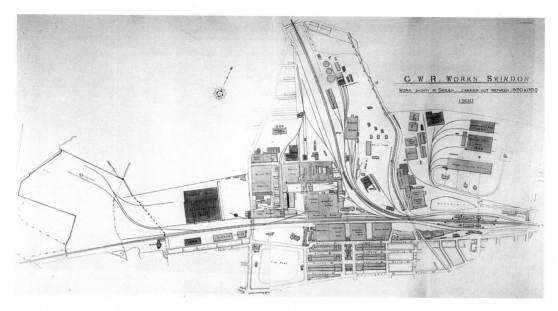

see in the next chapter, was to herald a development that, over the next two decades, was to shift the whole centre of gravity of the locomotive works (**Fig 147**).

NEW SWINDON

By 1880, the general trade depression led to a reduction in house building in New Swindon, although houses continued to be built on earlier developments and, from 1880, to the south of Cambria Place on the eastern part of J H Sheppard's Kingshill Estate (Albion Street, William Street and Red Cross Street) (see Figure 130). The western half of this estate had first come on to the market in 1870 but its remoteness from the core of New Swindon made it unpopular with prospective purchasers and substantial parts of the estate were still vacant in the mid 1880s. Further building plots were laid out in the area bounded by Farnsby Street, Carr Street and Catherine Street, but the large area of land owned by the Rolleston family (legatees of the late Colonel Thomas Vilett) remained undeveloped because of a legal dispute, serving as a barrier to the southward expansion of New Swindon until the estate was eventually put up for sale in 1885 (see p 125).[6]

THE SCHOOL BOARD

Despite the slowdown in house construction from 1878, the boom earlier in the decade had placed great strain on school accommodation. In 1876 the GWR schools, along with the parochial National Schools in old Swindon, had a combined estimated shortfall of 580 places.[7] This estimate was later substantially revised and the deficit put at 1,196. In the following year a school board was established to provide new schools and ensure at least an elementary education for all children in both old and New Swindon. The Swindon Education Board originally consisted of seven elected members, two of whom – James Holden and R L White – were senior GWR employees.

By the mid 1870s the expansion of New Swindon was such that the GWR no longer felt obliged to provide school places for all of the town's inhabitants. In October 1875, Armstrong suggested to the directors that the proposed school board should be offered the GWR's College Street schools provided that they built a new boys' school, thereby freeing the land occupied by the Bristol Street schools for works' purposes.[8] A plan of a suggested site for a new school was shown to the directors, who recommended that the GWR take powers in the ensuing session of parliament to enable the closure of the Bristol Street schools.

The school board moved quickly to provide temporary accommodation for pupils in a converted auction house in old Swindon and in the GWR's drill hall. The latter was rented by the board and fitted-up to take 200 children. Protracted negotiations between the board and the GWR over the transfer of the Bristol and College Street schools delayed the construction of new buildings. However, by the end of 1879 an agreement had been reached whereby the Bristol Street schools would be transferred to the board and then sold back to the GWR for the value of the land, set at £625. At the same time the College Street schools were transferred to the board for a nominal rental on a twenty-one-year lease.[9]

The board then took the opportunity to reorganise the existing school accommodation and to

Fig 147 *The railway works in 1900.*

Fig 148 *Gilberts Hill School, Dixon Street, one of three smaller board schools built in Swindon in 1879–81. The architect for these schools was Brightwen Binyon of Ipswich. Binyon was also responsible for the design of the Sanford Street Boys' School, the large extension to the Mechanics' Institution building (1891–3), and offices for the New Swindon Local Board in Regent Circus (1890–1).*

erect new buildings. In 1878 it purchased a plot on the corner of Sanford Street and College Street from Ambrose Lethbridge Goddard. A large central boys' school was built here by early 1881, replacing the Bristol Street schools, most of whose buildings were then demolished. The College Street schools then became the central girls' school.

New schools

Three smaller schools, each designed to accommodate approximately 250 infants and junior girls, were built in the most populous areas of New Swindon. The first of these was the Queenstown

School, completed in May 1880 for children living in the houses built on the new estates of the Swindon Permanent Benefit Building and Investment Society and the Oxford Building and Investment Company Limited, located to the south and south east of the railway station. Another was built on Dixon Street, on the Gilberts Hill Estate, and a third was erected on Birch Street, off Westcott Place, for the children temporarily accommodated in the drill hall. All three schools were completed by the end of 1881.

In March 1879 the board invited architects to send in plans for the Queenstown School, stipulating that 'the building is to be of a plain and substantial character and capable of enlargement at any future time'.[10] The successful candidate was Brightwen Binyon of Ipswich, a former pupil of the architect Alfred Waterhouse, who was given the contract on the strength of his having already built schools for six school boards. He went on to design all four board schools in Swindon.

The three infants' schools were built to the same plan. Two have since been rebuilt, but the Gilberts Hill School, though extended, survives almost unaltered (**Fig 148**) – a plain, red-brick building of two storeys with terracotta panels over the entrances (**Fig 149**). The Sanford Street Boys' School also survives, although parts have been demolished and the remainder has been converted to offices (**Figs 150** and **151**). Designed for 800 boys, it is considerably larger than the Gilberts Hill School and it has been treated in a more architectural manner with yellow-brick walls, red-brick dressings, and moulded brick and terracotta embellishments.

In 1878 a school for boys, girls and infants was built by the Stratton St Margaret School Board at Gorse Hill. A year later the Rodbourne Cheney Board erected a school for 350 children on Rodbourne Road in the rapidly expanding Even Swindon district. Designed by the local architects, Read and Drew, this plain brick school was extended in the 1880s and 1890s to cater for the growing population of the district. Both schools were brought under the control of the Swindon Board in 1890.

A larger brick school, in more flamboyant Queen-Anne style, was built for senior pupils on Clarence Street in 1897, and a training-school for local pupil teachers was built on an adjacent site in the same year. Also in 1897, another substantial building in Queen-Anne style was constructed to house the Swindon and North Wilts Technical Institute, on Victoria Road. Prior to the construction of this building all technical education in Swindon had been provided by the Mechanics' Institution. To help meet its continuing responsibilities in this field, the Institution building was extended to double its original size during 1891–3, through the

demolition of the octagonal covered market and the construction of a major new addition by Brightwen Binyon (see p 155).

CHURCHES

In 1881 the population of New Swindon reached 15,086, almost double that of 1871. New Swindon's churches and chapels could no longer cope with such a rapid increase in population, and in 1880 the new ecclesiastical district of St Paul was created to the south of the Wilts & Berks Canal. To serve the St Paul's parishioners, a temporary wooden church, lined with varnished

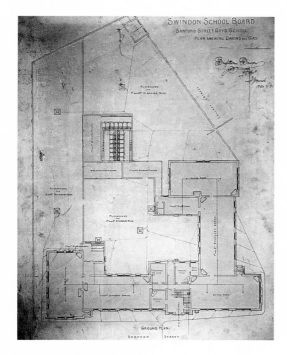

deal, was built by the GWR in Edgeware Road, off Regent Street. This continued in use as the church hall once a permanent brick church for 900 worshippers was opened in 1881.

THE ROLLESTON ESTATE

Overcrowding became less of a problem with the gradual development of new housing estates. The GWR were reported to 'have been considerably thinning out the tenants in their houses',[11] but there were still some alarming cases of over-crowding in other, privately owned, houses. In 1880, for example, six families were found to be living in a seven-roomed dwelling; thirty of the occupants were children.

When parts of the Rolleston Estate finally came on to the market in 1885, several building soci-eties and speculators began to erect terraced houses for working-class families. *The North Wilts and District Directory* for 1885 was quick to appreciate the implications of the new building land:

> For years the difficulties in obtaining any portion of the Rolleston Estate for building purposes stood in the way of the progress of the town in a symmetrical form. It seemed but natural that the stretch of land lying between Rolleston Street and Faringdon Street should be built upon, filling up a void and making the town a compact whole ... The Rolleston Estate – or rather, a portion of it – is now in the market for building purposes, and a great impetus is likely to be given to building.

The directory's prediction proved correct, as the entire centre part of the estate was covered with houses by 1901, thereby joining the two Swindons together.[12] In addition, a 54-acre (21·6-hectare) area of land, to the west of the old Drove Road, was subdivided for housing from 1897. The prin-cipal thoroughfare in this development was Manchester Road, so named after its Manchester-based developers, Maxwell & Tuke.[13] Comparing the railway estate with the numerous brick terraces which engulfed it, John Betjeman later wrote 'the model village of the eighteen-forties has developed a red brick rash which stretches up the hill to Old Swindon and strangles it'.[14]

NEW SWIMMING BATHS

In 1885 a section of the Rolleston Estate, immedi-ately opposite the GWR hospital on the south side of Faringdon Road, was sold to the trustees of the GWR Medical Fund Society for £999 as the site for a new dispensary and swimming baths. The old dispensary at the rear of the accident hospital was oversubscribed and the swimming baths of 1868

Fig 149 *(opposite bottom) A detail of the façade of Gilberts Hill School showing two of its three terracotta panels. Brightwen Binyon's name can be seen etched into the left-hand side of the panel to the left of the picture.*

Fig 150 *(above left) The plan by Brightwen Binyon for Sanford Street Boys' School, built in 1881 opposite the College Street schools of 1873. This was the first large school built by the Swindon School Board.*

Fig 151 *(left) The former Sanford Street Boys' School from the south east. The building is now used as offices.*

Fig 152 *A view of the town hall from the north west, built as the New Swindon Local Board office in 1890–1. By the late 1930s the council staff had become too large for the building, and new offices were built in Euclid Street to accommodate most departments. The town hall now houses the Swindon Library, the offices of Thamesdown Media Arts and a suite of dance studios.*

were without adequate changing facilities, as well as being inconveniently located within the works' site. The new dual-purpose building (begun in 1891 and opened in 1892) was, together with the extension to the Mechanics' Institution, the last major building erected under the auspices of the GWR in Swindon outside the works (for a detailed discussion of the building, with a plan and illustrations, see pp 166–9 and Figures 215–220).

LINKS BETWEEN OLD AND NEW SWINDON

In the 1880s the unification of Swindon's old and new towns was seen by many as inevitable, but constant bickering and lack of co-operation between the local boards delayed amalgamation. The eventual unification of the towns was prophesied by *The Illustrated London News* in 1845,[15] and, in an address to the GWR Clerks' Annual Dinner in 1877, William Dean stated that 'he hoped to live to see the day when it [Swindon] would be united' (his wish came true since he lived until 1905).[16]

Once before, in 1871, the two boards had combined forces to build a joint isolation hospital to the west of the quarries in old Swindon. They came together again, in 1881, to develop a new cemetery for both towns following the closure of the burial-ground of St Mark's church. In the following year old Swindon was linked to New Swindon by a railway line which branched off the main line at Rushey Platt. The line, which continued to Marlborough (and, from 1883, to Andover), approached old Swindon from the south west before connecting with a station located to the south of Newport Street. This line was closed in 1961.

Road links were also improved in 1888, when Victoria Road was constructed through the Rolleston Estate, passing downhill from the centre of old Swindon, to Regent Circus; this, despite its name, was a small square built at the same time as Victoria Road, at the southern end of Regent Street.

The New Swindon Local Board office

Soon after this, the New Swindon Local Board erected a substantial new office building for itself in Regent Circus (**Fig 152**). Opened on 21 October 1891, it was designed by Brightwen Binyon and cost £9,000.[17] The building, influenced by 17th-century Dutch architecture,

has a clock tower near its north-western corner and is built of red brick with stone dressings. Its grandiose appearance, and construction on a site approximately midway between the two towns, suggest that it may have been conceived as a future town hall for a unified Swindon. Its location at the end of Regent Street symbolises a shift in the focus of New Swindon away from the railway village to a neutral position closer to old Swindon. The building also represented the emergence of a new-found sense of local identity and civic pride.

Towards borough status

In 1894, the local boards became urban district councils, and on 9 November 1900 the two towns were incorporated as the municipal Borough of Swindon. The New Swindon Local Board offices in Regent Circus became the town hall, as anticipated, serving as the civic centre for what was, by now, the largest town in Wiltshire, with a combined population of 45,006, according to the 1901 census. The first mayor to be appointed under the new borough charter was the GWR locomotive works' manager, George Churchward, though the creation of the borough brought to an end the direct involvement of the GWR in the affairs of the town. Despite this, the company's influence and, indeed, its control over the lives of the inhabitants, was scarcely diminished: the GWR remained by far the borough's largest employer, and the fortunes of the works were, at this time, inextricably linked with those of the new borough.

7 *A New Century, 1900–1995*

The turn of the century proved to be a milestone in the history both of the town – now elevated to borough status – and in the development of the locomotive works, which was about to embark on a twenty-year building campaign. Most of this expansion was to take place to the west of Rodbourne Road, where additional land had been purchased in 1895 to consolidate the holding acquired at the time of conversion of the rolling stock. The expansion of the locomotive works was accompanied by further additions to the carriage and wagon works, both on the site to the north of the station and on land to the west of Rodbourne Road on both sides of the main line. By the time the GWR was nationalised in 1948, a century of development had resulted in the creation of a works estate that stretched for over 1·5 miles (2·4km) from east to west and totalled more than 325 acres (130 hectares) in extent, of which 77 acres

(30·8 hectares) was covered in workshops and offices.

Most of the buildings put up during the 20th century have since been demolished. As this book is principally concerned with the buildings that have survived, their history will be dealt with in outline only. Fuller discussion of the development and operation of the works during this period can be found in Alan Peck's work, more than half of which is devoted to the 20th-century history of the GWR.[1]

CHURCHWARD TAKES OVER

During the latter part of the 1890s, William Dean's health began to deteriorate (he was described as suffering from premature senility – perhaps Alzheimer's Disease) so that he was no longer fully in control of affairs at the Swindon works towards the close of the century. George

Fig 153 *An aerial view from the south west of the combined 'A' shops in 1987. The 1901 shop is the lower building to the east, with the extension of 1921 formed by the taller building in the centre and the lower building in the foreground.*

Churchward was made Dean's chief assistant in 1897 and in July 1899, whilst retaining the chief assistant's title, he received a large increase in salary. As Peck argues, this suggests that Churchward had already taken control of the works even though Dean did not officially retire until 1902 (he was to die three years later, at the age of sixty-five).[2] In his previous role as locomotive works' manager, Churchward would already have been involved in the detailed planning of the works' expansion and soon, as Dean's successor, he would also be involved in the boardroom politics surrounding the funding of the programme.

The new 'A' shop

By far the most important element of the new development was the construction of a huge erecting shop, designed to relieve pressure on the existing locomotive erecting and repair activities and to free further space in 'V' shop for boiler-making. The older facilities could not, in any case, cope adequately with the larger and heavier locomotives that Churchward was developing.

Authorisation for the £33,000 funding for the project was approved in June 1900 and the building itself was completed two years later. Structurally, and aesthetically, it was quite unlike any of the other works' buildings, owing nothing to the building traditions of the previous century. Designed in-house, it was an austere building with a steel-framed skeleton, brick panel walls, large windows and a north-lit sawtooth roof, very much designed for the streamlined assembly, repair and testing of locomotives. In contrast to previous generations of buildings, no attempt was made to present an imposing façade to the main line; gone was the architectural embellishment with which GWR designers, from Brunel onwards, had graced their buildings.

The new building was almost square, measuring 480ft by 485ft (146·3m by 147·8m). The southern portion was occupied by the erecting shop, known as 'A' shop (**Figs 153** and **154**), which took up most of the building and measured 415ft by 306ft (126·5m by 93·3m). To the north was a machine and fitting shop ('AM') and a wheel shop ('AW'). The erecting shop had two pairs of lifting bays, each bay with twenty pits and twin 50-ton (50·8-tonne) overhead cranes. Each pair was served by an electric traverser and there was a further traverser outside, to the east of the shop. In a series of ten articles describing the works of 1910–11, published in the *GWR*

Magazine, A J L White pointed out that most of the components were prepared elsewhere in the works to preserve the eighty pits in 'A' shop purely for erecting engines. He claimed that, at the time of writing, some sixty to seventy new engines could be turned out each year and some 600 repaired.[3]

At the eastern end of the shop was an innovatory engine-testing plant, designed by Churchward, and of such interest that, when it was commissioned, it warranted a separate feature in the *GWR Magazine* of October 1904. 'A' shop also had its own power station, with three vertical gas engines operating three 150kW generators; as well as providing direct current for lighting and for driving the machinery, this was also connected to the 1,500psi (103·4 bar) hydraulic system which powered the presses in the wheel shop.

Fig 154 *The interior of the 1901 'A' shop in 1987.*

Extensions to 'A' shop

Though the new 'A' shop represented a great advance on the previous facilities – in providing more spacious working conditions and greater lifting capability – it was soon to prove inadequate for the new classes of engine that Churchward was designing. Accordingly, as early as 1911, plans were prepared for a massive extension to 'A' shop and, after much deliberation by the board, authorisation for the first phase was given in December 1913. Before construction had started in earnest, however, World War I intervened, and, though sizeable sections were built to accommodate munitions work, the complex was not to be completed until 1921, with its final fitting-out taking another year.

This extension was comparable in area to the existing 'A' shop but it dwarfed the latter in

Fig 155 *(above right) The southern elevation of 'A' shop, showing the difference in height between the 1902 and 1921 sections. In the foreground is the restored diesel railcar No 4, built in 1934, and on the left is a 'Warship'-class diesel locomotive.*

Fig 156 *(right) The interior of the 1921 'A' shop in 1987.*

Fig 157 *(opposite top) The weigh house in 1987, viewed from the east.*

Fig 158 *(opposite centre) The interior of the weigh house, looking west, showing the instrument cabin and balance tables.*

Fig 159 *(opposite bottom) One of six balancing machines in the weigh house (see also Figure 192).*

massing by virtue of its third rank of windows (**Figs 155** and **156**). The sixty pits in this new erecting shop were 100ft (30·5m) long, served by 75-ft (22·9m) span 100-ton (101·6 tonne) capacity overhead cranes. These cranes, as an article in the 1922 issue of the *GWR Magazine* proudly boasted, 'are so powerful that "The Great Bear" – the largest engine in Great Britain – when complete for the road, can be lifted and carried over any intervening engines to any position necessary'.

Piecemeal developments

Several other piecemeal developments took place in the years either side of World War I. In 1911, in the north-eastern corner of the western site, a steaming-shed for testing boilers had been built, connected to the boiler shop on the opposite side of Rodbourne Road by a tunnel with a hydraulically operated lift at either end. Such was its success that it was more than doubled in size within two years. Somewhat earlier, around 1906, a lightly framed weigh house, for balancing locomotives, had been built to the south west of the site. This was rebuilt more substantially shortly afterwards, enlarged in 1918 and re-equipped in 1930, by which time it contained a 1930 balancing machine, made by Henry Pooley & Son Ltd of Birmingham and London, with six sections each capable of gauging axle weights of up to 13 tons (13·2 tonnes) (**Figs 157** to **159**).

Churchward had also been anxious to upgrade the gasworks, as these supplied the gas needed by the engines driving the electricity generators, as well as the gas for lighting and heating the works and the railway village. His plans were once again to be frustrated by the war, and it was not until 1920 that work commenced on a massive enlargement of the gasworks.

On the central locomotive works' site there was considerable reorganisation of functions but comparatively little new building, apart from a northerly extension of 'B' shop in 1913, and a major extension eastward of the iron foundry in 1923. This building campaign proved to be the last major development on the locomotive works, and the facilities provided saw the works through until steam-locomotive manufacturing ceased altogether on the site.

The general offices

Significantly, the general offices building was completely remodelled between 1904 and 1906. A third floor was added to provide a unified drawing office, replacing the existing six drawing offices that were spread around the site. This would have given Churchward direct oversight,

and hence better control, of all the disparate operations under his management. The addition of the drawing offices involved a considerable heightening of the first floor, along with alterations to the offices and the replacement of staircases. The general offices building, with its central corridors screened by high wooden partitions, now assumed the appearance, redolent of Edwardian working conditions, that was to last until the closure in 1986 (**Fig 160**).

These offices, it should be remembered, served more than just the Swindon works. Although the GWR had its headquarters at Paddington, many of its important functions were based in the general offices building, which stood at the geographical hub of a railway empire that stretched from Cornwall to the Mersey and from London to west Wales. The pressure on office space at Paddington was so great that most of the mechanical engineering department was based in Swindon,

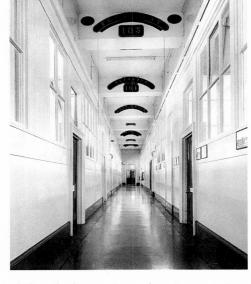

Fig 160 *(right) The first-floor corridor of the general offices showing the heightening created by the addition of the third-floor drawing offices in 1906. The name-plates of famous GWR locomotives, seen on the beams above the corridor, have been preserved in the Great Western Railway Museum.*

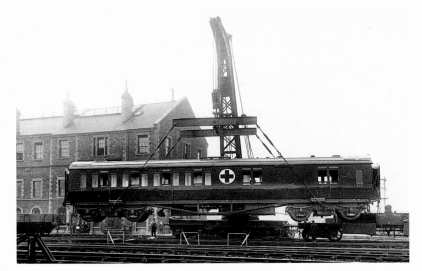

including the locomotive and carriage superintendent's office and staff (on the first floor of the eastern wing) and the outdoor superintendent and his staff (on the ground floor). The carriage department accounts office was located on the ground floor of the northern wing, with the locomotive department accounts and the mileage department on the floor above.

Such was the growth in traffic and staff during this period that the upper floor of the original fitting shop was converted into offices for the enlarged pay staff, while further offices were built on the site of the boiler house. In 1913, the pay-staff offices were connected to the southern range by a high-level covered walkway. In 1926 the gap between the two ranges was linked by a four-storey block, thus providing a sorely needed increase in office space for an office staff that now exceeded 1,500 in number.

The carriage and wagon works also continued to expand during the first three decades of the century, with major extensions to the wagon-lifting shop in 1907 and to the carriage brake shop in 1910. The last significant development, the No 24 carriage shop, a vast building 600ft by 400ft (182·9m by 121·9m), was completed, to the north of the eastern works, in 1930.

War work

World War I, which proved a turning point in railway history nationally, had a great impact on the GWR and the Swindon works. For the first time the operation of the railway itself came under direct government control, and the War Office made considerable use of the works' facilities for the construction of specialised rolling stock and, even more importantly, for munitions production. The works were thus involved in the specialist manufacture of ambulance carriages

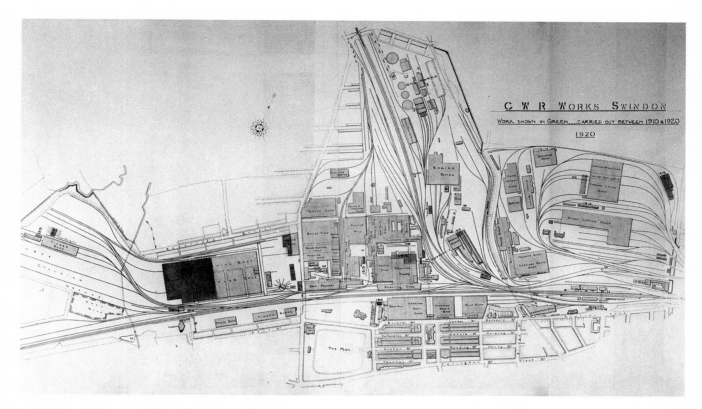

(**Fig 161**), the mass production of millions of high explosive shells, guns, gun carriages and howitzers, and the supply of road wagons and water carts for army use.[4]

All this extra work had to be undertaken alongside, and to the considerable disruption of, routine railway work, but the additional plant and machine tools, paid for by the Ministry of Munitions, was to be a significant bonus when normal work resumed in peacetime. The war also greatly increased the employment of women in clerical posts, an arrangement that was to survive once the war was over (**Fig 162**).

Churchward's retirement
Peacetime brought about a profound change in relations between workers and employers, and this was to hasten Churchward's retirement, which took place in December 1921. His fierce independence and strict paternalistic management style was out of phase with the times and out of favour at Paddington. Despite this, Churchward had presided over a doubling in the size of the works (compare Figures 147 and **163**). His design and production ideas had been innovative and up to date, and his insistence on the standardisation of parts had enabled the works to produce very reliable locomotives in prodigious numbers. Tim Bryan, in his review of this period, has calculated that some 888 Churchward-designed locomotives were produced during his twenty-five-year reign,

and that 586 of these were still in use in 1950.[5] Ironically, it was a descendant of one of these locomotives, the *Berkeley Castle*, that was to kill the seventy-six-year-old Churchward on 13 December 1933 as he crossed the main line close to his home, Newburn House (the company had allowed him to retain this house in his retirement, which took place some twelve years earlier).

THE COLLETT YEARS

Churchward was succeeded by his deputy, Charles B Collett, who had previously been the locomotive works' manager. Collett steered the works through the difficult days following the 1923 grouping of the national railway network into four companies, resulting in the addition of almost 1,000 non-GWR engines to the fleet. The maintenance and repair of so many varied types of engine was to pose problems in the works for years to come, but this did not hinder the development of some of the most famous of the GWR locomotives, including *Caerphilly Castle* (1923), the first of the 'Castle' class, and *King George V* (1927) the first, and most famous, of the 'Kings'.

A notable event in the history of Swindon took place on 28 April 1924, when King George V and Queen Mary visited the town, the king travelling on the footplate of the *Windsor Castle*. This was commemorated by a supplement in the *Swindon Advertiser* and, in the works itself, by the casting

Fig 161 *(opposite) A carriage from a continental-gauge ambulance train, pictured in front of the eastern end of the general offices during World War I. The carriage and the sling being used to lift it were both made in the works.*

Fig 162 *(opposite bottom) A GWR photograph of female clerks at work in the Mileage Office, Swindon in 1936. Note the overprinted 'restricted use' instruction, a measure perhaps designed to protect the privacy of the women portrayed in the picture (by courtesy of the National Railway Museum, York).*

Fig 163 *(above) The railway works in 1920.*

of a message of welcome in the iron foundry in the presence of the king and queen (**Fig 164**). This huge plaque has survived and is to be used as an adornment in the refurbished buildings.

Despite the recession that began at the end of the 1920s the GWR recorded its highest annual locomotive mileage in 1929, clocking up over 97 million miles (155 million km), worked by 3,858 engines (an average of just over 25,000 miles/40,288 km per locomotive).[6] The recession was to develop into the Great Depression and it was not until the mid 1930s that production of new engines significantly recovered. The 'Hall'-class, which had been introduced in 1928, was now followed by the 'Grange' and 'Manor'-classes in 1936 and 1938 respectively. Little in the way of new building was undertaken during this period, though, in 1929, under a government relief scheme, funds were borrowed to modernise 'B' shop. The work to the southerly extension of the shop involved the demolition of the original running shed of 1841, which had served as a workshop for many years (**Fig 165**).

During World War II, the works returned to manufacturing munitions of a very varied nature, including bombs, midget submarine superstructures and massive mountings for cross-Channel guns. Collet's retirement (at the age of seventy) also took place in 1941, an event many would claim was long overdue. In later years, the reclusive Collett, whilst maintaining a high degree of production efficiency at Swindon, does not seem to have encouraged innovation among his design staff, to the detriment of locomotive development.

HAWKSWORTH AND NATIONALISATION

Collett's successor, F W Hawksworth, was born in Swindon to a railway family and had entered the works as an apprentice in 1898. He rose through the ranks of the drawing office, first under the influence of Churchward and then of William A Stanier (works' manager, then assistant to Collier). When Stanier left in 1932 to take up the post of chief mechanical engineer to the London, Midland

Fig 164 *(above) King George V and Queen Mary watch the casting of a plaque in their honour in the iron foundry during their royal visit of 28 April 1924.*

Fig 165 *Work in progress on the extension of 'B' shop in 1930. This required the demolition of the 1841 running shed, as can be seen in the middle distance, where the wide entrance to the traversing-table bay is in the process of being taken down (by courtesy of the National Railway Museum, York).*

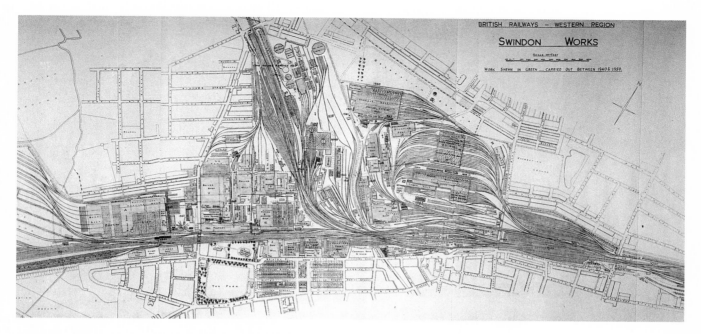

Fig 166 *(above) The railway works in 1950.*

Fig 167 *HRH The Princess Elizabeth on the footplate of the 'Star'-class locomotive No 4057, The Princess Elizabeth, which brought the royal train from Paddington to the Swindon works on 15 November 1950. During her visit, Princess Elizabeth gave the name* Swindon *to the last 'Castle'-class locomotive to be built (No 7037).*

and Scottish Railway, Hawksworth was appointed as assistant to Collett. Now, at the age of fifty-seven, Hawksworth assumed the top Swindon post in inauspicious circumstances, with the works placed on a munitions footing, and with no funding for new developments. By the time Hawksworth retired, eight years later, the GWR was merely a region of the newly nationalised railway system. He, meanwhile, had been constantly frustrated in his attempts to advance locomotive design and had been given no opportunity to effect significant changes to the works' site, which reached its maximum extent at this time (**Fig 166**).

The great many changes to the operation of the works that followed nationalisation in 1948 had surprisingly little impact on the buildings themselves. Initially, work was reorganised within the existing buildings. An exception was the new points and crossings shop, which was built in 1959 at a cost of around £500,000.

In 1950, Swindon once again received a royal visitor (**Fig 167**). On 15 November, H R H The Princess Elizabeth made a tour of the works and, in a moment laden with poignancy, gave the name *Swindon* to Locomotive No 7037, the very last of the 'Castle'-class to be built, in commemoration of the town's fiftieth year as an incorporated borough. The visit was again commemorated in the works by the casting of a plaque in the foundry, and the event was greatly appreciated by a town just emerging from post-war austerity.

At the close of the steam era, the Swindon works were accorded the honour of manufacturing the last steam locomotive ever to be

produced under the aegis of British Railways. The BR Class 9F 2-10-0 Locomotive No 92220 was appropriately named *Evening Star* in an 'out-shopping' ceremony on 18 March 1960 (**Fig 168**).

BEECHING, BREL AND THE CLOSURE OF THE WORKS

In 1960, a *General Plan for the Future of Swindon Works* was produced, but most of the investment finally approved was devoted to alteration and re-equipping, rather than for the provision of any new buildings. In any event, the proposals fell foul of changing policies introduced when Dr Richard Beeching became chairman of the national railway system in 1961.

The 1960s subsequently witnessed a complete reorganisation of railway locomotive works nationally. The Swindon works were separated from the Western Region in 1962 and were grouped, together with all the other main railway works, to form the workshops division of British Rail, with its headquarters at Derby. Steam haulage was rapidly phased out, and fifteen of Britain's thirty-one main workshops were closed. The Swindon carriage and wagon works were disposed of and the locomotive works were modernised following the demolition of considerable numbers of redundant buildings, including most of the northern ranges built in the 1840s.

British Rail Engineering Ltd (BREL) was formed in 1970 to operate British Rail's workshops, which were now free to tender for outside work. This move resulted in a temporary reprieve for the Swindon works which, under the former regime, had been withering away. Staff numbers had fallen to 2,000 in 1973, but they rose again to 3,800 by 1980, amid much optimism about the future.[7]

Alas, this was to prove a false dawn. In the early 1980s the works struggled to win outside orders and to retain a share of the diminishing British Rail work. BREL, while not unsympathetic to Swindon's plight, was faced with a similar situation at all its main works. Some have suggested that BREL was more receptive to lobbying from local authorities closer to its Derby base, and from towns less well placed to face a future without a railway works than Swindon. In any event, despite constant management assurances that the future of the works could be secured if the staff accepted cuts in their numbers, the Swindon railway works were finally closed on 27 March 1986.

THE FUTURE OF THE WORKS SITE

In 1984, the older buildings making up the historic core of the works were listed, some at Grade II* and the remainder at Grade II. Following the departure of BREL, these buildings were given additional protection by Thamesdown Borough Council when this part of the works was included in an enlarged conservation area in 1987.

In June 1987, after the closure of the works, the BREL property, consisting of some 142 acres (56·8 hectares) of land located to the north of the main line and to the west of the Gloucester line, was sold to Tarmac Properties Ltd. British Rail retained

Fig 168 *The naming ceremony of* Evening Star, *the last steam locomotive to be built by British Railways in 'A' shop, Swindon, on 18 March 1960.*

the small area to the east of the Gloucester line and the carriage works' site to the south of the main line. British Rail also retained ownership of the Mechanics' Institution, but most of the other buildings of the village, including the swimming baths, had long since been transferred to local authority ownership.

In December 1987, Tarmac announced plans for what was described as 'the most ambitious, challenging and exciting scheme undertaken in Swindon since Brunel's original development'. Proposals were drawn up to develop the area between Rodbourne Road and the Gloucester line as a 'historic village', with a mixed retail, office and residential development focusing on the surviving historic buildings. The plan envisaged a series of office-lined malls and courtyards, together with a railway heritage centre, cinema, hotel, restaurants, public house and wine bar, a market place and shopping gallery, and housing. The area to the west of Rodbourne Road, some of which required land reclamation involving the removal of millions of tons of ash, was to be developed for supermarket retailing, industrial units and housing.

DEVELOPMENTS IN THE 1990S

The collapse of the commercial property market in 1988, following the boom of the mid 1980s, delayed implementation of the project. During the recession that followed, only a few individually funded projects were undertaken within the context of a modified and less ambitious development scheme. These projects included a large supermarket at the north-western end of the site, the refurbishment of the works' manager's office for Tarmac's own use and the conversion and extension of the general offices building to house the headquarters of the Royal Commission on the Historical Monuments of England and its public archive, the National Monuments Record.

At the same time, most of the unlisted buildings, including the massive 'A'-shop complex to the west of Rodbourne Road, were demolished. The other loss in these years was 'B' shop, which was gutted to provide a central car park leaving the southern gables and Armstrong's 1874 arcaded wall as screening. 'B' shop had one final moment of glory prior to demolition when, throughout the summer of 1990, it housed the collections of the National Railway Museum while the main hall of the parent museum in York was being rebuilt. 'B' shop proved an eminently suitable substitute, and the spectacle of many of the nation's most illustrious locomotives and carriages, marshalled in ranks in this historic shed, will never be forgotten by any of the thousands of visitors who came to see the exhibition.

In January 1994, the pace of development began to quicken with planning approval being given for a £20-million development, called the Great Western Factory Outlet, to be housed in Armstrong's 1874 locomotive works. In January 1995 agreement was finally secured for the creation of a Railway Heritage Centre on the site, incorporating the existing restoration workshops. Modern developments such as these have radically altered the traditional focus of the site. The works were designed for rail access, with only limited pedestrian access, provided by gates and subways, and only rudimentary access for road vehicles. Now the site has been divorced from the railway and much-improved road access has been provided from the north. This involved dismantling the listed metal-framed machinery store of 1899, for re-erection on a preserved railway in west Somerset, and the demolition of later accretions to the 1870s locomotive factory.

THE RAILWAY VILLAGE IN THE 20TH CENTURY

From the turn of the century, the GWR's building activity outside the works' boundary was greatly diminished. Branches of the Mechanics' Institution reading-room were built at Gorse Hill, Bath Road and Rodbourne, and the last of these, dated 1904, has survived. Turkish baths were added to the Medical Fund dispensary and swimming baths in 1904–5 (see p 126). The old washing and Turkish baths were then used as a rifle range and bicycle shed, and as a store house for the Fund's shillibier, or horse-drawn hearse. In May 1931 the company opened a new sports ground, of about 13 acres (5·2 hectares), in Shrivenham Road, on the north-eastern outskirts of the town. In addition to a cricket pitch, this incorporated a bowling-green, tennis courts, and a pavilion with a skittle alley and bar.[8]

Refurbishment by Swindon Borough Council
The most important event to affect the railway village this century was its purchase by Swindon Borough Council from British Rail in 1966. In 1963 the borough architect, J Loring Morgan, had prepared detailed survey plans of the different cottage types in the village as a prelude to a comprehensive scheme for the modernisation and conversion of the buildings. The cottages were in a bad state of repair and it was clear that a great deal of money would have to be spent to bring them up to standard. For a while their fate hung in the balance, but fortunately the Swindon Borough, and its successor from 1974, the Borough of Thamesdown, decided to carry out an ambitious refurbishment programme, which was eventually completed in the early 1980s.[9] The

amount of work involved was considerable, as some of the cottages still lacked bathrooms and internal toilets. Rear extensions were run-down and, in some cases, vermin-infested. Such modernisation was not always welcomed by the tenants as it meant an increase in rent.

The first stage, which was finished at the end of 1970, involved the refurbishment of twenty-three cottages on the northern side of Taunton Street. The slate roofs were repaired, the stone façades of the cottages cleaned, and the individual garden plots replaced by a long strip of grass planted with shrubs and specimen trees. Unsightly external wiring was placed underground. In the rear yards of the cottages, kitchen/scullery extensions added prior to the mid 1880s were demolished (**Fig 169**). The extensions to the single cottages were replaced by a single lean-to, which ran the length of that part of the terrace, containing a new kitchen for each dwelling. The old external water-closets were demolished and rebuilt in concrete block as stores. These, and the concrete-block lean-tos were given a rendered finish to help them blend in with the stone walls of the cottages. The brick walls forming the alley were retained and the ends of the new stores facing the alley were given a brick skin to ensure a uniform appearance (**Fig 170**).

Internally, the stairs were enclosed by a new partition wall. The fireplaces were blocked up, those downstairs being fitted with gas heaters. A new bathroom and an adjoining linen cupboard were built next to the first-floor landing, thus slightly reducing the size of the single bedroom.

The double cottages at the east end of the row, which were being used as two-bedroom cottages, were given a different treatment. Old and unsanitary accretions at the back were demolished and replaced by new kitchens built in pairs between the projecting stair towers of each cottage. The privies in the yards were, again, replaced by stores built to the same dimensions. New bathrooms were created upstairs.

The Taunton Street terrace provided the model for improvements to the cottages in the western half of the village and work progressed in a northerly direction through the early 1970s. The cottages in the shop blocks and end blocks refurbished in a similar manner.

The refurbishment of the larger cottages making up the eastern half of the estate took place in the second half of the 1970s. Again, the principal alterations involved the provision of new kitchens and internal bathrooms and toilets. Great care was taken to preserve the rear-yard walls forming the alleys, especially the Swindon-stone walls of the narrow alley between London Street and Oxford Street. An exception to this was the alley between the cottages on Oxford Street and Reading Street, which was removed and replaced by a wide paved area broken up by brick planters. The line of the alley, however, is perpetuated in the paving and surface drainage pattern. A brick store attached to the back wall under a lean-to roof was added to the rear of each of these houses. The former GWR hospital, which was at that time being used as a working men's club, was converted to a community centre for the village.

Fig 169 *Kitchen/scullery extensions in the rear yards of the cottages between Exeter Street and Taunton Street prior to the refurbishment programme of the early 1970s. During the refurbishment, these were demolished and rebuilt, partly using existing materials.*

Fig 170 *The rear alley of the block of cottages between Exeter Street and Taunton Street after refurbishment in the early 1970s. Nineteenth-century extensions in the rear yards were replaced by a single lean-to containing a kitchen for each dwelling. The former external privies were rebuilt for use as stores, and the concrete blocks used for reconstruction were given a brick skin on the gable ends to help retain the original appearance of the alley.*

The scheme did include some demolition work. The twelve 'A'-class cottages and one 'C'-class house on the south side of Taunton Street were demolished in February 1970 along with the former washing and Turkish baths. The back yards of the cottages were visible from Faringdon Road and were probably felt to be unsightly. The stone wall enclosing the rear yards has been retained to mark the position of each of the demolished cottages. The triangular plot between Faringdon Road and Taunton Street is now partly used for parking, partly as landscaped open space. Six cottages built in the 1860s in Emlyn Square, to the north of the former GWR hospital, were also demolished. These were similar in plan to the five-roomed houses in Reading Street and Faringdon Street. The last of the six cottages, at the easternmost end of the row, had been designed by Thomas Lansdown and completed by company workmen in 1866.

Listing, recognition and awards

Despite these demolitions the refurbishment scheme secured the preservation of almost the entire village. In 1970 all the buildings in the village were placed on the List of Buildings of Special Architectural or Historic Interest. Their ownership by the local authority has ensured that the cottages have subsequently been well-maintained and kept free of the damaging incremental alterations which have had such a detrimental effect on the appearance of Swindon's other early railway estate, Cambria Place.

The village refurbishment scheme involved relatively little alteration to the original internal arrangements of the cottages, apart from essential changes designed to provide them with basic modern facilities. Original building materials were retained or reused wherever possible. The scheme was regarded as an exemplar of contemporary conservation practice and won several national awards. In 1971 *Country Life* wrote 'if the whole scheme is carried through on the same sound lines as it has begun, it may well become as exemplary a conservation scheme, as, at the outset, it was a model village'.[10]

Today the village is a quiet, attractive area of inner-city housing which, along with the surviving part of the works, remains the most tangible link with Swindon's development as a mid 19th-century railway town. Compared with Crewe, Wolverton, or Derby – all of which have lost many of their early buildings – it is an unrivalled example of an almost complete, planned railway settlement of the 1840s and early 1850s.

Whilst overcrowding and poor sanitation ensured that the village was something less than a workers' utopia, the GWR was able to build houses of considerable architectural dignity and sophistication of planning (particularly of the later cottages) that were well in advance of most contemporary artisans' dwellings. The Swindon railway village remains one of the best-preserved and visually most cohesive collections of early railway housing, an archetypal railway settlement of both national and international importance.

8 *The Building Legacy*

Most of the details we have of the appearance and use of early works' buildings, and the way they have changed through time, have come from descriptive tours, the first of which was published in 1852 in *The Illustrated Exhibitor*. After this came various, often floridly written, articles published in the *Swindon Advertiser* from 1861 onwards, as well as more restrained entries in various editions of *Astill's Original Swindon Almanack*, published in the 1870s. The GWR furnished most of the technical details for these notes and in later years published its own guides to the works, continuing to do so into the 1950s, after it had become the Western Region of British Railways. For much of the works' lifetime, the GWR also used to offer public tours, on Wednesday afternoons, for a nominal entrance fee.

In the same spirit as those early tours, this book concludes with a guide to the works and railway village as they were in 1994. Key sites on the works' tour are given in bold type in the text that follows, along with a number. This number refers to **Figure 171**, which also indicates the sites of significant buildings that have been demolished. Cross references are also given in brackets to pages earlier in the book where the structures are discussed in more detail. Many of the structures described below are visible from public footpaths and highways, and it is to be hoped that more will become accessible when the development of the works' site is completed.

A TOUR OF THE WORKS

From 1870 onwards tours invariably started at the **works' entrance (1)** opposite the Mechanics' Institution in Emlyn Square. The wide-arched opening, piercing the cliff-like façade of the former carriage works of 1870, is flanked by two smaller openings and leads to the subway, which passes beneath the carriage works and main line. In the last fifty years this entrance has undergone several changes in identity, from the anonymity of GWR days, when no sign was considered necessary, through a huge name-board in 1950, rather pedantically announcing 'British Railways Workshops, Swindon, Locomotive Carriage and Wagon Works', to the more elegant cast nameplate of the 1970s bearing the inscription 'British Rail Engineering Ltd'.

Nothing now remains of the iron turnstiles that once regulated the flow of pedestrians; the turnstiles were removed so that light vehicles could use the tunnel. To the east, the former mess-room, which early in the century could provide hot meals for 1,000 employees, was later downgraded to a cycle shed, then converted to offices. The frontage, running eastward along London Street, has heavy windows with cast-iron mullions, and the workshops behind, only two bays deep, are occupied by a variety of small businesses. **The carriage works (2)** (see pp 88–90), situated above these workshops, were constructed mainly on ground that had been substantially raised to enable rolling stock to enter and leave the works at the same level as the main line. This allowed most of the power transmission, ventilation and heating ducts, along with other services, to be accommodated below the main floor, and there are several entrances giving access to this labyrinth of tunnels. This section of the carriage works did not pass to BREL in the 1970s, being retained and developed by British Rail as a light industrial estate, with the buildings of the eastern end, closest to the station, being demolished to create space for car parking.

At the western end of the site all but the westernmost bay of the sawmills' building was demolished to provide a works' car park, but the water tower (surmounted by a later, less elegant, tank) survives (see p 90), as do the fire-station building and the laboratories on the site of the original Bristol Street schools of 1844 (see p 123). The central blocks of the carriage works retain their tall cast-iron columns, proclaiming their date of construction in the early 1870s, though the covered sheds are now much subdivided and the layout of the traverser in the yard immediately over the tunnel is scarcely discernible.

The 1870 **subway (3)**, some 380ft (115·8m) long, 15ft (4·6m) wide and 7ft (2·1m) high, is roofed with brick jack-arches springing from cast-iron beams (**Fig 172**). It still provides the main pedestrian access to the works' site, and is expected to pass from Railtrack PLC to local-authority control in the near future. It emerges north of the main line at the western end of the general offices building. Until 1992, an early 20th-century extension of the subway continued northwards under the office block to an open junction in the yard behind; from there it continued, by tunnel, to the general stores building beyond the Gloucester line.

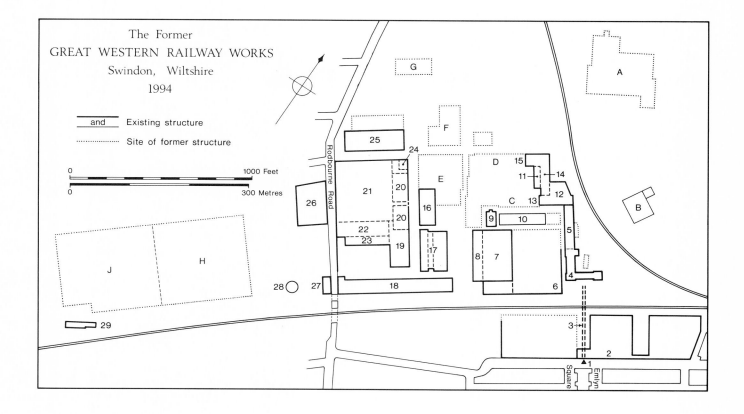

The Former
GREAT WESTERN RAILWAY WORKS
Swindon, Wiltshire
1994

and ———— Existing structure

········· Site of former structure

Fig 171 *(above) The railway works in 1994. Structures now mostly demolished are:*
A engine shed;
B general stores;
C boilermakers' shop;
D steam-hammer shops;
E rolling mills; F 'X' shop;
G machinery store;
H 'A' shop; J 'A' shop extension.

Fig 172 *The subway, looking south*

THE GENERAL OFFICES

The **general offices building (4)**, now named the National Monuments Record Centre (NMRC), played a central role in the evolution of the works and in the development of the GWR itself. In its new role, the building houses the head office of the Royal Commission on the Historical Monuments of England (RCHME) and the architectural, archaeological, air-photographic and maritime archives that make up the National Monuments Record (NMR) (**Fig 173**).

The building has a complicated history, having been extended, heightened and remodelled numerous times in the last 150 years. The main phases are illustrated by a sequence of five block diagrams (**Fig 174**).

The oldest part of the building is the north–south range which formed the southern half of the eastern boundary of Brunel's 1842 works (details of the original arrangement are given in Chapter 2 (see pp 22–4)). Little of this range – other than some window details, the northern doorway and lobby, the main party walls and the central room on the first floor of the southern pavilion – has survived the alterations of the last 150 years. Even so, the Bath stone used in the construction of the original building contrasts strongly with the stone used in later extensions and alterations, so that the outline of the original pavilions is still discernible, the southern elevation with its Venetian-style openings being particularly well defined.

Originally, in 1843, this façade contained two doorways – a central door giving access to a hallway and stairs that led to the locomotive department offices, and, to the left, a separate door to the timekeeper's office. Both these doors have long since been altered to windows. Elements of the ground floor of the ashlar-faced western elevation (which had been obscured by the addition of a later wing) have been revealed internally in the latest conversion. The 100-ft-long (30·5-m) central range was originally a two-storey storehouse, built of pier-and-panel construction,

but the distinctiveness of the piers was obscured when the wall was rebuilt at the end of the century when the range was converted to offices. Recent stone-cleaning has caused the outline of the piers to re-emerge.

Internally, the plaster stripping that took place during the recent rehabilitation work revealed large painted letters (identifying storage bays at both levels) and the outline of an archway in the eastern wall, created to allow rail access but subsequently blocked. The 1842 design drawings provided for such an archway in the western wall, but this was not built: obviously a change was made to the intended rail circulation before the building was finished. Very little survives of the original internal arrangement of the northern pavilion, apart from the entrance hallway.

Armstrong's additions

In 1869 Armstrong more than doubled the size of the office by adding the east–west block fronting the main line. This twelve-bay range was originally of two storeys with a hipped roof. The ground floor still retains its two ranks of cast-iron columns with the inscriptions 'GWR WOLVERHAMPTON NOV^R 1868' or 'GWR WOLVERHAMPTON DEC^R 1868' (these were made in the Wolverhampton foundry as the main iron foundry at Swindon had not yet been built). Externally, the building repeated the architectural detailing of the existing pavilions, but it was more substantial in its massing and it was built of a different stone. Nevertheless, a late 19th-century photograph shows that this wing was still relatively small in scale, with an eastern pavilion balancing the southern pavilion of the earlier range.

Recently discovered drawings show that by the end of the century the 1842 northern pavilion had been extended eastwards by two bays and heightened to three storeys. These alterations, which included a new iron stair, destroyed most of the original internal arrangements. Intriguingly, the drawings also show that, by this time, the central stores block had a glazed clerestory roof which might indicate that the upper floor was being used as a drawing office.

Churchward's additions

The present appearance of the general offices building results, however, from Churchward's addition of a second floor to both ranges in 1904–6. This high and spacious top floor was built to accommodate all the works' drawing offices and it was, in itself, a major engineering feat. Designed in-house, and using structural elements first used in 1892 in the Faringdon Road swimming baths, the heightening was achieved by resting a metal-framed cage on the existing walls. The steelwork of the lower tie was so deep that it

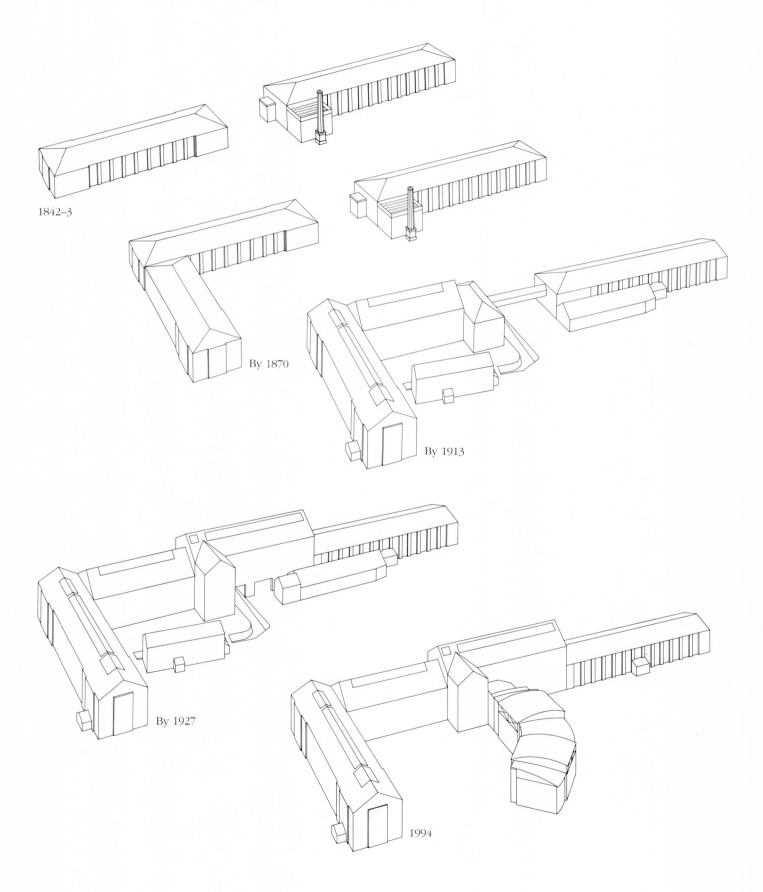

1842–3

By 1870

By 1913

By 1927

1994

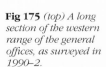

Fig 175 *(top) A long section of the western range of the general offices, as surveyed in 1990–2.*

Fig 176 *(above) The drawing-office of 1906, as restored in 1994 to house the National Monuments Record.*

added some 5ft (1·5m) to the existing height of the first floor, while the top floor was a further 31ft (9·5m) high to the roof apex. Both wings of the top floor are framed by arched metal ribs with a rail-profile lower member.

The long section of the building, drawn in 1992 before conversion (**Fig 175**), shows the generous proportions of these upper floors. Subsequently, the conversion of the top floor (to serve as search rooms for the National Monuments Record) has revealed these impressive rooms to the public for the first time (**Fig 176**). As part of the 1906 conversion scheme, the top floor was linked by a covered bridge to a suite of photographic darkrooms built above the engine-erecting bays of the 1874 'B' shop to the west. These were demolished in 1992 when 'B' shop was cleared for a car park.

Set into the southern façade of the east–west range are two bas-reliefs, depicting broad-gauge engines. These were relocated in 1906 from the near-derelict 1841 running shed to this more prominent position, over the porch that formed a new entrance at the eastern end of the building (**Fig 177**). The panels depict a 'Firefly'-class locomotive, designed by Gooch in 1840 and built in a variety of forms by different suppliers. The model selected for immortalisation was one of the engines (possibly *Centaur*), built by Nasmyth, Gaskell & Co in 1841.[1]

As part of the same Edwardian development a two-storey block (heightened within five years to three storeys) was built in the angle behind the ranges, aligned with the subway cutting, to serve as a paper and plan store, with a laboratory and toilets on the ground floor. At the same time a single-storey block was built on the site of the boiler house, adjacent to the former machine-shop range, to serve as a regional pay office. Both these buildings were demolished in 1992 to make way for the new NMR archive store.

Subsequent changes

In 1913, the northern pavilion was linked, by means of a covered bridge, to the enlarged accounts offices in the upper floor of the northern range. In 1926 Collett effected a further expansion of the general offices building by replacing the 1913 bridge with a four-storey linking block incorporating the northern pavilion of the original office range and the southern bays of the machine-shop range. Most of the ground level of this block was open, preserving eastern rail access to the site and vehicular access to the subway. Iron staircases were inserted at both ends of this extension, rising the full height of the building and matching those of the Churchward heightening (it is probable that the same foundry patterns were used – **Fig 178**). All four staircases have been retained in the latest conversion, complete with the original teak inserts in the metal treads.

The northern part of the continuous range thus created was built in 1842 as the **original machine and fitting shop (5)**, which is a good example of pier-and-panel construction. Most of the original floor trusses (see p 25) and almost all the wooden queen-post roof trusses have survived, whilst two walls of the beam-engine house have been exposed to reveal enough evidence externally to make clear the functional relationship with the former boiler house to the east. The metal bearing-box, conducting the line shaft to the smiths' shops beyond, has survived in the northern gable, but the southern bearing-box, in the former engine house, is hidden by later alterations. One section of the ground floor of this northern range remained in industrial use, as a wire-rope shop, until 1956, when it too was converted into offices and the range was given new metal-framed windows.

Taken together, these developments, spread over a period of more than fifty years, had the effect of converting the entire eastern side of the original works of 1842, totalling some 460ft (140·2m) from north to south, into offices serving both the works and the GWR's railway network.

The National Monuments Record Centre

The last main element in the development of this corner of the works was the construction, in 1992–4, of the NMR archive store, sited to form a landscaped courtyard and car park to the east of the offices. This building, designed by D Y Davies Associates, consists of two linked wagon-shaped pavilions, which provide environmentally controlled storage for archive materials and photographic negatives. The archive store formed part of the development that resulted from the decision to relocate the RCHME from London to Swindon. The general offices building was refurbished for the RCHME between 1992 and 1994, to provide

offices for its staff and public search rooms where visitors may study the large collection of heritage archives that make up the NMR.

Public access to the NMRC is through a doorway and reception area in the south-western corner of the building. This stands adjacent to the original timekeeper's office which, for so many years, was used to record the ingress and egress of the works' labour force. To the west of this door, the **screen wall (6)** to the new public car park is all that survives of the 1874 'B' shop (see p 94), which, by various extensions, had incorporated the sites of the erecting shop, the engine house and the running shed of the original works.

THE REMAINS OF 'R' SHOP

At the far side of the car park, the western wall of Brunel's engine house has survived to form the eastern wall of the historic **'R' shop (7)** (latterly known as '20' shop). This, in 1995, was appropriately being used for the restoration of historic railway rolling stock, retaining some early

Fig 177 (*opposite bottom*) *Bas-relief panels of a 'Firefly'-class broad-gauge locomotive (possibly* Centaur*). Originally adorning the 1841 running shed, they are shown here repositioned over the porch at the eastern end of the general offices.*

Fig 178 (*above*) *The first-floor staircase in the general offices.*

It retains its queen-post roof and some early fenestration in its eastern wall. The contemporary single-storey smiths' shop to the south was heightened and reroofed when it was converted to a power house at the turn of the century, but its pier-and-panel construction is still clearly evident. It was latterly used as the main electrical substation for the site.

CHURCHWARD HOUSE

To the north of the 'R' shop complex is the **works' manager's office (9)**, now called Churchward House. As mentioned in Chapter 6 (see p 122), the manager's office started as a small suite in the south-eastern corner of the 1846 iron store, expanding to occupy the entire building by the end of the century. During Tarmac's refurbishment of the building, in 1989–90, the central atrium was retained with its iron-framed central stair (**Fig 180**). The atrium is lit from above and the framing of the glazed roof is provided by wooden king-post trusses of lesser scantling, and of finer finish, than those of the separately framed roof over the original manager's office to the south.

Immediately east of Churchward House is a now-truncated **traversing table (10)**, the only one surviving on the site (**Fig 181**). It is of no great age and was first installed to the west of the old carriage works in 1959, before being moved to its present position when the rail and pit alignment in 'B' shop was altered by 90° in the mid 1960s.

Fig 179 (above) 'R' shop, with wagon wheel-sets awaiting turning.

Fig 180 (right) The atrium and staircase in Churchward House.

Fig 181 The traversing table in 1985, before the demolition of 'B' shop.

machine tools (**Fig 179**). It may be recalled that 'R' shop was created by roofing over, in two stages, the courtyard to the west of the original engine house (see pp 86–7). The columns of both the 1865 and the 1872 phases survive, as well as stub walls of the first phase.

The western boundary of 'R' shop is formed by the 1846 **machine and fitting shop (8)** (see p 25). This was originally a two-storey range, of pier-and-panel construction with a hipped roof. Subsequently the building was truncated to the north and the floor was removed (see Figure 35).

THE TEST HOUSE AND SPRING SHOP

To the north of the traverser yard is the **test house (11)** of 1874 (see p 94). The test house has not changed to any great extent in appearance, equipment or function since its construction. It retains its original fittings and most of its original machinery which, at its peak, during the 1950s, could test some 300,000ft (914km) of chain and rope annually.[2] Some loss of plant and fittings has occurred since the works closed in 1986, but the complex still retains its Victorian atmosphere (see Figures 103 and 104).

The nearby **spring shop (12)**, to the south east, has fared rather worse, even though it, too, operated until the 1986 closure. In the 1950s this shop supplied British Rail Western Region's entire requirement for springs, with an annual output of some 45,000 laminated springs and 93,000 coil springs.[3] In 1984, the RCHME photographed coil springs being manufactured by hand using skills unchanged since the beginning of the century (**Fig 182**). Little now survives other than a section of the southern wall, the bearing-box of the drive from the beam engine in the range to the south, and, to the west, the **gable wall (13)** of the original boilermakers' shop. However, the **smiths' range (14)** to the north, built in 1846 to house further forges, retains its original metal-framed hipped roof supplied by Fox Henderson. Nothing, apart from an extra-wide **gable wall (15)**, survives of the hammer shop; this building, together with the boilermakers' shop, was demolished in the reorganisation of the works that took place in the 1960s.

'Q' AND 'K' SHOPS

Proceeding westwards, the present open space to the north of Churchward House was formerly the site of further steam-hammer shops, the rolling mills and the central boiler station. The next building encountered is the former **'Q' shop (16)**, which incorporates part of the 1846 wagon works' smiths' shop (see pp 32–3) in its western half. The

Fig 182 *Springs being made by hand in 1984. (top) The workman on the right is forming the 'tang' (flattened end) of the spring to ensure that it sits flat after coiling. On the left is the furnace for heating the bar end. (centre) The spring is being coiled as it emerges from the furnace. In the foreground are the height-setting table and tools. These were used to adjust the height and verticality of the spring while it was still hot. (bottom) Grinding the end of the completed spring to ensure that it 'sits' vertically. In the foreground is an older laminated spring.*

west wall of this building preserves a long section of early pier-and-panel construction.

To the south is a block with a complicated historical development and function. It contained **'K' shop (17)** (coppersmiths), the white-metal shop, and the brass shop and store, all of which served these functions from the 1870s (see Figures 33 and 116), though they incorporated two earlier buildings of the 1846 wagon works in their fabric. These earlier buildings were built of pier-and-panel construction, as is still clearly evident.

The south-eastern corner formed the original wagon paint shop, with the Fox Henderson iron-framed hipped roof mentioned in Chapter 2 (see p 33) while the whole western portion of the building was part of the main western range of the wagon works. In about 1877 these were converted and extended for non-ferrous metal-working as part of Armstrong's new locomotive factory, but they remained physically separate. In 1890 the space between the buildings was roofed over to form the present single rectangular block. Despite the use of masonry for all these extensions, the different phases can be identified by changes in the type of stone used.

LATER EXPANSION

Fig 183 *The foundry (also known as 'J1' or 'No 9' shop) in 1987.*

All the remaining area of the historic site to the east of Rodbourne Road is occupied by Armstrong's new locomotive works of the 1870s.

The southernmost building is the **foundry (18)** (see p 96; also known as 'J1' shop or 'No 9' shop), stretching for 640ft (195m) east to west. The twenty westernmost bays of this building date from 1873–4, but the remaining twelve bays to the east were built in 1921–2. Externally, it is very difficult to identify the change in date as considerable care was taken to match the stonework of the later extension with that of the earlier building. Doubtless, the building's prominent position alongside the main railway line accounts for the use of masonry for its façade and for the subsequent attention to detail.

Internally, the building has two aisles, 40ft (12·19m) wide, separated by a rank of columns, and the change of date in construction is very apparent. The earlier section, 400ft (121·92m) long, has thirty structural bays of two-tier cast-iron columns, while the later 240ft (73·15m) section has only six structural bays of composite steel uprights (**Fig 183**). There is now no evidence of the intermediate phase in which the original building was extended eastward by a few bays in the early 1890s.

The cupola furnaces were sited in a building to the north of the middle bays of the original section. The heavier castings, such as cylinder blocks, were undertaken in the aisle next to the furnaces and moved around by overhead cranes. At its peak the foundry could produce some 10,000 tons (10,160 tonnes) of finished casting

per annum, the largest castings normally being in the region of 12 tons (12·2 tonnes). Exceptionally, larger castings were produced, the record reputedly being an anvil of 65 tons (66 tonnes).

The foundry was closed in the early 1960s when all such work was concentrated at British Rail's Horwich works. 'J1' shop became 'No 9' shop in the 1965 post-Beeching reorganisation and was extensively refurbished for diesel-engine repairs. This activity required three main work areas: stripping and cleaning at the eastern end, engine assembly and component fitting in the centre and machining at the western end. At this time, the furnace and coke-oven range, at the rear of the building, was replaced by brick outbuildings, and the western elevation was rebuilt.[4]

North of the foundry all the other buildings of the Armstrong era are built of brick and characterised by a degree of architectural pretension. The main eastern façade, for example, is a balanced composition with finely detailed panels of blind arcading using roll-moulded outlining and masonry keystones. The boundary wall to Rodbourne Road (large sections of which incorporate the gables of the main boiler shops) is a *tour de force* in brick (see Figure 105 and p 96).

The southern end of this originally T-shaped complex was the **brass foundry (19)** and some of the detail of the furnace vents has survived in the brickwork. Internally, an open arcade, supported on four squat cast-iron columns, reveals the arrangement of the casting floor (see Figure 111). The adjoining bays were structurally altered in the late 19th century to provide a clearer working space, but the brass-machining shop to the north retains its six tall original columns inscribed 'GWR WOLVERHAMPTON AUG 1874'. The wide entrance in the centre of the eastern elevation is spanned by a lattice girder and is flanked by **machine shops (20)** with columns dated 'SEP^T 1874'. Originally eight of the western bays of the northern machine shop were open, thus giving access to the boiler shop.

'V' shop and its construction

The six original aisles of **'V' shop (21)** (see **Figure 184** and p 96) formed the stem of the T, stretching west to Rodbourne Road. The aisles were enclosed to the north by a brick wall, of which only short end sections survived the 1879 northwards extension. Enough remains – with different architectural detailing from that of the eastern range – to suggest that the construction of the two elements of the T may have been undertaken by different builders (see Figure 113). As the columns in the eastern range were made by the GWR itself, and those of the stem bear no identification, it seems likely that the GWR built the structurally simpler eastern range using its own materials, while the construction of the stem, with its two-tier cast-iron colonnades, was entrusted to a specialist contractor.

Fig 184 *'V' shop in 1994 before conversion to the Great Western Factory Outlet.*

Fig 185 *A 'walking crane' in the machine shop. The machine shop was built in the 1880s to the south of the original 'V' shop, and the embellished wall in the background, originally one of 'V' shop's external walls, became the machine-shop internal wall.*

The T shape of this complex was soon lost by the construction of the three-aisle northern extension in 1879 and the two-aisle **southern extension (22)** in the mid 1880s (**Fig 185**). As the latter extension was designed to accommodate the 'O' shop 'Tool Room', formerly located above 'R' shop, the southern wall of the original stem was retained. In 1924 a further structural bay was added to the south to house the **pattern-makers' shop (23)**, which had been displaced from the eastern side of the works. This late date accounts for the present rather unprepossessing elevation.

The 'Hooter House'

At the northern end of the eastern range is the **central power house**, or 'Hooter House' **(24)** (**Figs 186** and **187**), which supplied hydraulic power. Most of this block was remodelled in the 1920s, when an extra floor was inserted, but the accumulator tower to the north has survived intact. Originally there was a single 750psi (51·7 bar) hydraulic power system with steam pumps supplying the accumulator in the northern tower. By the early 20th century the power requirement had grown so much that the system was enlarged to provide two networks working at 800psi (55·2 bar) and 1,500psi (103·4 bar) respectively.

The three accumulators in the main engine house date from this alteration with two 88-ton (89·4-tonne) weighted accumulators to provide pressure to the 1,500psi (103·4 bar) system and a 47-ton (47·6-tonne) weighted accumulator supplementing the original accumulator to power the 800psi (55·2 bar) system. The present electrically driven hydraulic pumps replaced triple-expansion steam pumps in 1953, while the original water tanks on the roof were replaced by smaller internal tanks in 1959. The engine house to the west of the hydraulic engine house later contained compressors for the works' compressed air system.[5]

The tender and paint shop

To the north of the boiler-shop complex was the 1876 **tender and paint shop (25)** latterly known as the tank shop or 'L2' shop. This was served to the south by a traversing table and each bay originally had a round-headed double-leaved door, only one of which survives (**Fig 188**). The eastern elevation retains its original appearance, but to the west the building was truncated to provide improved access, while the northern elevation was mutilated when later extensions were built. Internally each of the 40ft-wide (12·19-m) structural bays was served by an overhead crane and though most of these have been replaced by later, more powerful, cranes, one more slightly built wooden crane survives, which is limited to a 15-ton (15·2-tonne) lift. The arrangement of this crane, with a wooden tie beam and underslung metal tensioning, suggests that it may be original (**Fig 189**).

Fig 186 *(top right) The hydraulic-power engine house (the 'Hooter House') in 1985, with the hooter in operation.*

Fig 187 *(right) The interior of the hydraulic-power engine house as remodelled in the 1920s, showing the later pumps in the foreground and three of the hydraulic accumulators in the background.*

Fig 188 *(below) The only remaining original double-leaved door of the tender and paint shop of 1876. The spring-loaded upper bolts allowed manual operation from head level.*

Fig 189 *(below right) The overhead crane in the tender shop in 1987.*

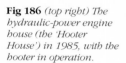

Fig 190 *(top) The roof of the 1911 steaming-shed in 1987.*

Fig 191 *(above) The surviving locomotive turntable as it was around 1987. All the buildings in the background have since been demolished.*

Fig 192 *(right) The engine weigh house in 1987, showing the 1930 Pooley balancing machines (see also Figure 159).*

West of Rodbourne Road

Across Rodbourne Road only four early structures of note survive. Facing the boiler shop is the **steaming-shed (26)** or 'P1' shop, the first structural bay of which was built by 1910, incorporating the existing boundary wall. In 1911 it was extended by two structural bays to the west and one bay to the north (**Fig 190**). The latter extension was designed to bring under cover the western end of a subway connecting with the boiler shop on the opposite side of Rodbourne Road. The subway was fitted with hydraulic lifts at either end whereby boilers could be transported on a special trolley to be tested – both hydraulically and with live steam – in the steaming-shed. This arrangement utilised an earlier pedestrian subway, built in 1890 to give secure access to the western site when this was first acquired for broad to standard-gauge conversion work. The steaming-shed was further extended in the 1920s to achieve its present extent.

The pattern store

To the south, dominating the Rodbourne Road cutting, is the heavily constructed 1897 **pattern store (27)** surmounted by massive water tanks (see Figure 146). The building is of fireproof construction with brick jack-arching supported by a steel framework supplied by P S & A Co Ltd Steel. However, as 'GWR 8/97' is scribbled in solder on some of the steel members, this would suggest that the works' own labour force may have been responsible for the erection of the building. Very little combustible material was used in the construction, the loading doors, internal doors and stairs all being of metal. It was heated by hot air ducted via brick piers from stoves in the basement. The basement was converted to a mess room in World War I and used again as a canteen from 1939 to 1960. Originally the upper floors were used exclusively for storing patterns on heavy-duty steel racking, but pattern-making was subsequently transferred to this building. The top floor contains much of the pipework associated with the four separate water tanks on the roof, which are reached by means of a metal spiral stair that emerges in a metal turret with a conical roof.

Turntable and weigh house

Immediately to the west of the pattern store is the only remaining locomotive **turntable (28)** on the site (**Fig 191**). This 65-ft (19·81-m) steel structure, in its brick-lined pit, is of a standard design produced at the end of the 19th century, but now rare enough to be worth protecting as a historic monument. The turntable was installed in 1902 to serve the new 'A' shop and in later years it

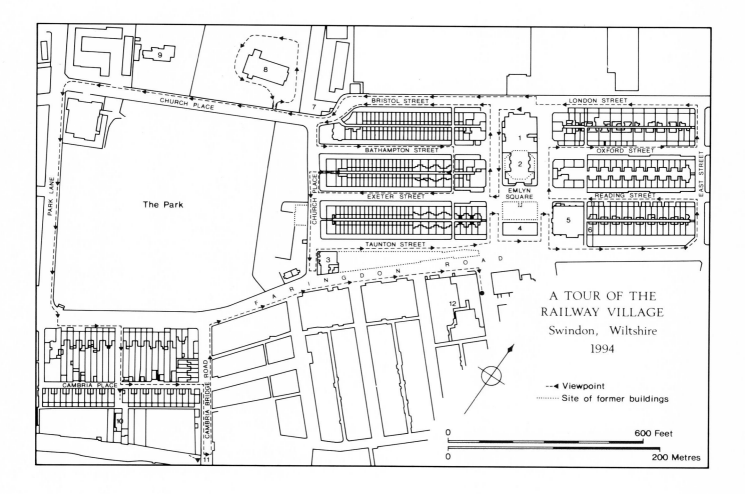

A TOUR OF THE
RAILWAY VILLAGE
Swindon, Wiltshire
1994

--◄ Viewpoint
······· Site of former buildings

0   600 Feet
0   200 Metres

became a favourite location for official photographs recording notable locomotives produced in the works.

Some distance to the west is the **weigh house (29)**, the sole surviving building of Churchward's 'A'-shop complex. An earlier weighbridge had existed at the eastern end of the works, but its plant was incapable of handling the new larger locomotives that 'A' shop was producing, and it was dismantled to be reused at Newton Abbot. The new weighbridge was erected in 1906, housing a set of Henry Pooley and Son's self-contained locomotive balancing tables in a light wooden shed. In 1919 this was replaced by a brick-built structure which survives as the eastern section of the present weighbridge. In 1930 the building was extended by a wider section to the west and re-equipped with the Pooley balancing tables that survive at the time of writing (**Fig 192**). The building is of considerable interest as such structures are now extremely rare.

A TOUR OF THE RAILWAY VILLAGE

This tour begins in front of the former **Mechanics' Institution building (1)**, located opposite the main entrance to the works (the route is shown in **Figure 193**, which should be used in conjunction with Figure 45, showing the sequential development of the various buildings; key sites are again given in bold in the text).

THE MECHANICS' INSTITUTION

The Mechanics' Institution (see pp 79–81) was built in 1854 and became vacant following the closure of the works in 1986. In 1995 it remained empty and in a bad state of repair. The ground plan of the original building is shown in Figure 85. It consisted of a central corridor running the length of the building to connect with a large reading-room in a cross wing at the southern end. Opening off the corridor were various rooms, the functions of which are marked on the plan. The

Fig 193 *Swindon village (New Swindon) in 1994 (based on the 1957, 1976 and 1970 1:1 250 maps for SU1484 NW, NE and SW with the permission of The Controller of Her Majesty's Stationery Office, © Crown copyright).*

Fig 196 (below) The Mechanics' Institution building from the north west in 1933, following the completion of the brick fly tower and the loading section between the 1854–5 building and the 1891–3 extension (by courtesy of the National Railway Museum, York).

Fig 199 (opposite bottom) The reading-room in the 1891–3 extension to the Mechanics' Institution, photographed in the mid 20th century (by courtesy of the National Railway Museum, York).

Fig 194 (above) Decorative ceiling plasterwork in the 1854–5 part of the former Mechanics' Institution theatre. This plasterwork was restored following a fire that occurred in late 1930.

Fig 195 (right) A detail of the art-deco plasterwork around the proscenium arch in the Mechanics' Institution theatre. This decoration dates from after the 1930 fire.

first floor of the original building contained a theatre, with a stage and associated facilities located above the reading-room. The stage area was destroyed by fire in late 1930. The plasterwork in the hall of the theatre was restored and the proscenium arch rebuilt in art-deco style (**Figs 194** and **195**). At the same time the old reading-room wing was replaced by a large, square-shaped fly tower and the ground floor converted into a dance hall.[6]

Apart from the construction of the fly tower, the exterior of the original building has undergone a number of alterations (compare Figures 85 and **196**). The tripartite entrance porch has been built up to the level of the sill of the large window above the gallery at the north end of the theatre, whilst a low spire, surmounted by a partially louvred cupola, has been added to the top of each of the towers. The side walls are now partly obscured by a series of single-storey additions, but it is still possible to distinguish the tops of the original buttresses.

THE COVERED MARKET

The octagonal **covered market (2) (Fig 197)** once stood to the south of the 1854 part of the Mechanics' Institution building, beyond the loading doors attached to the fly tower. The market had a slate-covered roof, measuring 40ft (12·19m) in diameter, supported by piers with glazed walls in between. A photograph of around 1890 shows that the southern half of the market was unglazed and consisted of half-length

columns resting on a 3-ft (1-m) high stone wall. There was a public fountain in the centre of the building around which were grouped thirty-two shops and space for thirty stalls.[7]

The market building was demolished around 1891 to make way for a major extension to the Mechanics' Institution, opened by Viscount Emlyn in 1893. The architect for the new building was Brightwen Binyon, who, at the same time, was engaged in designing the New Swindon Local Board offices in Regent Circus, and whose practice must have done extremely well out of the expansion of New Swindon. Like most of the single-storey additions to the old building, the 1891 extension was made with squared and snecked

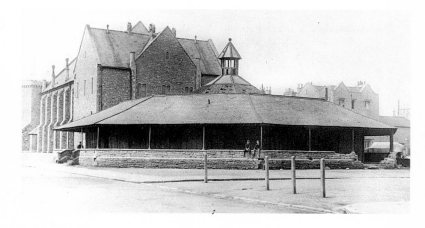

Fig 197 *(above) A view of the octagonal covered market from the south west, taken shortly before its demolition (around 1891) to make way for the extension to the 1854–5 part of the Mechanics' Institution building. The posts in the road, to the south of the market, are an indication that it was owned and maintained by the GWR, like most of the roads in the village.*

Fig 198 *(left) The extension to the Mechanics' Institution building on the site of the octagonal covered market. The latter was replaced by an open-air market in Cromwell Street. The main entrance to the extension was at the southern end where a marble staircase led to a large reading-room amply lit by canted bay windows.*

Pennant stone with Bath-stone dressings. The main entrance to the new building was placed between projecting square bays on its southern side (**Fig 198**). The extension housed a new reading-room (**Fig 199**), a smoking room, games rooms and a variety of other facilities, including a lecture room. The extra space also allowed the theatre in the original building to be provided with chorus room and dressing-room facilities, situated on the first floor above the new reading-room.

THE BRISTOL STREET COTTAGES

The west side of Emlyn Square, leading north to Bristol Street, retains its two shop blocks of 1845 (see p 57). Bristol Street leads westwards past a former shop, on the corner, an eight-room former lodging house and a double cottage. At the end

Fig 200 *Class 'E' houses, built in 1853–4, at the western end of Bristol Street. The house facing Church Place (on the right) was occupied by C B Collett, chief mechanical engineer, in the 1930s.*

Fig 201 *(below) The ground plans of the two class 'E' houses with the angled opening between them which led to the rear alley. The peculiar plan of these houses was necessitated by the awkward bend at the western end of Bristol Street where it meets with Church Place.*

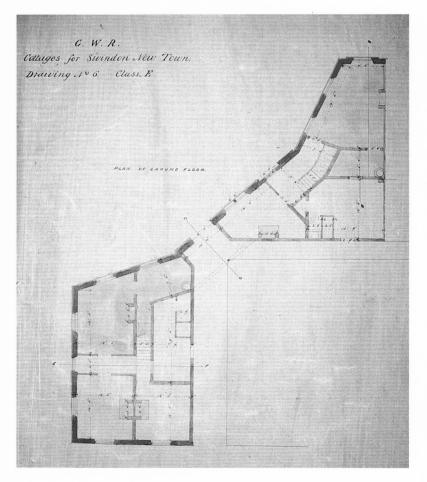

of the block, an alley runs north–south and separates the shop blocks from the earlier cottage terraces. Further west, the Bristol Street cottages are enlivened by shallow window bays under small gables. This is the earliest row of cottages in the village, designed by Brunel and completed by the end of August 1842.

At the west end of this terrace is a single class 'A' cottage which marks the beginning of the extension built in 1853 following the realignment of Church Place. Thirty-four cottages of this type (see pp 78–9) were built as part of the 1853–4 building programme carried out for the company by the contractors, May & Son. The class 'A' cottages are identical in plan to the five-room houses built in Oxford, Reading and Faringdon Streets in 1846, though slightly taller (see p 54).

CHURCH PLACE

Just to the west of this class 'A' cottage, Bristol Street bends southwards to meet the northern end of Church Place. Here an eccentrically planned pair of larger houses, known together as a class 'E' dwelling, were built to fill the awkward corner site (**Figs 200** and **201**). Two alternative and undated plans exist for this end block and the two to the south. One scheme shows Church Place on its original oblique alignment suggesting that this is an earlier plan, pre-dating the 1847 retrenchment phase. The elevations drawn as part of this earlier scheme are almost identical to those of the type 'A' to 'E' houses built in 1853.

These two houses, comprising type 'E', are separated at ground-floor level by an obliquely angled archway. This leads through to the rear alley running between the two cottage rows that make up the Church Place block. The northernmost house of the two is entered via a doorway in the Bristol Street façade and it originally had seven rooms, one of which ran over the alley archway. The house to the south is of a similar size, but its main entrance is through a centrally placed door on the Church Place façade. Canted bay windows and an entrance porch were added to this elevation early in the 20th century. A two-storey bay window has also been added to the Bathampton (formerly Bath) Street side of the house.

BATHAMPTON AND EXETER STREETS

On Bathampton Street, the cottages on the south side of the street are plainer than those to the north, lacking window bays, except for three cottage pairs at the east end of the terrace. The canopies over the doors of the cottages on the northern side have been replaced by drip moulds on the southern side. The easternmost five cottages on this southern side were built as larger, four-roomed dwellings, referred to by the company as 'double cottages'. The projecting stair towers to the rear of these double cottages can be seen from the alley running south between the cottages and the adjacent shop block.

The houses on the south side of Exeter Street,

completed by the beginning of 1844, are even plainer in their external treatment. The rough, squared blocks of Swindon stone used for the walls gives these cottages a vernacular appearance, reinforced by the virtual absence of ornamental features. Even so, the symmetrical articulation of window and door openings along the terrace owes much to the same Georgian tradition that underlies the architecture of the whole village and imbues it with considerable dignity.

CHURCH PLACE AND THE PARK

At the west end of Exeter Street, there are two class 'A' cottages on the north side, and a class 'D' cottage on the corner with Church Place. Another pair of class 'D' cottages stands to either side of the archway through to the centre of the block in Church Place (**Figs 202** and **203**). The gable above the arch is used to emphasise the centre of the block, an effect balanced by identical gables at each end of the elevation. The brick walls of these substantial eight-roomed houses, along with the L-shaped brick courtyard at the rear, can be viewed by walking through the archway.

On the west side of Church Place is the main entrance to the former GWR park, once known as Victoria Park, but now known simply as the Park. Formal gardens were laid out on the eastern side of the Park from 1871, but little evidence of these remains. The park-keeper's lodge, built on the southern side of the entrance, has also been demolished.

Fig 202 *A view from Church Place of a pair of class 'D' houses, built in 1853–4, at the western end of the Bathampton (Bath) Street/Exeter Street block of cottages. The back alley, with the brick walls enclosing the rear yards, can be seen through the archway.*

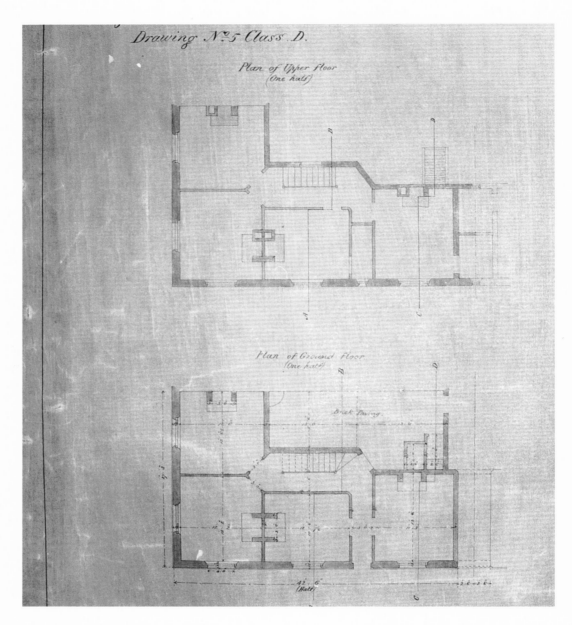

Drawing N<u>o</u> 5 Class D.

Plan of Upper floor
(One half)

Plan of Ground Floor
(One half)

Brick Facing.

At the western end of the block of cottages between Exeter and Taunton Streets are two class 'B' houses (**Figs 204** and **205**). From Church Place these houses look very similar to the class 'D' houses in the end block to the north, though they are, in fact, much smaller, owing to the limited size of the original building plot at the end of the block.

Further to the south, in Church Place, is the main entrance to **Park House (3)**, a large yellow-brick building erected as a dwelling and consulting rooms for the company's chief medical officer, G M Swinhoe, in 1876 (see p 113 and Figure 135). Later, it became familiar to generations of GWR men who came here for a medical examination before obtaining employment in the

works or as footplate staff. Park House replaced a class 'C' cottage, a four-roomed house built at the west end of a row of twelve class 'A' cottages demolished in 1970. Although it was much smaller, the Church Place façade of the class 'C' house was designed to harmonise with the larger houses in the end blocks to the north.

TAUNTON STREET AND THE GWR HOSPITAL

In Taunton Street, it is possible to identify the sites of cottages on the south side of the street, demolished in 1970, because the gateways to their rear yards are preserved in the boundary wall on the south side of the Park House car park. A class 'C'

Fig 203 Plans of the class 'D' houses built at the eastern and western ends of the village.

house stood at the east end of the twelve class 'A' cottages here, being the last surviving example of this plan type in the village. This house had a formal garden, on the east side of which was the Medical Fund limehouse. The latter was attached to the Medical Fund's washing and Turkish baths, begun in 1868 and also demolished in 1970 (see p 111). Before these buildings were constructed, the triangular plot had been the site of the company's slaughterhouse and bakehouse, both built in 1847–9 (see p 58).

On the corner of Taunton Street and Emlyn Square is a block of eight class 'A' cottages, and a pair of class 'D' houses facing the former GWR accident hospital. This site was originally earmarked for a block of cottages similar in appearance to the shop blocks to the north, except that the shops here were to be replaced by three-storey houses. These plans were interrupted by the recession of 1847 and the present houses were built on the site in 1853.

The south side of the former hospital (see p 113 and Figure 134), now the **Village Community Centre (4)**, has an ashlar façade, of Bath stone, flanked by the more rustic Swindon-stone cottages that once formed part of the hospital. Originally the façade was fronted by a formal garden, enclosed by iron railings. The hospital was established in 1871 by converting an existing building, the 1862 armoury of the XI Wiltshire Volunteer Rifle Corps. Immediately to the north of the hospital, on what is now a car park, stood a small terrace of six stone cottages built between 1862 and 1866.

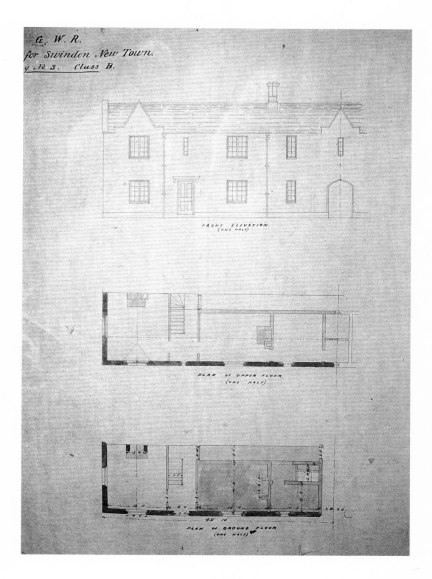

Fig 204 *(right) Elevation and plans of the class 'B' houses. Although externally these are virtually identical to their class 'D' neighbours, they are much smaller because of the restricted size of the end plots on which they were built.*

Fig 205 *(below) A GWR elevational drawing for the end block of class 'B' houses at the western end of the Exeter Street/ Taunton Street block.*

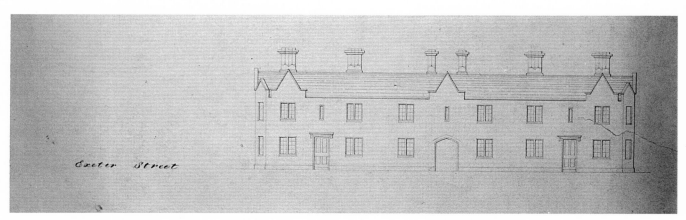

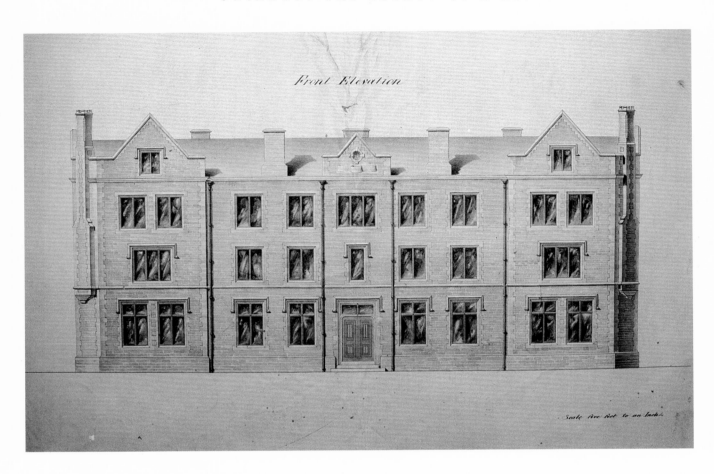

Front Elevation

Scale five feet to an Inch

Fig 206 *Brunel's original design (of around 1847) for the High Street (Emlyn Square) façade of a barracks for single men. This design was never executed, because of the 1847–9 recession. When building work recommenced in 1854, the Barracks were constructed to a completely different plan (see Figure 207).*

THE GREAT WESTERN RAILWAY MUSEUM

Opposite the hospital, on the eastern side of Emlyn Square, is the large and somewhat forbidding edifice built as a model lodging house for single men, and currently used to house the **Great Western Railway Museum (5)** (at the time of writing, plans exist to transfer the Great Western Railway Museum to a new site within the former railway works, and to rehouse the Swindon Museum and Art Gallery in this building). Brunel designed the building, originally known as the Barracks, in what was described on an elevational drawing as an 'Elizabethan design' (**Fig 206**). The three-storey structure was designed to match the style of the nearby shop residences. Work began in 1847, according to plan, but the contractor had only got as far as erecting the ground-floor walls when the 1847–9 recession took hold and the GWR ordered the cessation of all building work (see p 64).

When work on the building recommenced in 1854, it was to a completely different design. Massive four-storey towers, supported by buttresses, were built to each side of the main façade fronting the High Street (now Emlyn Square). Five gabled bays, each of three storeys in

height, were placed between each tower. Two rear wings, separated by a courtyard, abutted the front range to create a U-shaped building. The eventual architectural style of the building can best be described as Gothic. The windows are much smaller than those shown in Brunel's 1847 elevation and in general the building has a more austere and institutional appearance (**Figs 207** and **208**).

The Barracks

In 1855, Joseph Robinson, a GWR Inspector of Police in Swindon, applied to the company to rent the recently completed Barracks. The company agreed to the proposal, renting the building to Robinson for £160 per annum for an eighteen-month term.[8] In an advertisement in the local press, in March 1855, Robinson announced that he had taken the premises 'which he has fitted up in accordance with the original intention of the Directors of the Great Western Railway Company, viz the providing of comfortable and economical accommodation for the workmen of New Swindon; in addition to the furnishing of the rooms for the accommodation of lodgers, he has also opened in conjunction with this establishment, a coffee and eating house'.[9]

The building was said to have been modelled 'upon the plan of French lodging houses, to have a common kitchen and common entrance with a day and night porter'.[10] It contained over one hundred sleeping-rooms, each having a bed, a chest of drawers and a chair. There were also day rooms, a bakery and kitchens.[11] The construction of such a large hostel for lodgers was regarded as a laudable social experiment even though, in Richard Jefferies' view, 'it savoured not a little of communism'.[12]

Robinson had great difficulty in attracting lodgers and he gave up advertising the premises in July 1855. The forbidding appearance of the building and the institutionalised regime did not appeal to single men 'who clung to the home element in their off-work life, in so far as they could realise it, and preferred living in lodgings with families, to herding together in a barrack'.[13] The building appears to have remained empty until about 1861 when it was converted into two and three-room tenements for occupation by the Welsh families who had arrived in Swindon to operate the new rolling mills. At that time, according to Richard Jefferies, as many as 500 people were accommodated in the Barracks which 'was a vast place with innumerable rooms and corridors'.[14] The Welsh workers moved to

Cambria Place in 1864 and the building was again without a tenant until 1867, when it was purchased by the New Swindon Wesleyan Methodist congregation, of which Joseph Armstrong was a prominent member.

Conversion to a chapel
The purchase of the Barracks by the Methodists was a protracted affair. In April 1865 they had applied to the GWR for a piece of ground for a new chapel and it was decided to sell them a plot of garden land on the north side of Bristol Street for this purpose.[15] A few months later, following a protest by the Bishop of Gloucester who seemed to dislike the idea of a chapel being built so close to St Mark's church, the company offered the Methodists a plot of the same size on the north side of London Street. By the beginning of 1867, however, it was clear that this second plot would be required by the company for the new carriage works. In an ingenious solution to the problem, possibly devised by Armstrong, the company sold the empty Barracks to the Methodists for £1,600, thereby absolving it from having to carry out costly repairs to a redundant, and badly maintained, building while the site in London Street was reconveyed back to the GWR.

Fig 207 *The Emlyn Square façade (on the right) of the Barracks as eventually built in 1854–5. The Gothic-style windows were inserted in the Reading Street elevation at the time of the conversion of the Barracks to a Wesleyan Methodist chapel in 1868–9.*

Fig 208 *(right) The southern front of the former Barracks showing the stair towers added by Thomas Lansdown in 1869 during the building's conversion to a chapel. The glazed openings date from the 1960s, when the building was converted to form the Great Western Railway Museum.*

Fig 209 *(opposite top) The main exhibition hall of the Great Western Railway Museum in 1994. The ceiling, cast-iron columns and pointed-arched windows were inserted in 1868–9, when the Barracks was converted to a chapel. On the left of the photograph is a replica of* North Star, *a first-generation broad-gauge locomotive.*

Fig 210 *(opposite) The Glue Pot public house, originally a shop residence, built on the corner of High Street (Emlyn Square) and Reading Street in 1847 by the contractor Thomas Cooper. This is one of eight identical buildings erected in 1845–7 on either side of the 'grand promenade' of High Street. The first occupant of this shop was David Dunbar, a sculptor.*

The Barracks building was then converted into a chapel capable of accommodating at least 1,100 worshippers. The architect chosen for this difficult task was Thomas Lansdown. He turned the ground-floor rooms of the front (western) range into classrooms, vestries and chapel-keeper's rooms, with a large schoolroom on the floor above. The inward-facing side walls of the north and south wings were demolished, and the space between the outer walls, which included the 90ft-wide (27·43-m) courtyard, was roofed to form a single large room for the chapel. The eastern walls of the two wings appear to have been demolished and the whole eastern side of the block rebuilt to form the new side wall to the chapel. A new ceiling was inserted and supported by two rows of cast-iron columns. A vestry was created in the north-eastern corner of the chapel, whilst a dais, with a reading-desk and altar, was built at the northern end of the chapel, further to the west. A gallery designed to accommodate up to 500 Sunday School children was erected at the southern end of the chapel.

The chapel's new north–south orientation necessitated the creation of a new main entrance to the south, entered from Faringdon Road (see Figure 208). Lansdown built two towers to either side of the new door, each containing stone stairs up to the gallery. Larger Gothic-style windows, containing tracery of a late 13th-century type, were inserted along the north and south walls, at first-floor level, to provide more light and to highlight the religious function of the building. New windows, with pointed arches, were inserted at ground-floor level. The High Street (Emlyn Square) façade of the former Barracks remained unaltered. A chapel memorial stone was laid on 27 April 1868 and the building was opened in May 1869.

Conversion to a museum

In 1962 the building was converted again, this time to serve as the Great Western Railway Museum. The work, carried out by the borough architect, involved stripping-out the chapel and its gallery to create the main exhibition hall (**Fig 209**). Tracks were laid in the hall to take GWR locomotives and large glazed openings were created in the south wall of the chapel to enable them to be taken into the building. A large room on the ground floor of the west range was made into a room for the display of Brunel memorabilia, whilst the former schoolroom on the floor above was turned into a second exhibition hall. The museum houses an excellent collection illustrating the history of the GWR and its activities in Swindon.

Village life recreated

The cottage at **34 Faringdon Road (6)** forms part of the museum. In front of the cottage is a small garden, a feature that virtually all of the houses in the village possessed prior to the 1970s' refurbishment programme. The windows have the original multi-paned sashes, and the panelled front door and narrow window above have also been retained. Inside, the rooms have been restored to their appearance in 1900 (see Figure 65). The back scullery/wash house and external privy give an accurate impression of the arrangement of the rear yards in the 19th century.

At the east end of the row of five-roomed houses built in Faringdon Road in 1846 there is a pair of class 'D' houses facing on to East Street. This end block was not begun until 1862. An identical pair built in 1853 can be seen closing off the east end of the next block to the north.

PUBLIC HOUSES

On the corner formed by Reading Street and Emlyn Square stands The Glue Pot public house (**Fig 210**). This building (which sells beer brewed in part of the former carriage works) has operated as a public house for much of its existence. Emlyn Square was (until the building of the Mechanics' Institution in 1854) a large grassed area enclosed by iron railings. Four blocks of cottages, with three-storey shop residences on the corners, faced on to this open space. Three of the shops remain in use as public houses, but the other five have long since been converted to houses.

LARGER HOUSES AND VILLAS

The north side of Oxford Street is lined by a terrace of large, eight-roomed houses. At the east end of this row is a pair of class 'B' houses identical to the one at the west end of the Exeter/Taunton Street block. The large houses in London Street (see Figure 58) were the first to be built in 1845 on the east side of what was then High Street. With their gabled bay windows they are similar in appearance to the smaller houses in Bristol Street. Originally they faced on to the main line and the villas of the station superintendent and works' manager (demolished in the early 1870s to make way for the existing buildings – see p 59).

THE BRISTOL STREET SCHOOLS

Bristol Street heads westwards, past the cast-iron water tower of the railway works (see pp 90–91). It leads to the site of the company school of 1843–4 (see p 61) on the north side of the junc-

Fig 211 *A headstone in St Mark's churchyard commemorating Robert Hanks, a GWR employee, who was killed in an accident at the works in 1866, at the age of seventy-one.*

Fig 212 *(below) The nave of St Mark's church, looking east. The church was built in 1843–5 to the west of the railway village (see also Figures 71 and 72).*

tion with Church Place. The schoolrooms and master's house, designed by Scott & Moffatt, were set back from the road to the rear of an enclosed playground. A separate infants' school was built at the southern end of the site in 1857.[16] An agreement to close the schools was reached with the Swindon Education Board in 1879 and most of the buildings were demolished in 1881. The only survivor is the Swindon-stone **infants' school (7)**, later converted into the works' laboratory. In 1883 a single-storey building, used to store the company's horse-drawn wagons, was built at right angles on to the northern side of the laboratory.

ST MARK'S CHURCH

To the west of the former school site is **St Mark's church (8)**, also designed by Scott & Moffatt and consecrated in 1845 (see pp 61–2 and Figures 71 and 72). The burial-ground surrounding the church contains what amounts to a 'Who's Who' of early works' officers and shop foremen. Minard Rea, the much-respected works' manager of 1850–7, is buried next to his

brother, Stuart Keith Rea, the company 'medical man', in the north-eastern corner of the cemetery. Joseph Armstrong and members of his family are commemorated by a granite obelisk in the south-eastern corner. On the north side of the church are buried two workmen who were killed as a result of accidents in the works (**Fig 211**). Another former works' manager, William Frederick Gooch, is interred nearby.

At the north-western corner of the church stands the 140ft (42·7m) tower and spire. A contemporary reviewer in *The Ecclesiologist* considered that 'their position is affected and unnecessary, except for the too manifest object of producing an effect from the railroad'.[17] On the southern side of the church is the clearly

discernible addition carried out by Temple Moore in 1897 to lengthen the chancel and construct a northern vestry and southern Lady Chapel.[18] The interior (**Fig 212**), with its six-bay arcade, is light and spacious, and was praised as such by the same reviewer. The Lady Chapel and north aisle both have good stained glass by C E Kempe (1897).

To the west of the church is the Scott & Moffatt **parsonage (9)**, completed in 1844 (**Fig 213**). Made of Swindon stone, it had a cellar containing service rooms, an entrance hall, dining room, drawing room and study on the ground floor, and four first-floor bedrooms. A service range and stable yard were added to the west end of the building in 1880.

Fig 213 St Mark's parsonage was built in 1843–4 along with the church and the now mostly demolished Bristol Street schools. All three buildings were designed by Scott & Moffatt.

CAMBRIA PLACE

Church Place leads into Park Lane where, in the north-western corner of the park, the extensively rebuilt drill hall of the XI Wiltshire Volunteer Rifle Corps was erected in 1871 (see pp 83 and 114). South from here, on the opposite side of Faringdon Road, is the beginning of the Cambria Place development, built for Welsh iron-workers from 1864 (see pp 101–4 and Figures 117–121). In the middle of the estate is the **Baptist Chapel (10)**, built in 1866 to plans drawn up by the manager of the GWR rolling mills, Thomas Ellis. With its Swindon-stone façade and Bath-stone dressings, the chapel is similar to the surrounding cottages. The sides of the building are made of brick and the north side has been clad with slates to provide additional protection from the elements.

Cambria Place (which was once surfaced with ashes from the GWR works) turns into Cambria Bridge Road. The **bridge (11)** was built in the 1870s to carry traffic over the Wilts & Berks Canal. From the bridge there is an excellent view of the chapel and of the southern terraces of the estate, facing on to the canal (**Fig 214**), with their long thin strips of back garden.

THE DISPENSARY AND SWIMMING BATHS

Cambria Bridge Road leads north back to Faringdon Road where the large red-brick Health Hydro building stands on the corner with Milton Road. This was erected in 1891 as the

GWR Medical Fund dispensary and swimming baths (12) (Fig 215). The building housed a wide range of medical and recreational facilities, provided by the Medical Fund for the benefit of its members. As such it anticipated by several decades the medical centres set up by the National Health Service after World War II.

The background to the construction of the building, which at its opening was thought one of the best examples of its type in the country, is outlined in Chapter 6 (see pp 125–6). It was designed by the Swindon architect, J J Smith, in the Queen-Anne style and built for approximately £10,000. The bricks were supplied by the GWR from the company's own brickworks. The old main entrance, in Faringdon Road, opened on to a vestibule, with access on the right-hand side to the two covered swimming baths, and on the left-hand side to the dispensary (**Fig 216**).

The large bath was originally used by male swimmers and measures 136ft by 50ft (41·5m by 15·2m). There were changing boxes along each side and a viewing gallery above for 750 people (**Fig 217**). The coloured-glass windows at the southern end of the large bath, and throughout the rest of the building, were made by Mr T Rice, an employee at the works. The wrought-iron trusses supporting the roof over the large bath (**Fig 218**) were designed in the GWR drawing office.[19] The 60ft-long (18·3-m) small bath is sited on the eastern side of the large bath, and was originally used by women and children.

Fig 214 *This view, taken from the former canal bridge on Cambria Bridge Road, shows the southern terraces of the Cambria Place estate of 1864, the gardens that sloped down to the Wilts & Berks Canal, and the side of the Welsh Baptist chapel, built by Thomas Ellis in 1866.*

Fig 215 *A view of around 1910 showing the GWR Medical Fund dispensary and swimming baths, built in 1892 on the south side of Faringdon Road, opposite the GWR accident hospital.*

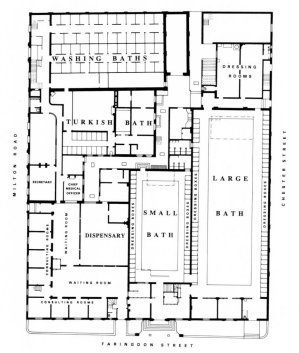

Fig 216 *Ground plan of the GWR Medical Fund dispensary and swimming baths, redrawn from a company plan of 1930 (PRO RAIL 258/411).*

The dispensary was located on the eastern side of the building. The waiting room, with its adjoining consulting rooms, had separate hatches for men and women through which medicines were dispensed (**Figs 219** and **220**). Above the dispensary area was a series of dentists' rooms. Most of the public rooms were lined at dado level with plain green ceramic tiles supplied by the Ruabon Coal & Coke Company. The floor tiles were made by Woolscroft of Hanley.

The building was provided with the most up-to-date sanitary arrangements and apparatus for heating and ventilation. Early in the 20th century a variety of more specialised services were provided for members, including a hairdressing department. The already excellent facilities were

Fig 217 *(above) An early 20th-century view of the large bath, looking south. Note the diaper brickwork on the end wall and the wrought-iron roof trusses.*

Fig 218 *(right) The large bath (in the centre) and small bath (on the right) during construction in 1891–2. The GWR Medical Fund washing and Turkish baths of 1868–77, on the northern side of Faringdon Road, are shown in the background (by courtesy of the National Railway Museum, York).*

supplemented by the addition, from 1897, of washing baths at the south-eastern corner of the building. New Turkish baths were built between these and the dispensary on Milton Road in 1904 and dressing rooms were added at the south-western corner of the site by the 1930s.

The complex was refurbished by Thamesdown Borough Council in the 1980s and, as part of this scheme, the roof supported on the wrought-iron trusses above the large bath was largely rebuilt. The total cost of the refurbishment was over £2 million. The building is now run by the council's leisure services department as a swimming pool complex combined with a health and fitness centre.

SWINDON RAILWAY STATION AND NEARBY PUBLIC HOUSES

Swindon railway station stands to the east of the village on Station Road, along with the Queens Tap and the Flag & Whistle public houses (see p 107). Only the northern block of Brunel's station of 1841–2 survives, and nothing remains of the once-famous refreshment rooms discussed in

Chapter 3 (see pp 36–41). Externally, the public houses on the southern side of Station Road, opposite the station, retain much of their original character, although the complex of outbuildings behind the Queens Tap has been demolished. Both buildings have been much altered internally.

Fig 219 *(above) Part of the dispensary waiting room in 1927. On the left are the doorways to the consulting rooms and, on the right, the hatches through which prescriptions were obtained from the dispensary on the other side of the partition (by courtesy of the National Railway Museum, York).*

Fig 220 *The dispensary in 1927 (by courtesy of the National Railway Museum, York).*

Notes

1 *'Furze, Rushes and Rowen'*
– a Greenfield Site

1 Jefferies 1875, 569–70.

2 Crittall *et al* 1983, 108.

3 MacDermot 1927*a*, 1–15.

4 Bourne 1846, 30.

5 Ibid.

6 MacDermot 1927*a*, 16–20.

7 PRO RAIL 250/82, report to Directors, 19 June 1838.

8 GWR Magazine, November 1890, 'Interview with Jim Hurst, the Great Western Railway Company's First Engine Driver'.

9 MacDermot 1927*a*, 58–60.

10 Quoted in MacDermot 1927*a*, 60.

11 PRO RAIL 250/82.

12 University of Bristol Library, Brunel Collection, GWR sketchbook 10.

13 PRO RAIL 1008/82, Gooch letters.

14 PRO RAIL 250/2.

15 PRO RAIL 250/2, Directors' Meeting, 3 November 1840.

16 Platt 1987, 54.

17 Simmons 1986*b*, 172.

18 Whishaw 1840, 238. Elsewhere (p 359) he notes that on one railway 'each engine is laid by every third day, to be thoroughly cleaned, examined, and repaired if necessary'.

19 Bourne 1839.

20 The following details are taken from Allen and Allen 1840, 34–5, and from Radford 1971, 15–16.

21 Bourne 1846, 47.

22 Francis 1851, vol II, 73.

23 PRO RAIL 253/334.

24 *Herepath's Railway Magazine* 1841, vol III, 989.

25 Drake 1840, 54.

26 PRO RAIL 250/94, London Traffic Committee minute book.

27 Vaughan 1977, 3.

28 Hallam 1939, 526.

29 PRO RAIL 250/2.

30 University of Bristol Library, Brunel Collection, GWR sketchbook 11.

2 *The 'Principal Locomotive Establishment', 1841–1849*

1 Brunel Report February 1841, quoted in MacDermot 1927*a*, 65.

2 Quoted in MacDermot 1927*a*, 74.

3 Bourne 1846, 47–8.

4 University of Bristol Library, Brunel Collection, GWR sketchbook 13, 1841.

5 PRO RAIL 253/334, Guard Book compiled by Daniel Gooch, 136–41.

6 PRO RAIL 250/110.

7 *Herepath's Railway Magazine* 1841, vol III, 1012.

8 PRO RAIL 253/107, Brunel letter-book, 31 October 1841.

9 Snell diary, 20 April 1846. The authors are indebted to Mrs Margaret Snell for permission to consult and quote from Edward Snell's unpublished diary 'The Life and Adventure of Edward Snell, 1842–1849'. They are also grateful to Dr Alan Platt for the initial reference and to Ms Shona Dewar of the State Library of Victoria, Melbourne, for assistance in locating the diary.

10 PRO RAIL 250/82, letter to Directors, 6 October 1841.

11 *Swindon Advertiser*, 27 February 1871 and 15 May 1871.

12 PRO RAIL 250/91, Finance Committee Minutes.

13 *Swindon Advertiser*, 31 July 1871.

14 PRO RAIL 250/102, Bristol Committee, 1 October 1841–2 January 1843.

15 PRO RAIL 250/120, 26 October 1843.

16 PRO RAIL 253/334, 102.

17 University of Bristol Library, Brunel Collection, Gooch sketchbook.

18 PRO RAIL 250/102; PRO RAIL 250/110.

19 PRO RAIL 250/3.

20 Lardner 1850, 108.

21 PRO RAIL 250/120, General Committee Minutes, 26 October 1843.

22 PRO RAIL 250/121, General Committee Minutes, 9 October 1843.

23 PRO RAIL 250/121, General Committee Minutes, 5 December 1844.

24 PRO RAIL 250/121, General Committee Minutes, 2 January 1845.

25 PRO RAIL 253/334, 158.

26 PRO RAIL 1008/2.

27 Ibid.

28 Snell diary – index of dates.

29 Platt 1987, 75.

30 PRO RAIL 250/123.

31 *The Illustrated Exhibitor* 1852, **1,** 103.

32 PRO RAIL 1005/414, General Manager's Brunel Collection, letter from Brunel to Gooch dated 19 January 1843.

33 Simms 1838. The authors are indebted to R J M Sutherland for this information and reference.

34 PRO RAIL 250/193, Finance Committee Minutes.

35 PRO RAIL 250/121, General Committee Minutes, 20 September 1844.

36 Snell diary, entry for 18 May 1849.

3 *The Creation of New Swindon, 1841–1849*

1 MacDermot 1927*a*, 72.

2 Ibid 75.

3 Bourne 1846, 47.

4 University of Bristol Library, Brunel Collection, Brunel letter-book 2b.

5 Bourne 1846, 47.

6 *Devizes & Wiltshire Gazette*, 15 July 1842.

7 Ibid.

8 J C Loudon quoted in Hawkins 1991, 76.

9 Bourne 1846, 47.

10 PRO RAIL 252/174, copy of sub-lease.

11 PRO RAIL 1008/34, letters of 1842–53 to the Secretary of the GWR.

12 PRO RAIL 250/121, General Committee Minutes, May 1844–February 1845.

13 Doyle and Leigh 1849, drawing no 21.

14 1851 census.

15 Meason 1852, 42–4.

16 Chandler 1992, 42.

17 *Swindon Advertiser*, 16 June 1877.

18 WRO, uncatalogued contract.

19 Peck 1983, 110.

20 University of Bristol Library, Brunel Collection, Brunel letter-book 2b.

21 PRO RAIL 250/5, Directors' Minutes, meeting of 25 March 1852.

22 PRO RAIL 250/3.

23 PRO RAIL 252/107, Brunel letter-book (business).

24 *Devizes & Wiltshire Gazette,* 31 March 1842.

25 PRO RAIL 250/82.

26 PRO RAIL 1008/34, letters of 1842–53 to the Secretary of the GWR.

27 PRO RAIL 250/3.

28 PRO RAIL 257/6.

29 University of Bristol Library, Brunel Collection, Brunel letter-book 2b.

30 Snell diary, entry for 1 March 1843 (also quoted in Platt 1987, 75).

31 PRO RAIL 252/107, Brunel letter-book (business).

32 PRO RAIL 250/3.

33 PRO RAIL 252/107.

34 *Devizes & Wiltshire Gazette,* 27 October 1842.

35 PRO RAIL 250/94, London Traffic Committee minute book.

36 PRO RAIL 253/94. general letter-book of the London Committee, 26 March–16 October 1841.

37 Pigot & Co 1842, 36.

38 PRO RAIL 250/122.

39 Quoted in Crittall *et al* 1983, 129.

40 The Fawcett List contains the names of all officers, managers, foremen and contractors, etc, employed at the Swindon works from 1843 to 1865. It is reproduced as appendix II in Peck 1983, 276–7.

41 PRO RAIL 250/121.

42 Ibid.

43 *Swindon Advertiser,* 1 May 1865.

44 WRO, uncatalogued lease.

45 PRO RAIL 250/125, General Committee Minutes, March 1847–July 1848.

46 WRO, uncatalogued lease.

47 PRO RAIL 252/334.

48 *Chambers's Edinburgh Journal* 1846, 78.

49 PRO RAIL 250/3.

50 PRO RAIL 1005/414, General Manager's Brunel Collection, letter from Brunel to Gooch dated 19 January 1843.

51 Ibid.

52 PRO RAIL 250/123, General Committee Minutes, December 1845–August 1846.

53 PRO RAIL 250/3, Directors' Minutes, 13 February 1843.

54 PRO RAIL 250/573, Paddington Committee for Swindon Church and Schools Minutes.

55 PRO RAIL 250/3, Directors' Minutes, 13 February 1843.

56 Cockbill 1992, 18–19.

57 Ibid, 23.

58 PRO RAIL 253/334.

59 PRO RAIL 250/573, Paddington Committee for Swindon Church and Schools Minutes.

60 PRO RAIL 250/2, Directors' Minutes, meeting of 1 December 1840.

61 PRO RAIL 250/119.

62 PRO RAIL 252/334.

63 PRO RAIL 252/334.

64 Ibid.

65 PRO RAIL 250/123.

66 University of Bristol Library, Brunel Collection, Brunel small sketchbook 25.

67 PRO RAIL 1008/34.

68 PRO RAIL 1008/18, reports and letters from Gooch to Saunders, etc, 1847.

69 Ibid.

70 Peck 1983, 5.

71 Snell, E 1849–59 diary, 101.

72 PRO RAIL 1008/27, Gooch letters.

73 PRO RAIL 250/126, General Committee Minutes, July 1848–August 1849.

74 PRO RAIL 276/22, papers relating to the New Swindon Mechanics' Institution.

75 PRO RAIL 253/334.

76 PRO RAIL 1008/1, Gooch letters.

77 Peck 1983, 54.

78 PRO RAIL 253/334, second Annual Report of the Council of the Mechanics' Institution, 6 January 1846.

79 PRO RAIL 250/125.

80 PRO RAIL 250/121, General Committee Minutes, May 1844–February 1845, meeting of 19 June 1844.

81 PRO RAIL 250/125, General Committee Minutes, March 1847–1 July 1848, meeting of 18 May 1848.

82 Chandler 1992, 50.

83 WRO, Deed 700/145.

84 Clark 1851, 2.

85 WRO, Deed 700/145

86 *Kelly's Post Office Directory...* 1848, 2831.

87 Crittall *et al* 1983, 110.

4 *Consolidation and Growth, 1850–1863*

1 PRO RAIL 1008/18, report to Directors, 22 September 1849.

2 PRO RAIL 1008/17, report by Gooch, 19 November 1849.

3 MacDermot 1927a, 218.

4 *Swindon Advertiser,* 20 February 1860

5 Ibid, 3 June 1861.

6 Simmons 1991, 125–6.

7 PRO RAIL 257/6, abstract of men employed at Swindon in 1849, Gooch list.

8 PRO RAIL 250/186, Expenditure Committee Minutes, November 1849–October 1852.

9 PRO RAIL 250/5, Directors' Minutes, meeting of 22 January 1852.

10 PRO RAIL 1005/454, notes compiled by E T MacDermot on the GWR Medical Fund.

11 PRO RAIL 250/187, Expenditure Committee Minutes, meeting of 3 March 1853.

12 Lee 1854, 9.

13 PRO RAIL 250/7, Directors' Minutes, meeting of 22 September 1853.

14 Lee 1854, 13.

15 PRO RAIL 250/7, Directors' Minutes, meeting of 6 October 1853.

16 *Swindon Advertiser,* 24 August 1857.

17 Lee 1854, 17.

18 PRO RAIL 250/6.

19 PRO RAIL 250/187, Expenditure Committee Minutes, meeting of 21 July 1853.

20 *Swindon Advertiser,* 31 May 1869.

21 A tender of £3,750 from Edward Streeter was accepted by the Company. *Builder* **12** No 591, 290.

22 *Swindon Advertiser,* 29 May 1854.

23 Ibid, 30 July 1855.

24 WRO G24/760/126, sketch plan of the estate.

25 *Swindon Advertiser,* 21 September 1857.

26 Crittall *et al* 1983, 130.

27 *Swindon Advertiser,* 1 April 1861.

28 Ibid, 29 October 1860

29 Backhouse 1992, 44.

30 *Swindon Advertiser,* 26 May 1856.

31 PRO RAIL 250/6, Directors' Minutes, meetings of 2 September and 23 September 1852.

32 *Swindon Advertiser,* 22 June 1857.

5 The Armstrong Era, 1864–1877

1 PRO RAIL 250/20, Directors' Minutes, 26 May 1864.
2 Quoted in *Swindon Advertiser,* 1 May 1865.
3 Ibid, 8 March 1869.
4 Ibid, 20 February 1871.
5 Pers comm J Walter.
6 *Astill's Original Swindon Almanack* 1872: Swindon New Town.
7 PRO RAIL 250/209, 19 November 1873.
8 PRO RAIL 250/27, Directors' Minutes, 19 January 1876.
9 Pers comm A Peck.
10 Peck 1983, 277 (Fawcett List).
11 WRO G24/760/388, plan of two houses built for L Ellis in Cambria Place c 1876.
12 *Swindon Advertiser,* 5 April 1879.
13 WRO 1461/933. In 1867 the County of Gloucester Bank was recorded as the owner of about fourteen of the cottages. Harvey 1994, 102, refers to the likely involvement of the Monmouthshire Baptist Association in the funding of the cottages.
14 *Swindon Advertiser,* 22 February 1869.
15 WRO 2515.
16 Platt 1987, 128.
17 WRO G24/2/1, New Swindon Local Board Minutes 1864–72.
18 PRO RAIL 250/186, meeting of 30 January 1867.
19 Reprinted in *Swindon Advertiser,* 1 May 1865.
20 PRO RAIL 253/131/2.
21 Jefferies 1875, 580.
22 Harvey 1994, 104.
23 *Swindon Advertiser,* 31 August 1868. House-ownership, as has been stated by Harvey 1994, 101, brought with it the right to vote, and the increasing enfranchisement of its workforce was no doubt viewed by the Company as an important means of securing greater political power.
24 Harvey 1994, 102.
25 Crittall *et al* 1983, 112.
26 WRO G24/2/1.
27 Harvey 1994, 103.
28 WRO G24/2/1, New Swindon Local Board Minutes 1864–72.
29 Crittall *et al* 1983, 112. Harvey 1994, 103, states that Haydon, Aylesbury, Gooch and Carlton Streets and Queen's Road were developed by a consortium of Swindon Permanent Building Society officers, Joseph Armstrong, Richard Strange (a grocer of old Swindon) and a Mr Kinnier (a solicitor of old Swindon).
30 *Swindon Advertiser,* 14 December 1878.
31 Peck 1983, 88.
32 Jefferies 1875, 572.
33 Ibid, 571.
34 *Swindon Advertiser,* 20 March 1871.
35 Ibid, 20 February 1871.
36 Jefferies 1875, 571.
37 *Astill's Original Swindon Almanack* 1877.
38 *Swindon Advertiser,* 20 May 1872.
39 WRO 1461/1981, lease.
40 Crittall *et al* 1983, 127.
41 *Swindon Advertiser,* 20 February 1871.
42 Ibid, 10 February 1877.
43 PRO RAIL 258/411/2, papers relating to the GWR Medical Fund.
44 *Swindon Advertiser,* 27 May 1872.
45 The men appear to have been paid on a weekly basis until at least the end of 1848. On 24 August of that year, tradesmen in New Swindon petitioned the directors to 'forbid the system about to be brought into use of paying the Mechanics employed at the Company's Works at Swindon once in every fort-night instead of weekly' (PRO RAIL 250/126). There is no indication in the General Committee Minutes that the petition was acceded to and it seems likely that fortnightly pay was introduced in late 1848 or early 1849.
46 *Swindon Advertiser,* 7 April 1877.
47 Ibid, 16 June 1877.

6 The Mature Works and Company Town, 1877–1900

1 Gooch 1892, 238.
2 Peck 1983, 102–6.
3 Malan 1892, 559–66.
4 Great Western Railway 1892, 18–29.
5 See, for example, Bryan 1991.
6 Crittall *et al* 1983, 112.
7 *Swindon Advertiser,* 3 April 1876.
8 PRO RAIL 250/27, Directors' Minutes.
9 *Swindon Advertiser,* 12 July 1879.
10 Ibid, 15 March 1879.
11 Ibid, 5 June 1880.
12 Crittall *et al* 1983, 113.
13 Peck 1983, 154.
14 Quoted in Chandler 1992, 60.
15 *The Illustrated London News,* 18 October 1845.
16 *Swindon Advertiser,* 17 February 1877.
17 Pevsner 1975, 510.

7 A New Century, 1900–1995

1 Peck 1983, 123–275.
2 Ibid, 122.
3 White 1911–12, 'Swindon Works' part No IX.
4 Peck 1983, 177–86.
5 Bryan 1991, 87.
6 Peck 1983, 214.
7 Ibid, 275.
8 British Railways 1950, 64.
9 *Country Life* 1971, 433.
10 Ibid.

8 The Building Legacy

1 There has been much discussion as to the identity of the engine depicted. Peck (1983, 149–52), after detailed argument, supports the view that the engine is *Premier* as claimed by G F Bird in his series of articles for 1901–3 (quoted in Peck 1983, 150). However Bird's drawing of *Premier,* which was built in 1838 to Brunel's specifications, would seem to show a locomotive identical to locomotive *Centaur,* built by Nasmyth, Gaskell & Co in 1841 to Gooch's specifications for the 'Firefly'-class. A detailed drawing of *Centaur* was supplied by the makers to illustrate E L Ahrons' classic work *The British Steam Railway Locomotive 1825–1925* and is reproduced on p 46 of that volume. As the latter ascription would seem to be firm, it would seem that Bird misidentified one of his illustrations and that that mistake has been perpetuated in subsequent derivative publications.
2 Pers comm J Walter.
3 Ibid.
4 Ibid.
5 Ibid.
6 Peck 1983, 216.
7 *Builder* 1854a, 290.
8 PRO RAIL 250/188, Expenditure Committee Minutes.
9 *Swindon Advertiser,* 12 March 1855.
10 Great Western Railway Museum nd, *Swindon and the GWR,* 15.
11 *Swindon Advertiser,* 31 May 1869.
12 Jefferies 1875, 569.
13 *Swindon Advertiser,* 1 May 1865.
14 Jefferies 1875, 569.
15 PRO RAIL 250/186, Expenditure Committee Minutes.
16 PRO RAIL 250/188, Expenditure Committee Minutes.
17 *The Ecclesiologist* 1846, 191.
18 Pevsner 1975, 508.
19 *Swindon Advertiser,* 11 June 1892.

Bibliography

Notes on sources

Many of the documentary sources consulted during the course of this survey are held at the Public Record Office, Kew, which has an extensive corpus of material relating to railways. The minute books of the GWR directors and committees contain much important information on the Swindon works and village in the 1840s and 1850s. Other important sources at the PRO are the correspondence of Brunel, Gooch and the GWR Company Secretary.

The Brunel Collection, at the University of Bristol Library, holds many of Brunel's sketchbooks, as well as a large number of his letterbooks. These throw light on Brunel's involvement in the design of many of the company's buildings. Company plans of both the works and the village are held by the Wiltshire Record Office, Trowbridge, and by the Records Manager of Railtrack PLC, Swindon. The WRO also has plans and drawings of most buildings erected in New Swindon from about 1866, along with numerous deeds and leases, and large-scale 19th-century site plans of the works and railway village.

Original GWR photographs of Swindon are held by the National Railway Museum in York and by the Great Western Railway Museum in Swindon. The latter also holds an extensive collection of artefacts and documents relating to Swindon. The Swindon Society has a comprehensive photographic archive covering all aspects of life in both Swindon old town and New Swindon in the 19th and 20th centuries.

Many original documents and photographs concerning the history of Swindon are available at the Swindon Reference Library, which contains a local-studies room. The Reference Library has an almost complete run of the *Great Western Railway Magazine* as well as a full run of the *Swindon Advertiser* on microfilm. Other newspapers with coverage of Swindon in the 19th century are available on microfilm from the Local Studies Library at County Hall, Trowbridge.

Works consulted and further reading

Ahrons, E L 1927. *The British Steam Railway Locomotive 1825–1925*

Allen, R and Allen, E 1840. *The Midland Counties Railway Companion*

Andreae, S 1979. 'Railway Towns'. In *Railway Architecture*, eds M Binney and D Pearce, pp 176–89

Astill's Original Swindon Almanack ... 1872, 1876, 1877, 1878, 1883

Backhouse, D W 1992. *Home Brewed, a History of Breweries and Public Houses in the Swindon Area*, rev edn

Barman, C 1950. *An Introduction to Railway Architecture*

Biddle, G 1973. *Victorian Stations*

1990. *The Railway Surveyors. The Story of Railway Property Management 1800–1900*

Biddle, G and Nock, O S (eds) 1983. *The Railway Heritage of Britain*

Bourne, J C 1839. *Drawings of the London & Birmingham Railway ... with an Historical and Descriptive Account by John Britton*

1846. *The History and Description of the Great Western Railway ... from Drawings taken Expressly for this Work and Executed in Lithography by John C Bourne*

British Rail Engineering Limited 1985. *Swindon Works and its Place in British Railway History*

British Railways 1950. *Swindon Works and its Place in British Railway History*

1954. *Swindon Locomotive and Carriage Works*

British Railways (Western Region) 1957. *Swindon Carriage and Wagon Works*

Britton, J 1814. *A Topographical and Historical Description of the County of Wilts ...*

Brooke, D 1983. *The Railway Navvy, 'That Despicable Race of Men'*

Brunel, I 1870. *The Life of Isambard Kingdom Brunel, Civil Engineer*

Bryan, T 1991. *The Golden Age of the Great Western Railway 1895–1914*

Buchanan, R A 1976. 'I. K. Brunel: Engineer'. In *The Works of Isambard Kingdom Brunel*, ed Sir A Pugsley, pp 5–23

Builder 1854a. 'A visit to Swindon New Town', **12**, No 591, 289–90

1854b. 'New Swindon Institution and Market', **12**, No 595, 346–7

Cardwell, D S L 1957. *The Organisation of Science in England*, rev edn, 1972

Carter, O 1995. 'Francis Thompson 1808–95 – an architectural mystery solved.' *Back Track* **9**, No 4, 213–18.

Chaloner, W H 1950. *The Social and Economic Development of Crewe, 1780–1923*

Chambers's Edinburgh Journal 1846. 'A day at Crewe', No 109, 31 January (New Series)

1850. 'A day at Crewe', No 338, 22 June (New Series)

Chandler, J 1992. *Swindon History and Guide*

Clark, D K 1855. *Railway Machinery*, 2 vols

Clark, G T 1851. *Report to the General Board of Health on a Preliminary Inquiry into the Sewerage, Drainage, and Supply of Water, and the Sanitary Condition of the Inhabitants of the Town and Parish of Swindon*

Cockbill, T 1988. *Finest Thing Out: A Chronicle of Swindon's Torchlit Days ...*, part 1: 1843–1873

1992. *A Drift of Steam, Being a Form of 'Who was Who' in New Swindon, Wilts. 1843–1853 ...*

Conder, F R 1868. *Personal Recollections of English Engineers.* (Reprinted 1983 as *The Men who Built Railways*, ed J Simmons)

Country Life, 19 August 1971. 'Restoring a railway village'

Crittall *et al* 1983. *A History of Swindon to 1965.* (Reprinted from the *VCH Wiltshire.* Vol 9, 1970)

Darwin, B 1947. *A Century of Medical Service: The Story of the Great Western Railway Medical Fund Society, 1847–1947*

Dickens, A L 1856. *Report to the General Board of Health on a Further Inquiry as to the Boundaries which may be most Advantageously Adopted for the Purposes of the Public Health Act*

Dore, A R 1864. *Swindon Almanack and Public Register*

Doyle, R and Leigh, P 1849. *Manners and Customs of Ye Englyshe Drawn from Ye Quick*

Drake, J 1840. *Drake's Road Book of the London and Birmingham and Grand Junction Railways*

Drummond, D 1986. 'Crewe – the society and culture of a railway town, 1842–1914'. Unpublished PhD thesis, University of London

The Ecclesiologist 1846. 'St. Mark, Swindon New Town, Wilts', **6**, 191–2

Eversley, D E C 1957. 'The Great Western Railway and the Swindon Works in the Great Depression'. *Univ Birmingham Hist J* **5**, No 2

1959. *The Great Western Railway Works*, Swindon. In *VCH Wiltshire* Vol 4, pp 207–19

Francis, J 1851. *A History of the English Railway: Its Social Relations and Revelations 1820–1845*, 2 vols

Freebury, H 1985. *Great Western Apprentice*

Fuller, F 1987. *The Railway Works and Church of New Swindon*

Gibbs, K 1986. *Swindon Works, Apprentice in Steam*

Gooch, Sir D 1892. *Diaries of Sir Daniel Gooch, Baronet* (ed Sir T Martin)

Great Western Railway 1892. *The Town and Works of Swindon with a Brief History of the Broad Gauge*

1935. *Swindon Works and its Place in Great Western History*

Great Western Railway Magazine. Vol **47**, No 9 September 1935. Centenary Number. (Reprinted 1985)

Great Western Railway Magazine 1908. 'Locomotive Carriage and Wagon Department' **62**. (Reprinted August 1984, Vol 1)

Great Western Railway Museum. *Guidebooks* (to museum and cottage – various dates)

nd. *Swindon and the GWR, introductory notes*

Griffiths, D 1987. *Locomotive Engineers of the GWR*

Grinsell *et al* 1950. S*tudies in the History of Swindon*. (Includes an essay by John Betjeman on the architecture of Swindon)

Groombridge, R 1840. *The London & Birmingham Railway: A Handbook for Travellers*

Hallam, W H 1939. 'Notes on the origins of the names of streets in modern Swindon'. *WAM* **171**, 523–9

1941. 'Swindon street names'. *WAM* **175**, 487–9

Harrod, J B 1865. *Directory of Wiltshire*

Harvey, M A 1994. 'The GWR and the Swindon Permanent Building Society'. *Back Track* **8** , No 2, 101–4

Hawkins, D (ed) 1991. *Wessex: A Literary Celebration*

Head, F B 1849. *Stokers and Pokers; or, The London & North Western Railway …*

Herepath's Railway Magazine and Commercial Journal 1841. Vol III, 'Wolverton establishment', 989

Hitchcock, H-R 1954. *Early Victorian Architecture in Britain*, 2 vols (Reprinted 1972)

Holcroft, H 1953. *The Armstrongs of the Great Western*

Hudson, K 1968. 'The early years of the railway community in Swindon'. *Transport Hist*. **1**, 131–52

The Illustrated Exhibitor and Magazine of Art 1852. 'The Great Western Railway Company's Locomotive Factory at Swindon', **1**

Jack, H 1988. 'Wolverton Locomotive Works'. *Railway World,* September 1988, 518–22

Jefferies, R 1875. 'The story of Swindon'. *Fraser's Magazine* **11**, 568–80

1896. *Jefferies' Land: A History of Swindon and its Environs* (ed Grace Toplis)

Judge, C W 1985. *Thro' the Lens: A Pictorial Tribute to the Official Work of the GWR Photographers*

Kelly's Post Office Directory of Dorsetshire, Hampshire, Wiltshire … 1848

Lardner, D 1850. *Railway Economy.* (1855 edn reprinted 1968)

Large, F 1932. *A Swindon Retrospect, 1855–1930*

Larkin, E 1992. *An Illustrated History of British Railways' Workshops …*

Larkin, E J and Larkin, J G 1988. *The Railway Workshops of Britain 1823–1986*

Lee, W 1854. *Report to the General Board of Health on a Further Inquiry as to the Boundaries which may be Advantageously Adopted for the Purposes of the Public Health Act*

Lloyd, D 1967. 'Railway station architecture'. *Indust Archaeol* **4**, No 3, 185–225

Lyons, E T and Mountford, E R 1979. *An Historical Survey of Great Western Railway Engine Sheds 1837–1947*

MacDermot, E T 1927*a*. History of the Great Western Railway. Vol I: 1833–1863. (Revised by C R Clinker 1964)

1927*b*. History of the Great Western Railway . Vol II: 1863–1921. (Revised by C R Clinker, 1964)

Maggs, C G 1983. *Rail Centres: Swindon*

Malan, A H 1892. 'A look around the GWR Works at Swindon'. *English Illustrated Magazine*, April

Marsden, C J 1990. *BREL*

Marshall, J 1978. *A Biographical Dictionary of Railway Engineers*

Measom, G 1852. *The Illustrated Guide to the Great Western Railway*

Meeks, C L V 1957. *The Railway Station: An Architectural History*

Morris, W 1885. *Swindon, Reminiscences, Notes and Relics of Ye Old Wiltshire Towne.* (The Tabard Press edn, 1970)

Morrison, B 1975. *Great Western At Swindon Works*

Mountford, E R 1985. *Swindon GWR Reminiscences*

National Railway Museum 1990. *National Railway Museum on Tour, Swindon 1990*

Nock, O S 1962. *The Great Western Railway in the Nineteenth Century*

1967. *The History of the Great Western Railway . Vol III: 1923–1947*

North Wilts & District Directory 1885, 1888

Ottley, G 1966. *A Bibliography of British Railway History* (up to 1962)

1988. *A Bibliography of British Railway History: Supplement: 7951–12956* (up to 1980)

Peck, A S 1983. *The Great Western at Swindon Works*

Pevsner, N 1975. *Wiltshire (The Buildings of England* series), 2nd edn revised by B Cherry

Pigot & Co. 1842, 1844. *Directory of Wiltshire*

Platt, A 1987. *The Life and Times of Daniel Gooch*

Radford, J B 1971. *Derby Works and Midland Locomotives*

Reed, B 1983. *Crewe Locomotive Works and its Men*

Richards, P 1962. 'The influence of the railways on the growth of Wolverton, Buckinghamshire'. *Records Buckinghamshire* **17**, 115–26

Robson's Commercial Dictionary 1839

Rolt, L T C 1957. *Isambard Kingdom Brunel, a Biography*

1963. *The Great Western Railway at Swindon* (Museum guidebook)

Russell, J K L 1983. *GWR Company Servants*

Sekon, G A 1895. *A History of the Great Western Railway; being the Story of the Broad Gauge*

Sheldon, P and Tomkins, R 1979. *Roadways: The History of Swindon's Street Names*

Silto, J 1980. *The Railway Town: Description of Life and Events in Swindon from 22 January 1901 to 11 November 1918*

1981. *A Swindon History, 1840–1901*

Silto, W 1989. *Of Stone and Steam: The Story of Swindon Railway Village*

Simmons, J 1986a. *The Railways of Britain*

1986b. *The Railway in Town and Country 1830–1914*

1991. *The Victorian Railway*

Simms, F W 1838. *The Public Works of Great Britain ...*

Slater, 1852–3. *National and Commercial Directory*

Snell, E 1849–59. *The Life and Adventures of Edward Snell: The Illustrated Diary of an Artist, Engineer and Adventurer in the Australian Colonies*, ed T Griffiths with assistance from A Platt, 1988

Spencer, F H 1938. *An Inspector's Testament*

St Mark's Parochial Church Council, 1945. *Saint Marks, Swindon, 1845–1945*

Swindon Chamber of Commerce 1985. *Signals from the Past*

The Swindon Society, 1988. *Swindon in Old Photographs*

1989. *Swindon in Old Photographs: A Second Selection*

1991. *Swindon in Old Photographs: A Third Selection*

1993. *Swindon in Old Photographs: A Fourth Selection*

Tarn, J N 1971. *Working-class Housing in 19th-century Britain* (Architectural Association Paper No 7)

Tomkins, R and Sheldon, P 1990. *Swindon and the GWR*

Turton, B J 1969. 'The railway towns of Southern England'. *Transport Hist* **2**, No 2, 105–35

Vaughan, A 1977. *A Pictorial History of Great Western Architecture*

1991. *Isambard Kingdom Brunel, Engineering Knight Errrant*

West, W 1988a. *The Railwaymen of Wolverton, 1838–86*

1988b. *Trainmakers 1838–1931, the Story of Wolverton Works*

1988c. *The Moving Force 1838–88, the Men of Wolverton*

Whishaw, F 1840. *Railways of Great Britain and Ireland, Practically Described and Illustrated*

White, A J L 1911–12. 'Swindon Works'. Series of ten illustrated articles in *Great Western Railway Magazine*, **23–4**

1922. 'The "A" Erecting and Machine Shop at the GWR Swindon Works'. *Great Western Railway Magazine* **17–18**, 45–50

1927. 'The Swindon Works welfare institutions'. *Great Western Railway Magazine* **39**, No 5, 177

Whitehouse, P and St John Thomas, D (eds) 1984. *The Great Western Railway, 150 Glorious Years*

Williams, Alfred 1915. *Life in a Railway Factory* (Illustrated edn, 1984)

Williams, Archibald 1925. *Brunel and After: The Romance of the Great Western Railway*

Wilson, R B 1972. *Sir Daniel Gooch – Memoirs and Diary*

Index

Page references in **bold** indicate illustrations

A

'A' shop **128**, **129**, 129–31, **130**, **136**, 137, 152–3
Abingdon: planned branch line 3
accidents, work 65, 88–9, 113, **164**
  see also hospitals
agricultural labourers 10–11, 65, 104
Albert, Prince **38**
Albion Street 123
Allnutt, Richard (tenant) 58, **58**
Alzheimer's Disease 128
ambulance carriages **132**, 132–3
Andover, line to 127
Appleton, Peter (engine-driller) 75
architecture
  of Armstrong era 94–6, 149
  Brunel's style 44, 45, 58, 81, 84, 129
  of cottages 44, 45, **46**
  early 20th-century design 129
  of general offices 142
  and GWR styles 95–6, 129, 139
  styles
    17th century Dutch 127
    classical: Swindon station 38
    Elizabethan 160
      housing 13, **14**, 14, 44
    Georgian: housing 12, 157
    Gothic 160, **161**, 162
      housing 59
    Perpendicular style 81
    St Mark's church, Swindon 61
    Jacobean ('Jacobethan') 44, 45, 58, 81, 83
    Northern Italianate style: Baptist chapel 66, **67**
    Queen-Anne 124, 166
  see also roofs
Arkell & Son, Messrs (brewer) **107**, 107
Arkwright, Richard 11
armoury **82**, 83, **112**, 113, 114, 159
Armstrong, George 84, 116
Armstrong, Joseph 105, 121, 161, 172
  appointed superintendent 75, 84–5, **85**, 104
  additions to general offices 142
  era of 84–115 *passim*, 148–9
  and expansion/modernisation 85, **86**, 86, 88, 91, **94**, **96**
  impetus of 118
  residence 108, **109**
  and social welfare 113, 114, 123
  death 101, 115, 116
  commemorated 165
  legacy 1, 116, 137
Ashford: railway works x, 95
Astill's Original Swindon Almanack 87, 115, 116, 140
Atlantic: telegraphic cable across 105
Aylesbury Street 172

B

'B' shop **94**, 94, **95**, 95, 96, 144, 146
  extension & modernisation 131, **134**, 134
  as museum and demolition 137, 145, **146**
Bailey Shaw & Smith (contractors) 37
bakehouse **58**, 58, 77, 159
Baker, Orlando **110**
bakery, co-operative 76
Banbury: extension to 69

Baptists
  chapels
    Cambria Place 103, **166**, 166
    Fleet Street 66, **67**
    Monmouthshire Baptist Association 172
Barley Pegg & Co (subcontractors) 29
Barracks 64, 78, 79, 83, 101, **160**, 160–3
  converted to Methodist chapel 104, 111, 161, 161–2, **162**, **163**
  see also Great Western Railway Museum
Barrett, Exall & Andrews 27
Bath 7, 31, 59, 78
  carriage sheds at 56
  and GWR route 3
  line to Chippenham 16
  quarries 29
  Twerton 13
Bath (later Bathampton) Street 76
  cottages 47, 48, 49, 54
  shops 57, 58
Bath Road
  Mechanics' Institution reading-room 137
  Museum and Art Gallery 19, 160
Bath stone
  armoury 83
  Baptist chapel 166
  general offices 142
  housing 51, 54, 58, 78, 81, **82**, 103
  Mechanics' Institution 81, 155
  St Mark's church 62
  viaduct (Twerton) 13
  village community centre 159
  in works 29, 89
Bathampton (formerly Bath) Street
  housing **48**, **157**, 157
  shops **58**
baths, public
  early communal facilities 66
  Medical Fund (Faringdon Road) 112, 113, 114, 125, 139, 142, 159, 166–9, **167**, **168**
    added to (1904–5) 137
  planned provision for 80
  Turkish baths
    Barracks 111
    Milton Road 169
bay windows *see* windows, bay
beam engines 9, 25, 27, 32, 147
beam-engine house **18**, 145
Bedlington, Northumberland 4, 76
bedrooms 55, 57, 59, 103
Beeching, Dr Richard (chairman, BR) 136, 149
beer retailers 66
Belper, Derbyshire: planned housing 11
Berkeley Castle (locomotive) 133
Bertram, T H: succeeds Brunel 24, 74
Betjeman, John 125
Beyer, Peacock & Co 87
Binyon, Brightwen (architect) **124**, 124, **125**, 125, 127, 155
Birch Street: school 124
Birmingham
  engine sheds 9
  GWR and rival penetration 69
Birmingham & Derby Junction (B&DJR): workshop at Derby 9
blacksmiths 30
blacksmiths' shops: Derby 9
Bleat Lane (Fleetway) 2
  see also Fleet Street
Blisworth: cottages for workers 43
boiler house 27, 132, 144, 145

boiler shop 28, 32, 72, 73, 120, 131, 149
  of Armstrong's expansion 93, 96, **99**, 116
boilermakers 30
boilermakers' shop (original) **27**, 27, 31, 32, **35**, 147
borough status: Swindon 127, 128, 135, 137–9
Bourne, J C, *History and Description of the Great Western Railway* 3, **4**, **8**, 9, 10, **16**, 17, 22 28, 30, 38
Bowley, R 108
Box 3, 51
Box Tunnel 16, 24, 51
brake shop (wagon works) 118
brass founders 30
brass foundry
  original **28**, 28, 94
  of Armstrong's expansion 93, 96, **100**, 120, 149
  at Wolverton 9
brass shop 73, **102**, 148
Briary Close 107
brick
  and Armstrong's works 94, 95, 149
  and cottages 48, 51, 103
  GWR produced 166
  kilns 100
  later works' building 153
  manufacturing 81, **110**, 110, 118
  supply of 29
bridge: Wilts & Berks Canal 114, 166
Bridge Street 51, 114
  housing in 65, 67
  Methodist chapel 66
  and population expansion 83
Bristol 7, 13, 27, 61, 104
  birth of GWR 3
  building designs at depot 17
  journey time to Paddington 36
  line to Bath 13
  maintenance and repair facilities 69
  and route planning 6, 7
  and route to London (broad gauge) 4
  and standard gauge lines 93
  and supply of coke 28
  workers from 11, 76
Bristol & Exeter Railway 16, 116
Bristol Blue stone 114
Bristol Street
  cottages **48**, 51, 52, 58, 62, 155–6, **156**, 157, 163
    architecture 44, 45, **46**
    layout 46–7
    leasing 58
  footpath 77
  land for chapel 161
  schools 61, 123, 124, 140, 164, **165**
  shops 56, **57**, 57
  and water supply 65
British Rail 137, 147
  Horwich Works 149
  railway village sold 137
British Rail Engineering Ltd (BREL) vii, 136, 140
British Railways **136**, 136, 140
broad gauge
  carriages 87
  development 69, 73
  GWR allegiance to 31, 32, 74, 84
  locomotives **68**, **144**, 144
  peak of 116
  and standard gauge 3–4, 84
    conversion to 93, 118–20, 152
Brotherhood, Roland 78

Brunel, Isambard Kingdom vii, 11, 32, **36**, 36, **41**, 41, 42–3, 137
  accommodation for 59, 60–1
  appointment of Gooch 4–5
  architectural style 58, 81, 84, 129
  and Barracks **160**, 160
  chosen as engineer 3
  and engine design 31
  engine house **86**, **94**, 94
  and final building phase 79
  and first building phases 19, 20
  and Great Exhibition 69
  and GWR finance 30
  housing
    architect for **13**, 13–15, **14**, **15**
    design 44–5, **46**, 46, 47, 48, 54, 58, 59, 78
    early cottage-building 156
    provision 51, **63**, 63, **64**, 64
  impetus of 118
  and library and reading room 66
  and new Mechanics' Institution 80–1
  and roof construction 34
  shop provision 56
  Swindon station **36**, 37, **38**, 38, 39, 111, 169
  and trade depression 35
  and water supply 78
  works
    choice of Swindon site **6**, 6–8, **7**, 10
    construction 32
    design 16–18, **17**, 25, 30, 142
    precedents for 9, 10
  death 73, **74**, 74
  legacy/achievement 1, 67
  memorabilia (museum) 163
Bryan, Tim 133
Bucknall, F A 75, 84, 85
building societies 81, 83, **105–6**, 105, **107**, 107, 109–10, 124, 125
Bush & Beddoe, Messrs: contract for iron work 28
Butterfield, William (architect) 61
Byron Street 108

C

Cadogan, Frederick (Liberal MP) 113
Caerphilly Castle (locomotive) 133
Cambria Bridge Road **166**, 166
Cambria Place 101–4, **102**, **103**, **111**, 123, **166**, 166
  present private development x
  subsequent alterations to 139
  and Welsh workers 103–4, 161, 166
Cambridge, Duke of 40
Camden 3, 43
  Locomotive Engine House **8**
canteens
  carriage works 89–90, **90**, 140
  pattern store 152
  see also Swindon station
carbolic acid 114
Carlton, Samuel (works manager) 85, 105, 121
Carlton Street 172
carpenters 30
carpenters' shop 27, 28, 89, 94
Carr Street 123
carriage works x, 121, 163
  demolished 118, 140
  disposed of 136
  early 20th century expansion 132
  new building (Armstrong) 59, **88**, 88–90, **89**, 108, **109**

locomotives
    broad gauge phased out 119
    Churchward's designs 133
    GWR's annual mileage record 134
    manufacturing x, 20, 69, 72–3, 87, 93,
        116, 153
        early 8
        end of steam 131
        introduced 30–2
        last BR steam 135–6, **136**
        new factory (of Armstrong) 96,
            97–101, 100–1
        of standard-gauge 73, 84, 91
        westward expansion 93–4
        workforce 120
    works extension added 117
    Berkeley Castle 133
    Caerphilly Castle 133
    'Castle' class 133, **135**, 135
    Centaur **144**, 144, 173
    diesel 149
        'Warship'-class **130**
    Evening Star **136**, 136
    'Firefly' class **5**, 5, **16**, **144**, 144, 173
    'Grange' class 134
    Great Western 32
    'Hall' class 134
    King George V 133
    'Kings' class 133
    Lord of the Isles **68**, 69, 73, 120
    'Manor' class 134
    North Star 5, **163**
    Premier 5, 32, 173
    'Star' class 5, **135**, **136**, 136, **163**
    Swindon **135**, 135
    The Princess Elizabeth **135**
    Vulcan 5
    Windsor Castle 133
    see also Works (Swindon)
lodgers 55, 63, 75, 160, 161
London
    and Armstrong's death 115
    and birth of GWR 3
    contractors 37
    Duke Street: Brunel's office 18, 43
    engine sheds at 9
    'London Engine House' **7**
    overspill from x
    RCHME move from 145
    and route to Bristol (broad gauge) 4
    route to Swindon 93
    United Land Company Limited of London
        108
    workers from 11
London & Birmingham Railway
    Camden Engine House **8**, 9
    and cottages for workers 43
    engine sheds 9
    Fox as engineer 32
    planned junction with 3
    Wolverton 10, **11**, 12, 13
London & Greenwich Railway, viaduct on
    13
London & North Western Railway 31, 69,
    116
London, Midland and Scottish Railway
    134–5
London Street 140
    alley between houses 138
    housing 52, **53**, 53, 54, **79**
    land for chapel 161
    larger houses 59, **60**, 163
    occupiers in 75
    shops 59
    and water supply 65
Longsight (Manchester) 31
Lord of the Isles (locomotive) **68**, 69, 73, 120
Loudon, J C, *Encyclopaedia of Cottage,
    Farm and Villa Architecture* 38–9, 59
Lower Eastcott Farm 1

M
MacDermot, E T: *History of the Great
    Western Railway* 3
machine and fitting shops
    of 1840s 145, 146
    'AM' 129
machine shops 144, **150**
    of Armstrong 93, 96, **100**, **101**, 149
    machinery store **121**, 121
Maidenhead 4, 5, 37
Major, George 51, **53**, 59
Malan, A H 119–20
Manchester
    Longsight: railway stock manufacturing 31
    Salford: engine depot at 10
    see also Joseph Whitworth & Co
Manchester & Leeds Railway Office, Rochdale
    5
Manchester, Sheffield & Lincolnshire Railway
    75
Manchester Road 125
'Manor'-class locomotives 134
marble 38, 40
market, covered (octagonal) 79, **80**, 81, 125,
    154–5, **155**
Marlborough, line to 127
Mary, Queen 133–4, **134**
Mason, John Hawe (tenant) 58
masons 102
Matlock Bath 101
Maxwell & Tuke (Manchester) 125
May & Son (building contractor) 78, 79, 156
Measom, George 40
Mechanics' Institution **74**, 79–81, **80**, 89, 91,
        105, 108, 111, 140, 153–4, **154**,
        155, 155
    BR retains ownership 137
    building of 163
    extension to **124**, 124–5, 126
    original scheme for **64**, 64, 65–6
    reading-room 80, 137, 154, **155**, 155
Medgbury Road **110**
Medical Fund Society, GWR 65, 83, 111
    limehouse 159
    see also baths; dispensary
memorials
    chapel (Barracks) 162
    royal visits (foundry) **134**, 134, 135
Merrin & King: housing development 108
Mersey, River 73, 132
Merton Street 108
Methodists 66, 161
    Wesleyan 104, 111
    see also Barracks
Methuen, Lord 81
Midland Counties Railway: Derby workshop
        9, **11**
Midland Hotel, Derby 37
Midland Railway 90
Mileage Office **132**
Mill Street 108
millwrights 30, 94
Milton Road 166, 169
Monmouthshire Baptist Association 172
Moore, Temple 165
Morgan, J Loring (borough architect) 137
Morris, W E (private speculator) 114
mortgages 81, 102
Moulsford, Oxfordshire: housing **14**, 14
Munitions, Ministry of 133
munitions work 130, 132–3, 134

N
'N' shop 117
Napier, Mr 31
Napoleon III: invasion fear 83
Nasmyth, Gaskell & Co 19, 31, 32, 72, 144,
        173
National Health Service 166

National Monuments Record Centre (NMRC)
        vii, 137, **142**, 142, **144**, 144, 145
National Museum of Science and Industry 75
National Railway Museum 137
National Schools: old Swindon 123
nationalisation x, 128, 135
navvies, fear of 11
New Lanark: planned settlement 11
New Swindon Improvement Company 79, 80
New Swindon Local Board **124**, **126**, 127,
        155
New Swindon
    Armstrong era 101–15
    building legacy **153**, 153–69
    consolidation and growth 75–83
    creation of 36–67
    united with old 125, 126–7
    see also health; housing; old Swindon;
        railway village; Swindon station
New Swindon Wesleyan Methodist
        congregation 161
Newburn House 108, **109**, 115, 133
Newburn-on-Tyne 108
Newbury 58
Newcastle upon Tyne 5, 77
Newport Street: station to south of 127
Newton Abbot 153
Newton (Newton Abbot): South Devon
        Railway's works 73
Nicholson, William (foreman) 76
Nine Hours Movement 114
North Midland Railway 5, 9–10, **10**, **11**, **12**,
        12, 37
North Star (locomotive) 5, **163**
North Wilts Canal 2, **52**, 82, 118
The North Wilts and District Directory 125

O
offices
    of works manager 32, 34, 121–2, **122**, **146**,
        146
    see also general offices
old Swindon 2, 10, 42, 67, 81
    building 107
    chapels in 66
    company workers housed in 75
    Kingshill quarries 29
    National Schools 123
    and New Swindon 104, 125, 126–7
    Prospect Place 51
    quarries 38, 51, 103, 110
    water supply to 78
Oldham, E 29
Owen, Mr (local superintendent) 24
Oxford 3, 7, 69
    and carriage production 87, 104
Oxford Building Company 107–8, **109**, 111,
        114, 124
Oxford Street
    alley between houses 138
    housing 52, **53**, 53, **54**, 54
        additional 64
        eight-roomed 163
        five-roomed 156
        repairs 77
    occupiers in 75, 76

P
P S & A Co Ltd Steel 152
Paddington 13, 61, 62, 69
    engine house at 5
    as GWR headquarters 132
    journey time to Bristol 36
    line to Maidenhead opened 4
    line to Swindon 24
    rolling stock maintenance 87
    royal train from **135**
    station 42–3
    to Penzance (conversion of gauge) 119

paint shops
    Armstrong's plans for 89, 93
    tender and paint shop (1876) 100, **101**,
        102, **151**, 151
    wagon
        roof of **33**, 33, 34, **35**, 100–1, 148
        see also 'K' shop
Park House **113**, 113, 158
Park Lane 166
Park, The 114, **115**, 157
Parliament: and 'gauge question' 31
parsonage, St Mark's 61, **165**, 165
pattern store **122**, 122, 152
pattern-makers' shop (1924) 150
Peck, Alan 128, 129
Pennant stone 78, 155
Penzance 116, 119
Perris, William (tenant) **58**, 58
Peto, Sir Morton, MP (for Bristol) **67**
Philadelphia: American Centenary Exhibition
        117
Phillips, John Rouse 40, 82
pier-and-panel construction 29–30, 94–5,
        147–8
    machine and fitting shop 25, 145, 146
    and offices 24, 142
Pigot & Co's *Directory of Wiltshire* 51
Platt, A 8
Plummer, William (of Westcott Farm) 66
Pooley *see* Henry Pooley & Son
population
    and census returns 59, 75–6, 83, 104, 127
    contemporary 1
    early statistics 63
    increase 56, 76, 78, 82, 111, 125
    New and old Swindon (1871) 110
    of New Swindon 67
    and overspill from London x
    of unified town 127
Potter, William (GWR chairman) 74, 75, 84,
        87, 88
power house ('Hooter House') 96, 150, **151**
power, transmission of 27
Premier (locomotive) 5, 32, 173
Primitive Methodist chapel, Regent Street 66
The Princess Elizabeth (locomotive) **135**
privies 46, 48, 49, 54, 77, 103, 107, 163
    replaced 138, **139**
Prospect Place, old Swindon 51
Public Health Act (1848) 76, 78
public houses 163, 169
    Flag & Whistle **107**, 107, 169
    Queens Tap **41**, **63**, 63, 107, 169
    The Glue Pot **163**, 163

Q
'Q' shop 147–8
quarries 38, 51
    Bath 29
    Corsham 29
    of Goddard 111
    Kingshill 29
    old Swindon 51, 110, 127
    Swindon stone from 103
Queen's Hotel, Cheltenham 40
Queen's Road 172
Queen's Royal Hotel, Swindon 37, **63**
Queens Tap public house **41**, **63**, 63, 107,
        169
Queenstown School 124
quoins 29, 45, 51, 89

R
'R' shop (engine shop) 150
    Armstrong's era **86–7**, 86, 87, 93, 94
    in 1878 116
    in 1890s 120
    remains of 145–6, **146**
    see also engine houses